INTELLIGENT

THE ART & SCIENCE OF SELLING ONLINE

SELLING

KEN BURKE

Edward...!
Thanks for your interest
in MML. I hope you enjoy
the book.

Ken Burke

For information, contact:
Multimedia Live, 625 Second Street, Suite 100, Petaluma, California, 94952
Phone: 707-773-3434.

Visit Multimedia Live on the Web at www.intelligentselling.com.

Intelligent Selling™ is a trademark of Multimedia Live.

FIRST EDITION

Research Assistant: Kerin Schiesser
Edited by Peter Loughlin, Kerin Schiesser, and Rebeca Zaun.
Designed by Sean Dolinsky. Cover design by Sean Dolinsky.

Printed and bound in the United States of America.

ISBN: 0-9722871-1-6

Library of Congress Control Number: 2002111535

This book is dedicated to all the wonderful clients, partners, and most importantly the employees of Multimedia Live whom I have been so fortunate to work with. They have taught me more than I could ever have hoped for.

Contents

Introduction:
The Roots of Intelligent Selling

This book sums up my company's e-commerce development vision that has grown from our real-world experience in building e-commerce sites that work. The methodologies you find here were all born from actual website implementations, the ideas and input from our clients, and the careful evaluation of customer behavior. The Intelligent Selling approach has proven time and time again to offer real benefits to retailers, catalogers, direct marketers, and manufacturers selling their goods and services on the Web.

I founded Multimedia Live in 1995 with the vision of creating a better way to sell online. Back then, some people were already selling online but the idea of using merchandising techniques from traditional selling channels had not yet entered the mainstream world of Web design. The Web was still largely run by technicians who could make the Web machinery run, but did not understand merchandising or the customer experience. Sales were being made, the industry was learning very quickly, and new and better ways of conducting online transactions were being created all the time. But the vast majority of the population — and the buying power they represented — were not yet involved. Clearly, there were enormous opportunities if only someone could figure out the right approach. Something had to be done to make shoppers able and eager to use it.

Multimedia Live was created to change all this. Our mission was to help catalogers, retailers, manufacturers, and dot-coms integrate merchandising-centric e-commerce solutions into their overall business mix. The focus was to be on making the customer experience as good as it could be, so they felt as comfortable shopping online as at a local store. We set about designing websites and building e-commerce technology that could accomplish this.

Multimedia Live approached selling online from a different angle than most other e-commerce developers. When most were looking at technology as a means of making a cool website, we looked at the customers and their needs and adapted our website design and technology to keep them happy.

We started off with a solid base of traditional cataloging and direct marketing customer service and merchandising techniques. After a lot of experimenting, examining the actual results of our sites, and listening to the input of our clients, we found that there are eight core aspects to website development that contribute to successful sales and long-term healthy growth. When taken together these eight aspects offer the only truly intelligent approach to e-commerce.

It was from this real-world experience that the idea of Intelligent Selling was born. The chapters of this book offer a detailed and systematic examination of these eight aspects.

The term Intelligent Selling refers to the aggregated merchandising and customer service tools, techniques, and technologies that have worked so well over the years to help our clients:

- Increase conversion rates.
- Increase average order size and frequency of purchase.
- Improve customer loyalty and retention.
- Reduce abandoned cart rates.
- Decrease customer service costs.
- Improve the overall customer experience.

Distilled down to its basics, Intelligent Selling means:

- Creating a stellar customer experience,
- Optimizing all selling opportunities, and
- Rapidly analyzing and deploying change.

Intelligent Selling is an evolving thing. It has its roots in off-line merchandising, customer service, and data analysis, and it adopts solid new technologies that support any of its precepts or help the website integrate more smoothly with other sales channels. As customer expectations change, Intelligent Selling techniques also change in order to keep pace with them.

You do not need a high-priced e-commerce platform to institute an Intelligent Selling approach. You do not need to pay your e-commerce developer millions of dollars to obtain the optimal online customer service machine. What you do need is to take a careful look at your merchandising, your customers, and your approach to business to find out what changes you need to make to develop a deep-rooted customer focus.

I wrote this book to help you do just that. The Internet is one of the greatest sales tools ever invented, not just because it can help your company make money, but also because it can make life easier for your customers. An Intelligent Selling approach can make online purchasing easy and satisfying throughout any kind of transaction – B-to-C or B-to-B – regardless of the kind of business you run or the nature of the products or services you sell. And right now there are vast numbers of businesses and consumers who are being poorly served by websites that pass themselves off as customer-focused e-commerce destinations. Both groups deserve more.

Although every website for every company shares a number of basic traits and although certain rules of e-commerce apply equally to all of them, each one is different and offers its own lessons. At Multimedia Live we have been privileged to work with some of the finest companies in the country and are privileged to say that even through the so-called "dot-com shakeout" most of the companies that we have worked with are still growing and vital.

Many of the concepts in this book are best explained through images, so I have included many screen shots from actual websites that take an Intelligent Selling approach. And because there is such a huge amount of good information online I have included a list of Web addresses for reference sites at the end of each chapter. I am sure you will find them useful. If you should choose to visit any of these sites online, please keep in mind that the nature of a website is to grow and evolve. These sites could easily have been changed between the time of this book's publication and your visit, and any feature or page I refer to may look very different or be unavailable.

So I invite you to take a look at the inner workings of a system that has revolutionized the way many highly successful companies do business. You'll find that Intelligent Selling is not a single technology, a particular way of looking at data, a customer service tool, or a method of integrating sales channels. Rather, it is a holistic approach that encompasses all these and more, letting businesses build effective websites that serve their customers, support their brands, and provide a good return on investment. Intelligent Selling helps unite all aspects of the business into a cohesive whole. It is a philosophy that, in the age of e-commerce, helps move businesses in whatever direction they need to go.

Building the Customer Relationship

The Purpose of Your Website

The purpose of your e-commerce website should be to build a good relationship with your customer so they choose to buy from you. Intelligent Selling is wholly focused upon this, and therefore strives to place the customer at the center of the online selling experience. Everything your website does should have the sole aim of "wrapping your arms" around your customers, anticipating their needs, providing the products and information they want, and addressing their concerns in a respectful, thoughtful fashion.

If this sounds like the kind of treatment one should expect from a high-quality retail establishment or cataloger, then you already understand the main aim of Intelligent Selling.

Retailers and catalogers understand about serving customers. Those who do this best are those who understand that the customer is the focus of their business, and who build all their company's guiding principles, strategies, and tactics around this idea. Unfortunately, when it comes to selling online, even the best of these companies can be unsure of how to proceed.

The goal of this book is to show you how you can use Intelligent Selling principles to create a customer-centric website that not only showcases your goods and services, but primarily succeeds in the loftier goal of creating true customer satisfaction. Intelligent Selling is the key to leveraging your off-line selling successes and creating a great online customer experience.

Make the customer experience as good as it can be, and you are well on your way to creating a highly successful and profitable e-commerce site.

The customer-centric approach works. During the first several years of e-commerce, the focus of most sites was, pure and simple, to make money. This single-minded approach blinded these website builders and operators to a hard reality of real-world commerce: it's what your customers think of you that determines how much they buy, and therefore how much you make. Intelligent Selling addresses this issue by going back to marketing, merchandising, and customer service basics that have been relied upon for decades — even centuries — before the first website was ever launched. So it can be said that Intelligent Selling is not primarily about making money, but about building a successful online business that takes care of customers the way they want to be taken care of. Profits mount as this goal is realized.

Since you are reading this book it is fair to assume that you have some experience with selling online but that you don't consider the results wholly satisfactory. Or perhaps you're thinking of putting together your very first e-commerce website and you want to get off on the right foot. Either way, the question now arises:

How do I execute on this customer-focused approach?

Quite simply, whenever you look at your website with a view towards improving its ability to keep your customers happy, ask yourself this question:

What does the customer want from my site?

You need to understand their goals and objectives in visiting your site, just as a cataloger or direct marketer tries to figure out which customers are interested in what products based upon the data in their database. Are they looking for a specific product with specific features? The lowest price? Information on products they want to buy at a retail location? An easy way to track a catalog order? Or maybe just an interesting article to read?

Regardless, it is your job to construct your site in such a way that they easily find what they are looking for and come away from your site feeling happy with their experience. This is a complex project and it cannot be accomplished without a good set of guiding principles.

Guiding Principles

Your guiding principles are guidelines for everything that manifests on your website. They are the rules against which you measure the website and all of the results it generates. Your guiding principles exist to make all aspects of your website consistent with each other and with all other aspects of your business. They make the Web experience for each customer consistently rewarding from one visit to the next. Your guiding principles will be many and diverse. Some will be generic, common-sense practices used by hundreds of other sites, and some will be particular to your business and to no other.

All of your guiding principles must fit with the way you do business online and through other channels. So you need to know what the goals, objectives, and strategies of your entire organization are. Your website can and must be built in concert with these overall strategies, or you risk confusing the customer with mixed messages about your brand, products, and services.

Using your overall business strategies as a guide, create a list of guiding principles that reflect what you want your site to accomplish. Make sure that in one way or another they all revolve around what the customer wants from your website. Here's a short list of examples of guiding principles:

- Strengthen the customer relationship through customer registration, relevant messaging, and useful online support tools.

- Make all products easy to find.

- Provide easy navigation.

- Simplify and speed up the buying process.

- Provide relevant information about each product.

- Focus upon building customer relationships rather than selling products.

- Update all content often and regularly.

- Create a consistent brand image across all channels.

- Use the same product photos on the website and in catalogs.

- Use the same messaging, imagery, colors, and fonts as used in other company materials.

Notice that every one of these guiding principles revolves in one way or another around what the customer wants from your website. The last three on the list are heavily dependent upon your current business practices, and are focused upon providing the consistency your customers expect from one sales channel to another.

Primary Aspects of Intelligent Selling

There are eight core aspects to Intelligent Selling (fig. 1). Every one of them is directly related to improving your relationship with your customers, and therefore to supporting your guiding principles. They are:

- Personalization
- Online Campaigns
- Customer Service
- Data and Analytics

- Merchandising and Messaging
- Customer Loyalty
- Content
- Multi-Channel Selling

These are explained briefly in the following section and in far greater detail, one by one, in the other chapters of this book.

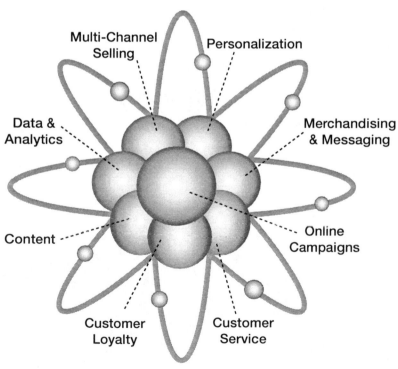

Figure 1

Personalization

Personalization is all about tailoring the shopping experience, making it relevant to the individual customer's wants and needs.

An online example: Someone sees an ad in the newspaper for an online special on casual office clothing. He launches his Web browser, and inputs the Web address that was listed in the ad. This takes him to a special homepage which prominently features the promotion discussed in the ad. He buys two shirts and a pair of slacks and as part of the purchase process he decides to register with the site. On subsequent visits, the site will recognize him and will be able to serve up images, offers, and other material calculated to be of interest to him based upon his past buying behavior. As he makes more purchases the website "learns" more and more about him and refines the assumptions it makes about his interests, enabling greater and greater accuracy in catering to his wishes.

An off-line example: Someone sees an ad in the newspaper for a special in-store special on casual office clothing. This person drives down to his local store and mentions the ad to a salesperson who then walks him over to the appropriate section of the store. The customer buys two shirts and a pair of slacks. He was satisfied with the purchase and the friendly attention of the sales clerk, so he returns to the store again and again to make other purchases. During these subsequent visits, the store staff gets to know him and his tastes better, and there is a proportional increase in their ability to anticipate his needs and recommend appropriate products.

The common element: in both cases, a customer wants a certain kind of product, and the merchant tailors its presentation for greatest accuracy based upon what it knows is relevant to the customer.

Merchandising & Messaging

Merchandising and messaging is all about placing your products, product information, and brand identification in such a way that customers find them, recognize them, and are encouraged to make a purchase.

An online example: the generic homepage for an online clothing store is set up to appeal to as many different kinds of people as possible. Unless the site has some clue as to who the current customer is as in the example above, there is no way to know what his interests are. So to make the customer experience easy and enjoyable there is an easy navigation system that lets anyone find the men's clothing section, the women's section, and so forth. There are also colorful images and attention-getting text links that connect visitors to special sections, promotions, and other interesting material. This is the first step in an optimal path to purchase that guides the customer smoothly to the final placement of an order.

An off-line example: the store-front of a retail location is set up to appeal to as many different kinds of people as possible. Unless a clerk is present at the front of the store to recognize and greet every individual customer, the customer will have to begin navigating the store on her own, using visual clues such as aisle names and flashy imagery on impulse racks to find what she wants. A salesperson may or may not be present to help. A good retail establishment will make sure that the merchandise is set up in a sensible fashion, that the most popular items are easy to find, and that everything is presented in a way that encourages the customer to buy more before leaving the store. The checkout stand will be easy to find, and there will even be items available for last-minute purchase right at the cash register.

The common element: in both cases, the store is set up to encourage the customer to find what she is looking for, browse for other items, and to take an interest in everything on display.

Online Campaigns

Campaigns are all about using the Web to unite all of your sales channels to draw attention to products, services, and other aspects of your business that may be of value to your customers. This could be a one-time only sale or your continuing commitment to excellent customer service.

An online example: in an effort to let customers know about an exciting new line of fashions available on its website, an apparel company sends e-mails and digital coupons announcing its new line to its existing customers, places ads on appropriate fashion websites, and puts a large new image and promotional text on its homepage. The company tracks the leads from every channel to see what works best in drawing customers to the site.

An off-line example: in an effort to draw attention to a new line of fashions, an apparel company places ads in newspapers and magazines, launches a series of television commercials that air over a three-month period, and places big signs about the new line in each retail location. Furthermore, it trains its retail staff to highlight these products during their sales pitches.

The common element: both merchants use whatever means they have to get their sales channels to work together to alert their customers about new products.

Customer Loyalty

High customer loyalty means that people are getting what they want from your website, that they are happy with your service, and that you are providing them something of value.

An online example: Our online clothing store wants to become the default shopping location for its customers. It therefore offers good pricing, a wide selection, prompt service, an online magazine that explains the latest styles, and personal accounts that can store information on the customer's size, color preferences, and tastes. Even though another website might have better prices, customers continue to shop here because the overall value of the experience is very high.

An off-line example: A retail clothing store wants to become the default shopping location for its customers. It offers good pricing, it trains its sales staff to be courteous and to ask key questions about the customer's interests and tastes, and it offers a range of styles from the newest to the most reliable old classics. The strategy is to provide value that is hard to match elsewhere so customers keep coming back.

The common element: Both merchants seek to provide exceptional value to the customer since it is easy to get beaten on price alone.

Customer Service

Customer service is all about making the shopping experience go smoothly and predictably before the sale, during order placement, and during and after shipping.

An online example: being fully aware of the concerns of many online shoppers, an online apparel store posts a clear and strict privacy policy regarding customer information. To help customers choose the right products and place their orders, they offer an online chat feature so customers can communicate directly with a customer service rep in real time. A detailed FAQ page is readily available, as is an e-mail link to someone in the customer service department. There are many useful options available during order placement such as multiple shipping addresses and gift wrap. To help out after the order the site features online order tracking. And in case the customer is unhappy with the product once it arrives they can ship it back to the warehouse or return it to a local retail location, whichever is most convenient.

An off-line example: the retail apparel store also wants its customers to feel well taken care of. They train their salespeople to be patient and attentive to customers. It is announced that the focus is to be providing the customer something he wants rather than selling the product that generates the most profit. Gift wrapping and shipping are available, and there is a generous return policy.

The common element: both merchants are trying to build a customer service program designed for the customer's convenience, not the store's.

Content

Content exists primarily to support the sale. It should always be designed to help the customer during the decision-making process.

An online example: because the customer can't actually see and touch the garment before buying it, the online retailer wants to leave as little doubt as possible in the customer's mind about the product they intend to purchase. Therefore, every product listing comes with extended information about fitting, materials, and care and cleaning. Images include fabric color swatches and front and back views of each garment. The site features an online magazine with articles and tips about the latest fashions, and even humorous stories about the history of clothing. Every page in the magazine has one or two links to related products on the site.

An off-line example: in a retail store, the customer has the garment right in front of her which reduces much of the need for product related content. However, our retailer is very thorough in providing extended information about the materials used in every product. They too have a fashion magazine, and have occasional fashion shows at selected retail locations.

The common element: both merchants seek to inform the client about their product line and to provide information that makes the customer comfortable with purchasing their products.

Data and Analytics

Data and data analytics give you a glimpse into the workings of your business so you can figure out which of your products and promotions are favored by your customers, and which need improvement.

An online example: the online apparel store carefully collects and tracks a large amount of information about orders from its site and the purchasing patterns of its customers. It finds one group of customers that tends to buy new items whether they are on sale or not, and another group that only buys discounted merchandise. It therefore adjusts its personalization tactics to provide each group with messaging and offers that are calculated to be most appealing to them. Furthermore, it finds that its online magazine gets a lot of readers and the decision is made to update it more often.

An off-line example: our friends at the retail clothing store decide to launch a catalog. They analyze their retail sales and find out what products sell the best. They also purchase data from a third party source so they can select groups of customers that are likely to be interested in their product line. As soon as sales start to come in from the catalog and call center, they analyze their sales and customer data to better improve their product offering.

The common element: both merchants seek out the best data available on what their customers like in order to refine their product offering and provide more of what their customers find appealing.

Multi-channel selling

Multichannel selling is about getting all of your sales channels to work together to serve your customers, advance your entire business, and provide a consistent brand image everywhere.

An online example: the online apparel retailer decides that its website has sufficiently proven itself, and that it can serve as the center of a major business initiative. In addition to e-mail and other online campaign strategies described above, it launches a small catalog of its own and uses its Web databases to drive order placement and customer service through its new call center. The company places ads in newspapers and magazines to help raise awareness of the new ways it can serve its customers. It creates targeted signage for use in its retail locations and trains its staff to help customers place orders online and to accept returns from online orders. The retail locations are also given online access to the website database. Now, no matter how a customer approaches this company, they see a consistent presentation of the same products, imagery, and messaging. This builds customer confidence, trust, and loyalty.

An off-line example: the retail apparel store takes a similar strategy to multichannel selling, but because it has a slightly different business model its goal is to drive sales at its retail locations. It upgrades its website to present its complete product line so its customers can research their options before visiting a store. It links its catalog operation, retail locations, and website to the same inventory and customer information databases to provide a consistent view of the customer across all channels. It includes a catalog quick order feature on its website to make it easier for catalog browsers to place online orders. It upgrades its advertising to emphasize the high quality of the overall shopping experience and to encourage customers to visit its stores.

The common element: both organizations use every tool at their disposal to make the shopping experience easier and more enjoyable regardless of the channel the customer chooses. Each element is tuned to support the overall goals of the organization.

Again, the one thing these all have in common is the attempt to serve the customer better. It is not just about selling stuff and making money. This will follow— as we all know—as a natural result of putting the customer first.

Your Website: A New Approach to Serving Your Customers

This focus on serving the customer is really what your website is all about. If you merchandise effectively, and help customers make selections that meet their specific needs, they are more likely to buy from you.

Unfortunately for most online merchants, their websites have fallen way short of the mark. Poor merchandising, lack of good organization, bad navigational systems, unfavorable privacy policies, just plain ugly site design, and a wide number of other serious problems have done nothing to promote a healthy customer relationship, and have even destroyed many good relationships that existed before.

Clearly, there is a great need for an entirely new approach. If you focus your attention on helping your customers, you can turn a potentially tedious or unpleasant shopping excursion into an enjoyable experience.

The finest retail locations have known how to do this for a long time. Take my recent experience at a well-known department store. I needed a new suit and

I knew pretty much what I wanted. I was greeted by a polite and pleasant sales associate in the men's suits department and after some careful questions about my needs and tastes, he helped me select the suit that was just right. I had expected to just buy it and leave, but he asked me if I also needed a shirt, shoes, or anything else. This reminded me that I did indeed need these things and that if I left now I would have to go shopping again to find them. To cut a long story short, I walked away from the store that day with a perfectly fitted, well-tailored suit, two shirts that coordinated with it and with other outfits, a tie, and a pair of shoes. This sales associate did not use a hard-sell to increase his sale. He was just careful to uncover my needs and help me meet them. And I was extremely happy with the entire experience, and I know where I am shopping the next time I need some good clothes.

That is the magic of retail. Good retailers build a strong relationship with their customers by understanding their needs and providing solutions that fulfill them. Customers leave the store feeling good.

Intelligent Selling is all about doing exactly that in the online world. Although a customer may enter your website, shop around and make a purchase without ever interacting with your staff, Intelligent Selling is not about "self-serve." The goal of Intelligent Selling is in part to emulate the presence of an attentive sales associate because online, that sales associate may never be there. And it is that personal attention which builds the customer relationship and generates sales.

The Web is a different medium from the off-line world. Intelligent Selling represents that medium in its best possible way. The tools that build the customer relationship online are very different from what you would find off-line, and they need to be assembled and coordinated in a different way. Intelligent Selling provides the paradigm for doing this properly. Intelligent Selling is the right way to build customer relationships and to do business in the online world.

Is this CRM?

A hot topic in the last couple of years has been Customer Relationship Management, or CRM. Whatever anyone has told you about CRM recently, you can probably ignore it. CRM is still a loosely defined term that means different things to different people at different companies and in different industries. This has led to a lot of confusion among retailers, catalogers, manufacturers. They ask what this new era of CRM means to them and how they can best incorporate it into their businesses, and they get complicated and conflicting answers.

The truth is that for these groups, appropriate CRM will consist of the website and all off-line channels merged together. Your entire presence must support the customer relationship. You cannot simply add a module to your business to handle CRM. So if you hear a lot of talk about CRM strategies and applications, don't let it mislead you. Intelligent Selling is the retailer's, cataloger's, manufacturer's, and direct marketer's version of CRM; it encompasses everything the customer wants in regard to his or her relationship with you, and provides the whole pattern for your customer interactions.

Real-World Roots

However broad the reach of Intelligent Selling may be, it is very specific and has a certain set of rules, best practices, and methodologies for building a solid relationship with your customers for the long term. Intelligent Selling is based upon successful strategies and principles borrowed from direct marketing, cataloging, and retailing. These have all been proven to work in the real world, both online and on the Web. Let's begin by taking a look at the relationship between Intelligent Selling and these principles and studying how they can be brought into the online world.

2

The Intelligent Selling Model

In this chapter I will discuss:

- Intelligent Selling is based upon the premise that E-commerce should revolve around the customer. If it does so appropriately, you will make money.

- Everything a customer does, looks at, and chooses while on your site can potentially contribute data that can further refine your knowledge of that customer. Use your knowledge to build a good customer relationship.

- Intelligent Selling practices help online marketers build a 360-degree loop of customer acquisition, conversion, and retention.

- The true test of your marketing campaign and site design is whether customers return for second, third, and more visits.

- How do retailers, brands/manufacturers, and catalogers/direct marketers differ in their approaches to selling online, and what can they learn from each other?

- Data — intelligently stored, tracked, and managed — is your secret weapon and your strongest tool.

Driven by Data

Intelligent Selling is driven by data. Intelligent Selling practices provide a framework that helps you:

- Look at data about customers, products, and sales and use it to improve and shape the relationship between your customer and your company.

- Apply your business practices to maintain and enrich that relationship.

- Make that relationship benefit from and contribute to the act of selling goods or services on your website.

In essence, selling on the Web is a variety of one-to-one direct marketing. The ideal of direct marketing is to efficiently determine what you have to offer, how to most efficiently complete a sale, and how to encourage new sales from that customer in the future.

Customers who truly want nothing you have to offer should be gently led elsewhere, so you can focus your resources on interested customers. This redirection should be done in such a way that — should their desires change — they will remember to come back to you. Customers who do want something you have should be allowed to find it as quickly and pleasantly as possible. Intelligent Selling practices are those which help your business:

- Attract the customer to your site.

- Find out what he is looking for.

- Determine what you have that could fit his needs.

- Determine what else you have that may interest him.

- Make his task of finding and buying as pleasant as possible.

- Encourage him to return to buy again.

Direct marketing methods are at their best when the right message reaches the right audience at the right time. In the old scope of direct marketing, obtaining the right list of potential customers was of enormous importance, and catalogers and other direct marketers would expend a lot of time and effort to get the best collection of names.

If the list was a good one, accurately containing a good proportion of people interested in the direct marketer's products, then successful sales and a profitable business were the usual result. If not, then the marketer's time and money, and the customer's time, were wasted. In direct marketing, profitability depends entirely on getting and keeping enough buyers to make the investment in a list worthwhile. Everything depends on the quality of the data that generated the contact list.

On a website, you have a number of advantages not available to most direct marketers. Your customer has come to you. You don't depend on the post office to get your message to the public, nor do your marketing materials have printing costs and finite print runs. But you still need the data that will let you personalize the relationship between your site and each individual visitor. The quality of that data determines how successful that interaction will be.

The Web itself is a huge data engine; everything a customer does, looks at, and chooses while on your site can potentially contribute data that your website can use to further refine your knowledge of that customer. In a practical sense, tracking every single thing that every customer on the Web does is not really possible. But we have learned some of the things that are important to track. When a customer is on your site, you have a special relationship with that customer, and special access to their behavior and preferences, even if you do not yet know exactly who that customer is.

Selling More is Satisfying the Customer

So what should your goal as an online merchant be? Quite simply, to improve your bottom line and make money. This sounds self-serving, but in fact it is actually as much for the customer's benefit as yours.

Customers want to buy. It is your duty as a merchant to make that sale possible. As an e-tailer, or any kind of merchant, you need to be aware that everything you do contributes to the buying experience. The buying experience does not end once the money is collected. Delivery, technical support, repair services, return departments, and other elements of your business continue to make an impression on the customer long after her credit card has been debited. Other aspects of your business influenced the customer long before she decided to visit your site. At some level every single action your business takes is a part of marketing to your customer.

A customer's primary reason to visit a selling site is not to read articles, play games, or admire artwork. Those things can be valuable in pleasing and supporting the customer, but they are only truly valuable to the extent that they support the site's real goal: making sales.

Customers visit your site to make a purchase. That purchase should be as easy and as pleasant to make as possible. It is your job to craft the site experience so that the customer enjoys buying online, is comfortable, interested, and feels that at all times he or she has all the help needed to initiate and complete the sales process successfully. Failing to do this will not prevent you from making sales, but it will keep you from selling as much. It will handicap you, and can leave your customers frustrated.

There are two tenets at the core of the Intelligent Selling methodology that should direct every stage of the development, analysis, and refinement of your website:

- E-commerce should revolve around the customer.

- If it does so appropriately, you will make money.

Everything else builds on these central principles.

But just because the customer is king doesn't mean that he rules alone. Your role is to guide. The customer is depending on you to anticipate his needs, suggest products based on your valuable expertise, lead him in new directions, answer his questions, and shape the visit into a successful interaction that either completes a sale or prepares for the next one. Application of the rules and techniques in this book will help you consistently deliver a high-quality customer experience like this, leading to higher customer satisfaction and increased sales. We will now take a closer look at the mechanics behind the customer-marketer relationship.

The 360 Degree Relationship Cycle

Intelligent Selling brings into play all the factors required to implement a successful, profitable e-commerce site. By uniting a number of concepts and developing appropriate supporting technologies, Intelligent Selling lets you build a 360-degree loop of customer acquisition, conversion, and retention (fig. 1).

Acquisition is the method by which you find your new customers, and bring them to your site. Acquisition issues include:

- Branding and brand support.

- Offline and online campaigns.

- Multiple channel support.

Conversion is the process of convincing a site visitor to make that first purchase and become a paying customer. After their first purchase, the odds increase dramatically that customers will return to buy again. It is often worthwhile to offer deep discounts with little or no profit margin to convince the customer to complete that first sale. Conversion issues include:

- Dynamic merchandising.

- Effective site tools.

- Personalization.

- Site promotions.

Retention refers to the effort required to keep your customers coming back to buy again. The true test of your marketing campaign and site design is whether customers do return for second, third, and more visits. An initial highly-discounted offer may bring customers to your site, but once they are there, it is up to your messaging, presentation, and personalization efforts to convince them to return on another day and to make a second purchase. Retention issues include:

- Customer loyalty strategies.

- Strategic campaigns.

- Advanced personalization techniques.

- Customer education: Why your product or service has value.

Figure 1

The Value of a Good Customer Relationship

It is between 2 and 20 times more expensive to acquire a new customer than it is to retain an existing one [e-Satisfy]. A study done by the Harvard Business School indicates that an increase of 5% in customer loyalty can increase profitability from 25% to as much as 80%. It is obvious that the rewards can be enormous for those businesses that dedicate themselves to learning more about their customers and how to build websites around the customer's needs and goals.

The goal of the Intelligent Selling model is to complete this loop repeatedly, and so successfully that customers return again and again. The Acquisition-Conversion-Retention cycle is the force that drives your Web business constantly forward.

Intelligent Selling is therefore a business philosophy. It applies to every stage of business operations and not just online. It is the customer-centric organization of your products, your services, your policies, and your entire customer relationship.

Who You Are Influences How You Sell

Before we get further into the specific details of Intelligent Selling, let's talk about you and your business. Identifying who you are and how you look at your business now may help you identify what your strengths and weaknesses are, what you are already doing right, and where your business might benefit from change.

In order to sell something, you must have a product or service to offer. Whoever you are, you are almost certainly more than an individual with a pile of widgets to market. Sellers fall broadly into three main categories, and which category you are in has probably influenced your outlook on what you sell and how you sell it. The three groupings are:

- Retailers

- Brands/Manufacturers

- Catalogers/Direct Marketers

These groups have slightly different behaviors and resources, and usually approach the art of selling (especially online) in different ways. Each has a part of the puzzle and some individual blind spots. To build the best possible website you will want to learn from the best practices of all three (chart 1).

The best sites will utilize the exhaustive product knowledge and advertising and marketing resources of the brand, the inventory and production resources of the manufacturer, the personal shopping relationship of the retailer, and the customer segmentation, fulfillment and customer service resources of the cataloger.

Business Type:

Retailers	Brand Manufacturers	Catalogers
Goals		
Support offline channels, increase sales.	Support Brand Identity and positioning in market. Online sales usually a secondary goal.	Serve customer, increase sales.
Strengths		
Retailers are experienced in dealing with customers. They are used to dealing with a wide range of products, and high volumes. They have good sources among manufacturers for their product range, and good distribution to distribution centers. They are experienced in face-to-face relationships and personal guidance in matching customers to products and the personal relationship that it takes to complete a sale.	Brands have the advantage of extensive knowledge of their particular products. They often have specific information on the wants and needs of those who use their products, including common complaints and reliable fixes. They usually have control of their own manufacturing schedules as well as control of the marketing and advertising that supports the brand. They often do have customer service departments and some data on who their customers are in general. Their strengths are inventory control and distribution resources.	Catalogers sell many brands from a variety of manufacturers, often a subset of items specifically selected to appeal particularly to their targeted audience. Catalogers have a range of specific information on their customers, and often co-related data on past buying behaviors with themselves and other catalogers or merchants. Catalogers' strengths are in gaining and retaining customers, mail-order type distribution and order fulfillment (much of which translates very directly to web sales) and in after-order customer service and support.
Weaknesses		
May not have much experience with to-the-door delivery. They may or may not have much in the way of customer service mechanisms; for many this is handled in-store, on a walk-in basis, and may not have after hour or weekend service.	Have little specific date on who individual customers are, or how to reach them. Little experience in leading customers to the sale, or interacting on a personal level.	May not have much specific data on their variety of products, or control over long-term inventory and availability of products. Harder to obtain warranty service and information.
Data Resources		
Sales figures on overall successful products in the brick-and-mortar environment	Sales figures on overall successful products, specific extensive information on the products themselves, and technical support and/or warranty data. Sometimes data on local outlet locations for specific products	Long term customer behavior data, detailed customer profiles both of groups and individuals. Often have years worth of data on campaign successes and other marketing data.
Tips for Improvement		
Need to learn how to gather and correlate data on who the customer is and what products interest which groups.	Need to learn how to gather and correlate data on who the customer is. Need improvement in after sales support and return sales generation.	Need to provide more extensive product data and support, learn to accomplish something more similar to the retail face-to-face service.

Chart 1

Each type of seller has access to a different segment of the data tools that are crucial to refining the customer/seller relationship and for improving the mechanics of good sales practices. The Internet is a special environment that, being computer-intensive, benefits from organized data as no market has ever been able to before. Data—intelligently stored, tracked, and managed—is your secret weapon and your strongest tool.

The Power of the Personal Relationship in Selling

What makes a good customer-merchant experience? Is it making sure that the transaction has been completed? That the customer got the lowest price? That the merchant made the most profit possible? Or is it simply that at the end of the transaction, both the customer and the merchant were happy enough with the transaction that they look forward to repeating it?

There are times when the lowest price or the highest profit do not result in the best buying experience. Customers may avoid buying from the place with the lowest prices if they have to put up with weak customer service, poorly trained staff, or rude sales people. Many will knowingly pay a higher price if it means receiving good service. Merchants may find that making the highest possible profit on one sale robs them of future profits when their customers search elsewhere for a better price next time around.

The single most powerful indicator of a successful buying relationship is the degree to which both parties look forward to repeating it. The intelligent way to structure the buyer/seller relationship is with mutuality in mind. The customer wants to buy; the merchant wants to sell. A good merchant is serving the customer best when making it as easy and as pleasant for the customer to find, buy, and return to buy again. The goal of Intelligent Selling is to create this kind of experience online.

Chapter 2 Links
Intelligent Selling and Direct Marketing Principles
These are general links, applicable to the universal issues of e-commerce.

http://www.the-dma.org
The Direct Marketing Association (DMA)
In recent years the DMA has become increasingly involved in e-commerce issues, and the organization's website has a lot of very valuable material regarding selling online. Take a look before you solidify your own marketing plans. Though some material is reserved for use only by DMA members, plenty is accessible to everyone. These sections of their site are particularly useful to email marketers:

- Consumer Help: see what the experts are teaching the public about their rights, privacy, and safety.

- Library: includes news, white papers, research resources, and other valuable material. The section on privacy is especially useful.

- Government Affairs: information on legislation.

- Professional Development: in particular their guidelines on ethics.

http://www.imarketing.org
Association for Interactive Marketing (AIM)
AIM is a non-profit trade organization devoted to helping marketers use interactive opportunities to reach their respective marketplaces. AIM is an independent subsidiary of the Direct Marketing Association.

http://www.retailing.org
Electronic Retailing Association (ERA)
ERA is the trade association for companies who use electronic media to sell goods and services to the public. The purpose of ERA is to foster the growth, development and acceptance of the rapidly growing electronic retailing industry worldwide.

http://www.nrf.com
National Retail Federation (NRF)
The world's largest retail trade association. NRF's mission is to conduct programs and services in research, education, training, information technology, and government affairs to protect and advance the interests of the retail industry. Their scope has naturally spread to the Internet.

http://www.shop.org
Shop.org
The leading trade association for online retailers. Shop.org, the E-Retailers' knowledge exchange, now serves as the NRF's online retailing arm.

http://industryclick.com
Primedia Business Magazines and Media
Publisher of a number of titles, including Catalog Age Magazine. When you get to the main Primedia site, click on the Marketing link in the main part of the screen and you will be presented with links to Catalog Age, Direct, and others. Though not specifically about e-commerce, these magazines regularly publish articles about e-commerce strategy and related subjects.

http://researchcenter.zdnet.com
ZD Net Research Center
ZD Net covers virtually everything about the integration of technology with business. This link takes you straight to their research section.

http://www.e-commercetimes.com
E-commerce Times
A part of News Factor Network, one of the largest e-business & technology news publishers in the U.S. News and comment about e-commerce issues.

http://www.catalogsuccess.com
Catalog Success Magazine
This magazine is directed at catalogers, but it regularly publishes articles about online selling, email marketing, and other pertinent subjects.

http://www.internet.com
internet.com
Internet.com serves as an index to a wide number of other Internet-related sites. Many of the sites in this list can be found there.

http://www.targetonline.com
Target Marketing Magazine
The Target Marketing site has a large number of current and archived articles relating to e-commerce.

http://cyberatlas.internet.com/markets/retailing
Cyberatlas on Internet.com
Section on marketing/retailing that provides articles and commentary on a variety

of related subjects, such as customer loyalty, retention, ROI, customer confidence and branding.

http://www.clickz.com/res/
Clickz Today
Comprehensive list of articles and white papers, on many topics pertaining to e-commerce. Keyword-searchable database with an impressive selection of material.

http://www.ftc.gov/bcp/menu-internet.htm#bized
Federal Trade Commission (FTC) Bureau of Consumer Protection
Look especially for the section on E-Commerce & the Internet: Business Information. Contains constantly updated information on legal, business, and consumer issues directly bearing on the problems and issues related to doing business on the Internet. Contains an online form, allowing consumers to file a complaint with the FTC directly from the site.

http://www.wilsonweb.com/
The Wilson Internet
Comprehensive portal site with exhaustive resources on every aspect of an e-commerce business. This site describes itself as "the largest collection of articles, links and resources on e-commerce to be found at any single place on the planet". Of particular use is the E-Commerce Research Room. Uses a database search tool to locate articles or whitepapers. Also provides a newsletter with articles, case studies and other valuable information.

http://search.darwinmag.com/
Darwin Online Magazine
Darwin has a searchable database of articles and very useful book reviews on a variety of internet subjects.

http://www.thestandard.com/
The Industry Standard, from IDG Net
"The Newsmagazine of the Internet Economy... written for senior-level executives who view the Internet as an opportunity to grow their business." A good source of e-commerce articles. The site has a robust search tool.

http://www.business2.com/webguide/
Business 2.0
Business 2.0 is an online magazine that discovers and reports on the smartest, most innovative business practices and the people behind them. Use the topic webguide or keyword search to find a comprehensive list of articles on branding, customer service, customer loyalty, marketing, and other e-business topics.

http://commerce.jmm.com/
Jupiter Media Metrix
This is one of the biggest names in research and customer metrics. Most of their reports are available only on a paid basis, but if you need specific, hard, rigorously researched data on customer behavior and segmentation, this is one of the top places to go. Click the "Featured Reports" link to find reports of high universal value, and often at somewhat reduced price relative to their other reports.

3

Personalizing the Customer Experience

In this chapter I will discuss:

- Personalization is the heart of Intelligent Selling because it makes the online experience relevant to the customer's needs and interests.

- Personalization is primarily an attitude and a way of looking at your data. Though reliant upon technology for its implementation, it is not a technology in and of itself.

- In 1999, Jupiter Research found that personalization of e-commerce sites increased annual sales by over 34%. But in the ensuing three years relatively few online marketers have figured out how to do it right.

- What parts of your Web pages should you personalize?

- Why should you personalize the product sort order, the product image, the nature of a discount, and other such details?

- How to assemble well-planned target customer groups, the key to effective personalization.

What is Personalization?

According to the Personalization Consortium, an advocacy group of businesses formed to promote the development and use of responsible one-to-one marketing technology and practices, personalization is:

> The use of technology and customer information to tailor electronic commerce interactions between a business and each individual customer. Using information either previously obtained or provided in real-time about the customer, the exchange between the parties is altered to fit that customer's stated needs as well as needs perceived by the business based on the available customer information. The purpose of this information technology combined with marketing practices specialized for the World Wide Web is to:

- Better serve the customer by anticipating needs

- Make the interaction efficient and satisfying for both parties

- Build a relationship that encourages the customer to return for subsequent purchases

Note the importance placed upon serving the customer better. A website lives or dies by the degree of satisfaction it instills in its customers, and because all your customers have differing needs and tastes, personalization can be crucial to making the customer experience better for every visitor.

Personalization is the heart of Intelligent Selling. Online merchandising is a form of direct marketing, and it is personalization that gives it its direct aspect. That is, personalization makes an otherwise generic site relevant to the individual customer's interests, emulating the one-to-one marketing practices of good direct marketers. So it can be said that personalization is primarily an attitude and an approach to addressing each customer, rather than a technology in and of itself.

True one-to-one marketing is still mostly a myth online. Though technologically feasible, it is very complex to implement. Instead, the goal is to create the illusion of one-to-one marketing by creating a number of iterations of your basic website and presenting the right one to each customer based upon what you know about his or her needs and interests.

In simple terms, personalization is nothing more than an intelligent application of market segmentation techniques. The basis of personalizing is knowing how to analyze the customer base, divide it into useful groups with similar tastes, and design different advertising images, product placement, and marketing campaign rules for each group.

By creating as many of these groups as possible, and by allowing customers to belong to more than one group, a site can come very close to individualizing its response to each customer. And it makes sense to meet as many of your customer's objectives as possible while meeting your own; the more of the customers' goals are met, the more valuable your site becomes to them.

What Does Personalization Do for the Web Experience?

The goal of personalization is to improve the customer experience by giving the customer the impression that the site was designed expressly for him or her. In short, personalizing a website allows an e-commerce store to be many stores for many people. Building a solid customer relationship through personalization is based on an old, reliable idea: in the long term, the more you know about your customers the better a relationship you can build with them.

As an example, consider the standard department store. Its marketing team has no doubt gone to a great deal of trouble to find out who their customers are, what attracts them, and what sort of images they identify with. Different departments have different audiences, and will have their own unique look and feel. Advertising images for the women's department have mature models and the petite sections usually have younger models. In the stores, the manikins will suggest different ages, and the decoration, signage, and other merchandising elements of that department will be designed to appeal to their target populations.

A store's advertising will attempt to use images that match the customer segment they are most strongly trying to reach. A sporting goods store trying to appeal to young adults will feature active sports and younger, early adult models. Campaigns targeted to older groups will feature products for less strenuous sports such as golf and walking. If a store must put out one advertisement to all customers, the advertisement for each segment must be prioritized for the largest segment of the population that will respond to it. But if the customer is known, a better match can be made in all departments.

If this sporting goods store knew that the recipient was an active, older outdoorsman, with a taste for hiking and rock climbing, even the more extreme products could be shown with mature models. If it knew that the customer was a younger man, it might show Tiger Woods and younger models in the golf section, rather than folks from the older crowd. The advertisement would show a different subset of golf clothing, designed to attract a younger audience.

What would be almost impossible for a physical store to do, and difficult for paper advertisement to achieve, is something the dynamic website can excel at: the personalized store, where every department is optimized to one audience.

If done well, personalization can improve the appeal of all departments, and increase customer interest by making each display more relevant. Even more useful, personalization can be used to prioritize product sort order so that relevant products are offered first, increasing chances that your site's visitors will find the products they want — or that you want to encourage them to buy — quickly and efficiently. By placing items of higher interest more prominently, the customer experience becomes more satisfying and rewarding, and the store's profits can be maximized.

Why do You Need Personalization?

In 1999, Jupiter Research found that personalization of commerce sites increased annual sales by over 34% - *Target Marketing*, 1999. Since that time, Web merchandisers have been struggling to understand, effectively implement, and profit from the promise of one-to-one marketing in e-commerce.

According to Melissa Shore, a senior analyst for Jupiter Communications: "Consumers return to sites where they receive tangible value for being loyal, whether the value is priority service, personalized offers, or email updates. Commerce players must create an online experience for users in which their customers see transacting on the Internet as a benefit, not deficit."

Other research seems to agree. A Rubric study (see summary on next page) found that leading e-commerce sites are not personalizing offers and are not leveraging the Internet as an interactive and personalized medium. While the sites made it relatively straightforward to buy online, "the experience was like shopping in a retail store, without the service."

How Does Personalization Increase Sales?

Every e-commerce website contains a mixture of messaging and product. It is already known that when customers can identify with the messaging, they respond positively and tend to buy more. Loyalty, retention, and sales increase when customers identify with a store.

But personalization can affect more than the store's lifestyle imagery and text messaging. Personalization allows the merchant to develop a number of simultaneous sales campaigns, and apply the most effective one to the current user.

Another advantage personalization offers is the chance to improve sales by product placement. Just as grocery stores put high-margin items on "end caps" (the displays at the high-traffic end of the aisles) so can websites use personalization to put items of their choice at the top of product lists. Whether the site's goal regarding an individual customer is to increase the chance of a sale, increase the amount of the sale, or something else, personalization can be used to present products in such a way as to meet those sales objectives.

Building a Solid Customer Relationship through Personalization

Although the rewards can be enormous, delivering a personalized site can be a challenge. Only a small percentage of sites currently make more than the most basic

Rubric Study Finds Many Sites Not Meeting Personalization Goals

E-commerce sites are not proactively promoting and cross-selling products:
- 47% of the sites did not ask buyers if they would like information on related products and promotions.

- Only 16% of the sites sent a follow-on email offer within 30 days.

E-commerce sites did not attempt to build ongoing customer relationships:
- When buyers took advantage of a follow-on offer, only 25% of the sites recognized the buyer as a repeat customer.

- Only one site allowed the purchaser to schedule a purchase reminder email.

E-commerce sites are not effectively communicating with customers:
- While 57% of the sites provided a self-service way for customers to check the status of their order via their website, 40% of the sites did not respond to the email inquiry.

- One company left a voicemail indicating that an email reply was forthcoming but it never arrived.

Customer Feedback:
Buyers indicated that personalization and effective cross marketing can influence their propensity to purchase:

- 90% of the buyers indicated that personalization would increase their likelihood to purchase from a site again.

- 94% said that they would be more likely to respond to offers related to their purchase and interests.

-- Rubric Research --

effort to personalize their stores. In time, nearly every successful website will offer some level of personalization. Those that do it well will have a huge advantage over sites that offer nothing but the plain-vanilla generic site.

Personalization is one of the most powerful ways to build a solid relationship with your customers. Initial segmentation will allow you to offer a range of products tailored to the customer's general demographics. As the customer responds and begins to buy, you will learn more about her through customer services, follow-up messaging, and subsequent purchases. Your relationship with her can begin to deepen and develop until you can serve up offers suited to her personal interests, and not just the general interests of her demographic group.

Task Items for Personalization Development:

1. Examine your site critically. Identify some areas where it would benefit from personalization. Find out what data your business now collects from the site, and what personalized response the site is currently capable of. What levels of personalization could you implement...

    *   immediately?

    *   with a little effort?

    *   with a major programming effort?

2. Estimate the level of personalization your competitors use, if any. How effective do they seem? (You may need to enter the site in various ways — through search engines, from banner ads, from direct URLs — to detect any differences.)

2. How would the ability to personalize affect how you message and merchandise to your Web customers? Do you already know some ways that you could arrange and group products and offers to appeal better to different groups?

4. How can you adapt your website to take advantage of the customer information and research you already have? How many store "variations" do you already employ (if any)? If you could build a unique store for 5 main target groups, how would they be different from your "generic store?"

5. Keep the underlying goal of personalization in mind; maximizing sales. Evaluate every idea for personalizing against these criteria:

    *   Will it increase sales directly?

- Could it increase sales indirectly?

- Will it improve customer relations?

- What resources will it require, and Is resource consumption reasonably proportionate to its benefits?

The Foundation of Personalization

The foundations of personalization are very simple. In a sense, you are slicing and dicing your database or segmenting your market to create specific customer groups, and then applying the traditional tools and techniques used for decades by direct marketers. There's no mystery to the theory behind personalization: the difficulties can be in the implementation. But it is important to realize that at the bottom, it's not a terribly difficult idea.

Personalization is not artificial intelligence. Some software that offers personalization may use advanced computational methods to analyze customer behavior and chose from the e-commerce site's marketing options, but on the merchant's side, personalization requires common marketing tasks:

- Researching the customer base

- Segmenting the customer base into functional groups

- Developing marketing campaigns for those groups

- Creating "if-then" business rules to determine your site's responses to customer behavior and interests as indicated by their customer group

While you could do all your personalizing the hard way (building a separate, hard-coded site for each group), that is a time-consuming, laborious method that fails to utilize the computing resources and flexibility of the Web. While it might be a good place to start for companies needing a quick-and-dirty solution in the short term, it is completely unsuited for any company that wants a serious Web presence that will hold up over time.

If you want to start personalizing right away because you have a couple of high-reward initiatives you want to put into place immediately, building a special splash page, home page, or category gateway page may be worth it. Such pages are good for greeting customers responding to special banner promotions or peer programs. In fact, a few of these may be a great way to do some quick preliminary testing on different responses to different programs. It really is true that personalization — as a part of your Intelligent Selling guiding principles — is primarily an attitude, and not a technology.

Figure 1

An Example

If a pet supply site knew with certainty that its three largest groups of customers were cat owners, dog owners, and exotic pet owners, in the very beginning of their personalization efforts they might construct a splash page with choices leading to 3 different home pages (fig. 1). Links from specific banners, such as from the Cat Fancier magazine site, would take customers into the cat home page directly, and customers book-marking the site would be book-marking the home page for the link they had chosen.

Being aware of the major groups that your customers fall into can be useful even at the most basic levels of personalization. Appropriate static pages at specific locations or alternate home pages can add appropriate customization touches.

Personalization often works best when it is determined by customer behavior, and it can be enhanced through use of pertinent demographic information. Let's look at two examples of personalized home pages from a real website.

The first home page (fig. 2) is personalized for a person whose past purchasing behaviors indicate an interest in gadgets: tools, electronic equipment, and so forth. Your records indicate that he is a man, about 35 years old, and that he is not price-sensitive since he buys whether products are on sale or not.

In our second example (fig. 3), we have a home page for an older woman who typically shops in the women's clothing section, and since she buys primarily sale items, she is apparently price-sensitive.

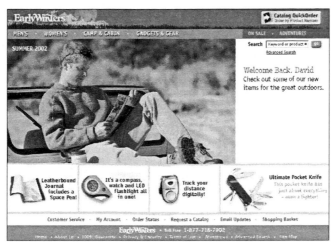

Figure 2

Since good personalization starts from the moment the customer clicks on the home page, you will immediately notice the difference between each person's Web experience.

In the first example the camping theme is backed up by offers for all kinds of gadgets and other accessories that could make a stay in the woods more fun and exciting. Personalized product kickers include a completely waterproof camera for rainy days or swimming in a lake, and a pocketknife that even includes a lighter. Note that there are no price-based incentives. Even the text-based links are customized to appeal to this customer: great gadgets for the campsite, deerskin gloves for climbing or working, and rough and ready packs.

In the second example (fig. 3), the campsite image is dispensed with and instead we see a picture that showcases the comforts of the vendor's apparel. Because the customer typically buys sale items, only products that have been marked down are featured in the kickers. The text links are calculated to be more to her liking as well: stay cool in our desert cotton shirt, light sweaters for cool summer nights, and rugged footwear for the adventurous.

You might have dozens or even hundreds of customers like these two in your database, and it could be worth your time to designate specific customer groups that reflect their interests. Therefore, anyone who seems to have similar interests to these two will see the same home pages.

Anyone familiar with website construction will see that creating pages like these by hand throughout the site would be a nightmare, and site maintenance would be worse. For this reason intelligent personalization uses dynamic Web pages and other programming tools to drive personalization whenever possible.

Figure 3

But your understanding of your customer and interpretation of data will always be the foundation of any customization effort. Just remember that the essence of personalization is the idea, not the machine.

Personalizing Page Elements

Before we examine the details of assigning personalized material to different segments of your database, it is useful to take a look at the things on a website that lend themselves to personalization. Use the following list as a frame of reference when going through the remainder of this chapter, and you will start to develop interesting personalization ideas for your own site.

- **Site Messaging**
  Many sites greet customers by name when they log onto the site. This is accomplished by recognizing a cookie file stored on the customer's computer (more on cookies later). This is one of the easiest and most trivial forms of personalization and although it is in common use, beware of relying on low level personalization like this to accomplish much. While many people do like being addressed by name, not all customers are comfortable being addressed by the first name by their shop clerk – or by a website.

  Whenever possible, allow customers to choose their own form of address. In addition, mail merge and cookie recognition has become common enough that customers are becoming somewhat blasé about it. The greatest uses for site messaging are to indicate that your site has some awareness of your customers' likes and dislikes, or to otherwise acknowledge who they are.

An example would be the greeting you give new customers entering from a banner link on a known site. You might use a message like "Welcome Cat Fanciers!" when customers enter a pet shop site from a cat magazine's web-site. Even more effective would be to recognize that the customer was a new visitor, and point the customer to the on-site bulletin board of localized cat show events.

- **Images / Displays**
  In addition to product shots, many sites have illustrations or lifestyle images that are analogous to a retail store's window display. These images can be provided in a variety of styles to appeal to different demographic segments or different buying types. Advertisements (kickers, etc) are also present on many pages, and a personalization engine can be used to choose the most appropriate of these for each target group. Even product images for certain high-margin or popular items may be used. For example, you could sell the same sporting goods to young and old shoppers by using different product images.

- **Product Sort Order**
  Products can be sorted according to any number of rule sets. The rule set you use could vary by customer segment. If you are dividing customers by past buying behavior or site history, sorting the most popular items to the top can help inspire that first sale for new customers or those who have never yet bought onsite. Customers who continue to return but have not yet bought might be worth trying a new sort order on, in the hopes of stimulating a sale by presenting a different group of products first. Customers who have responded best to discounts, closeouts, and bulk-rate upsells should probably be offered products in a price-related sort order that puts less expensive items nearer the top, whether they are markdowns or not. Quality or luxury minded shoppers should be shown brand-names and higher-priced items first. As with so many aspects of online selling, you can ask your customer what he is most interested in through a customer survey. This is the equivalent of a sales clerk at a store asking "So what can I help you with today?"

- **E-Mail**
  Newsletters, product updates, consumer information, and other pertinent materials provide a legitimate excuse for contacting your customers directly.

E-mail campaigns can be highly personalized. Different wording, imagery, targeted offers, and links can be sent through emails, offering a multitude of personalized offers. For example, separate Valentines Day offers for men and women will yield far better responses than will generic messaging to the whole population.

A Mother's Day jewelry ad may contain images that place a woman at the center of the family, show her receiving a gift, and emphasize her role as "mother." Messages targeted to men may show a man and woman together, emphasize the relationship between them, and illustrate him presenting a gift. Even in simple text emails, links can be differentiated to go to different special pages with targeted imagery and descriptive text designed to appeal to a different segment for each.

- **Discounts and promotions**
  Different things appeal to different groups. Some groups may respond best to "$10 off a minimum $100 order," while others buy more when given "10% off the whole order." The two discounts may be identical on the same $100 order, but in one segment, the $10 off promotion might cause the customer to increase the order to $100, while with another segment, a 10% off deal might lead to buying more, even above the $100 mark. Try a number of different promotions, and correlate them with your customer segments to see which are most effective.

- **Pricing**
  Personalized prices should be used with caution; companies such as Amazon.com have had public relations problems after it became known that they were automatically offering higher or lower prices across the board to certain target groups. However, pricing specials can be very effective with segments shown to be especially bargain-conscious, and such groups can be very responsive to up-sells or bulk savings offers. Also, sites that offer products through regional fulfillment centers have an excellent reason to use localized pricing structures that reflect the true cost of items in the customer's local delivery area. Grocery and quick-delivery items are particularly appropriate for this type of personalization.

- **Customer loyalty tools**
  A very wide range of loyalty tools is possible (see Chapter 9, Customer Service, for examples) and nearly all are prime candidates for personalization. And customers are more willing to tell you their personal preferences and demographic information in return for the use of tools that

help streamline their lives or improve their quality of life.

Even when using tools that do not require login or registration, the choices customers make reveal a lot about themselves. You can increase the effectiveness of loyalty tools and boost sales through judicious use of personalization that enhances the use of these tools. But always remember that the purpose of these tools is to improve the customer experience; if they become too highly merchandised, they may fail as loyalty tools. With a nicely-tuned balance, these areas can be a benefit to both customer and merchant.

- **Content**
  Content is an especially useful place to personalize, for two reasons. First, a customer's choice in content gives you some information about them, and therefore increases the chance that personalized offers made there will be well received. This holds true even if the customer is new, has never bought on the site before, and has not registered. For example, if a customer goes to a gardening site and asks for information on begonias, it is a good bet that an offer for a sampler of begonia bulbs or perhaps begonia food might be appealing.

  Second, if you already know something about the customer, items of higher relevance can be offered first. While the entire catalog of content should always be available to users, a content page is made far better if you include some prominent links like "You might be interested in" or "Top picks in your favorite categories." If you successfully bring items to the customer's attention without requiring the customer to go on long searches, the customer will come to value your recommendations and the section itself.

- **Category structures**
  Different customers have different shopping methods, and the way customers view your products can be highly individual. On complex sites with many subcategories, allowing customers to choose which categories are important to them, or automatically prioritizing categories, can help to ensure that customers see the parts of your site they are interested in first. Consistent navigation should not be compromised, but the order in which categories are presented, and especially their sub-categories, can be very helpful.

  When a male customer enters a sports gear website, the men's sportswear section should be a prominent part of the sportswear category. The women's section should not be invisible; the customer might want to buy something for a friend or relative. But the men's section could be offered first, as well as showing more prominently the sub-sub-categories that he habitually shops in. A female customer might see a similarly-prioritized array, but with women's sportswear and subcategories prominent, and a smaller link to the men's sections. For some sites, complete customization may be appropriate, especially where the site potentially has a huge number of categories and sub-categories. Such sites might allow the customer to deliberately design his or her own "store within a store."

An example might be a hobby site, which allows customers to design a store based on the hobbies that interest them: a train modeler with side interests in woodworking and gardening would end up having a very different "store" than a quilter with side interests in watercolor painting and flower arranging. This sort of personalization works best for stores with a large number of customers having widely varying interests and little product overlap. Even so, the site should make it possible to find any product in the whole store when necessary. Unused categories might be displayed smaller or moved to a pull-down menu, but it is rarely a good idea to remove them entirely.

- **Product Selection**
  Product Selection can be personalized either from the merchant's end, or from the customer's. Just as with the personalized category structure in the previous example, the products offered within categories might be personalized. The hobby store above might list only certain kinds of paint for the model railroader and other kinds for the watercolor painter.

  If a customer shopping at a clothing website had registered and given her size (for example, tall size 18) that site might choose to only present products for size 18, or even just tall 18. When a store has many, many products, choosing not to show the products that can't fit the customer can be a very effective way to avoid frustrating her. The shopper might otherwise select product after product from the index page, only to find that none were available in her size.

  However, the navigation bar might then offer a link to "petite styles" or "more products" to indicate to the customer that there are other products not being shown. Should it develop that the customer is looking for products for someone else, then the product winnowing should stop. Indicators to watch out for might include putting a smaller size into the cart, or boy's clothes, or using a shopper tool and asking for items in a very different size.

- **Thank You Page**
  Thank you pages are an excellent opportunity for personalization. After a customer has purchased an item you know their name and a little about the products they like, even if they are not registered. The post-sale thank you page is a good place to offer a next-sale coupon, to direct the customer to particular relevant site content, to offer to save the current information into an account, to sign the customer up for email notification of product launches, newsletters, and discounts, or any number of other ways to maintain and strengthen the customer's relationship with you.

- **Cross-sells**
  Cross-sells benefit from personalization more than most marketing. While upsells and accessories are closely attached to a particular product, cross-sells can be very dependent on the customer's interests and situation. A blouse may call for a skirt with one customer group, or for trousers with another. A good cross-sell for some people may be jewelry, while others favor shoes or even jackets. Cross-sells can be targeted to the customer's taste and be responsive to past buying histories, as well as to information from collaborative filtering.

- **Product Stories**
  Products might have qualities that appeal to different populations. An example might be a natural fiber blouse. If this is a popular item, it might be worth while to have several product "stories," or expanded text content available for customers interested in getting more information on a particular product. The fact that the natural fiber contains no bleaches or dyes might appeal to the hypoallergenic shopper. The fact that it was locally made might be important to another. The fact that it is light and travels well could appeal to travelers. If the product text came in three sections, personalization could choose which of these three sections to offer a target group first; the customer could read all the sections by hitting a "more" link, but the one most likely to be applicable would be offered first.

Understanding Target Customer Groups
How to Segment Your Database

How do you decide what special messaging to apply to each of these elements? Each one will contribute its own part to the overall customer experience, but you need to decide who your customer is and how you will treat them before personalization can really begin.

Start by identifying your target customer groups. Your customer database can be divided into target groups in an infinite number of ways; the critical task is to identify the divisions that are significant to customer buying behavior.

- First, determine how many group-related campaigns your site can support simultaneously.

- Second, analyze the data you currently have on general customer trends

Criteria for segmentation vary widely, and will depend on your products and customer base (chart 1). Determining factors can be as abstract as demographic information, or as specific as currently observed behaviors. Some examples include: gender, age group, income levels, previous buying history, working/ retirement status, marriage status, geographic region, rural/urban, products already in their cart, referring site, and pages visited.

Examples of Segment Criteria:

Demographic	Site Stored Facts	Offline Campaigns	Current Behavior
Age	Past Order History	Catalogs Used	Site entry link
Gender	Gift / Wish Lists	Frequency of past orders	Pages viewed
Location	Preference Settings	Amount of past orders	Navigation choices
Marriage Status	Survey Answers		Categories visited
# of Children	Registration Info	Response to past campaigns	Content viewed
Income Level	Customer Service Requests	Offline specials/ offers responded to	Links chosen
Culture			Items in basket
Associations			Tool use

Chart 1

You can personalize based upon very broad segments, such as gender or new/returning visitor. Or you can use many narrow segments with multiple criteria: middle-aged women who answer "yes" to specific survey questions and who have bought before. It all depends on what information is necessary to identify a group sufficiently well to market to that group effectively. It is not necessary to construct a plan for every permutation of sub-segments: identify those for whom a marketing effort will be most rewarding, and use the generic campaign for other customers. But re-examine your customer information frequently, and be alert to new trends and behaviors that might indicate that a new group is emerging that should be addressed.

Significant segments will fall into two broad categories:

A. Good customers that you wish to maintain and encourage

B. Under-performing groups that analysis suggests can be converted to good customers with the correct marketing effort.

Note that not all cross sections of demographic/buying information may be critical. While it may be useful for some businesses to have a full-blown plan for every cross-section of multiple criteria, for many websites, only some groups will be significant enough to build a separate campaign for. All others may perform similarly when offered the generic campaigns, or may return so little sales for the effort, that maintaining a separate Web campaign for them is not cost-effective.

However, it is worthwhile to be aware of which segments do have a high level of interest in the site and low current value. It may be worthwhile to aim a future campaign at converting likely groups of high-interest visitors into first-time customers who may become high-value customers in the future.

Customizing for Segments

Once significant groups have been identified and the goals have been written for each, it is time to begin working on your personalization plan. For each group, you will want to decide how and what to personalize, and to begin designing the personalized marketing messaging for each group.

Many areas of personalization overlap with marketing and messaging areas. The power of personalization is in its ability to improve marketing and messaging on the site. I'll examine these areas more in Chapters 5 and 6, but for now, start thinking about the customer's onsite experience, and refine your personalization tactics later as you develop your site and your marketing campaigns.

A personalization grid (chart 2) is a simple planning tool that can help you map out your tactical personalization efforts. Chart 2 shows a sample blank grid. You should fill out one grid for each target segment. The number of site areas you address will depend upon your site's capacity for personalization, but you should think carefully about the effects of your personalization on all areas of the site.

Your actual plan will have many more site areas, and probably more segments than in the example given here.

How Personalization Works

A personalized website can rely on technology as simple as static Web pages, or as complicated as proprietary analytical software operating in real time to observe and track individual customers' online behavior. But the most common forms of personalization involve two techniques: the cookie, and the registered customer.

Target Segment   A blank Personalization Grid

Site Area	Images	Kickers/Offers	Featured Product Tools	Market Goal
Home page				
Gateway pages				
Product pages/ product index pages				
Content pages				
Shopping cart/ Thank you page				

Chart 2

Segment: Generic Visitors   An Example of Segment Personalization Plans

Site Area	Images	Kickers/Offers	Featured Product/tools	Market Goal
Home page	Mixed group of customers	Season specials	Seasonal items Shopping buddy	Convince first time visitor to buy and return customers to register. Slightly geared towards potential "best customers"
Gateway pages	Category image	Category lead item	Seasonal category item	
Product pages/ Product index pages	Feature popular item	Offer $10 off on $75 order	Sort most popular items to top	
Content pages	Mix	Offer discount on featured item related to newest (seasonal) content	Seasonal article	
Shopping cart/ Thank you page	N/A	Free shipping for minimum order	Popular items offered as cross sell. Percent-off coupon code offered on thank-you page if info saved in a registration	

Chart 3

Charts 3 - 6 show the basic procedure for different kinds of customers, or customer groups. At this point, start thinking from the customer's point of view. What can you offer to improve the customer's experience? Which of your customers' goals can you make easier to meet? Where would personalization efforts be most effective? Later, you will expand on the basic personalization ideas to form your messaging, marketing, and campaign planning.

Segment 2: Men 35 and above, who have visited and bought before

Site Area	Images	Kickers/Offers	Featured Product/tools	Market Goal
Home page	Male customer matching "best customer" demographics	Kicker/offer on product designed to appeal to segment	High margin item with high segment appeal	Reinforce relationship, foster continued sales
Gateway pages	Category image with male using item	Segment lead item	Seasonal category item Special "Gateway" page for target group Targeted Cross-sell items	
Product pages/ Product index pages	Targeted cross-sells	Free targeted item with $200 order	Offer Advanced Search tool for quick/easy gift suggestions	
Content pages	Put targeted content first	Offer discount on items referred to in content	Item targeted to segment	
Shopping cart/ Thank you page	N/A	Free item	Offer automatic reorder/ automatic gift programs	

Chart 4

Segment 2: Previous buyers in the 25-35 age group

Site Area	Images	Kickers/Offers	Featured Product/tools	Market Goal
Home page	Young people, mixed genders	Kicker/offer on product designed to appeal to segment	Specials and closeouts, good deals, items aimed at young professionals	Reinforce relationship, foster continued sales, increase average order size
Gateway pages	Young adults using items	Segment lead item	Seasonal category item Special "Gateway" page for target group Targeted Cross-sell items	
Product pages/ Product index pages	Targeted cross-sells	Choice of $10 off or free shipping w/ minimum order	Seasonal item targeted at young adult/active group	
Content pages	Put targeted content first	Offer discount on items referred to in content	Direct customers to "Active Adults" section	
Shopping cart/ Thank you page	N/A	Free item	Offer free gift for signing up to "Specials" email list	

Chart 5

Segment 3: Women w/ 1 item, never bought previously

Site Area	Images	Kickers/Offers	Featured Product/tools	Market Goal
Home page	Women lifestyle images w/ strong branding	Great price on item of high popularity with women	High margin item with high segment appeal	Encourage completion of the first sale, completing registration
Gateway pages	Women using category items	Segment lead item	Gift finder tool, with messaging to "help find what men want"	
Product pages/ Product index pages	Targeted cross-sells	Choice of $10 off or free shipping w/ minimum order	Items of interest to women sorted first, featured in promo placements	
Content pages	Put targeted content first	Offer discount on items referred to in content	Articles of Interets to women sorted to top	
Shopping cart/ Thank you page	N/A	Free item	Offer free gift for saving info into registration, coupon code for next visit	

Chart 6

The Cookie Alone

In simple terms, a cookie is a little file that the customer's browser writes to his computer's hard drive, in a very constrained way which protects his privacy and limits the cookie's file size. The cookie serves as a key that enables your website and the user's computer to recognize each other.

Technically speaking, cookies are a general mechanism which server side connections (such as CGI scripts) can use to both store and retrieve information on the client side of the connection.

Certain kinds of information can be stored on the customer's computer, and then fed back to the site when the customer returns. The presence of the cookie tells the site that someone using this particular computer and browser has visited before, and whether any personal information such as their name or address was provided. Cookies cannot identify individual users.

The website can store observations of online behavior in the cookie, and retrieve this information once the browser connects to the site again. For example, a customer may have visited the tall men's section of a clothing store five times, and if the cookie was programmed to store this information, the site could read it. The site could then automatically place a promotion on the home page featuring a tall men product, under the assumption that such an offer would be interesting to that particular customer.

The Registered Customer

Customer registration is another way to gather and store customer information. Using registration information is better than using only cookies, since registration information is more detailed and can be used to serve up better targeted campaigns, improved product sorts, and more well-targeted personalized messaging.

This method also uses a cookie, but the cookie references more detailed information stored by the user on the site. It is usually necessary for the user to log in to enable use of such information. Customers logging in from another location are also able to access their account.

When a registered user returns to a site and logs in, the site recognizes her as a past customer, and taps into whatever information is on file about her. Identification of the individual customer is more certain than it is with a cookie alone. This allows the site to make offers with a higher degree of confidence, as well as giving the user access to personal information in wish lists, contact information files, and other site features that require privacy protection.

The Personalization Cycle

A visit to a website triggers a chain of events that leads to the automatic personalization of the site (fig. 4). In this example, we will assume that the site visitor has been to the site before and that the website server has planted a cookie on the visitor's computer.

1. When a customer visits a site, her browser connects to the site's server.

2. The browser detects that it has a cookie stored for that site's URL and sends the cookie file to the site's server.

3. The server reads the cookie, and sends pertinent information in the cookie to the personalization engine of the site.

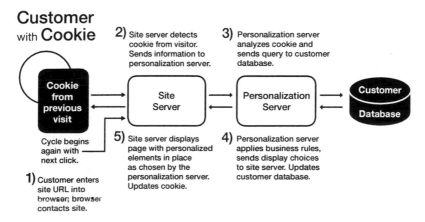

Figure 4

4. Whatever analytical tool the site uses will look up that customer in the site database, place the customer in the appropriate group or groups as determined by pre-determined rules, and make certain display choices appropriate to the URL of the page being served.

5. The site server then displays the dynamic page according to the programming choices made by the personalization engine.

The customer sees the page, and then makes some sort of response. Whether the customer clicks on a kicker, a link, or leaves the site, the site server updates the customer's cookie, if appropriate. As long as the customer stays on that site, the cycle is repeated with each click from the customer. Personalization is achieved by feeding the customer behavior through the analyzing tool before each new page is generated, and by updating the information in the customer record and on the customer cookie whenever appropriate.

The mechanism itself is relatively simple: the difficulty for the merchant is in creating the marketing campaigns and business rules that will be effective. On the programming side the challenges lie in creating analytical tools which intelligently interpret customer behavior and apply the business rules, and to dynamically build each page accordingly.

Data Gathering

A solid data collection strategy is the cornerstone of an effective personalization and profiling effort. You probably have access to a great deal of data about your customers. Your initial data is almost certainly going to come from a number of disparate sources, and in the beginning your website will be retrieving information from databases throughout all parts of your business. Data sources can be purchase histories, campaign response figures, customer demographics, inventory reports, and much more.

Eventually, you will want to move towards developing one integrated database that merges data from multiple sources into a single system. This process lets you mine rich sources of both online and offline data to feed each other, which will make your personalization efforts much more effective. Moving customer data onto a dedicated customer database will probably allow your site to be a lot more efficient and speed up the analysis process.

But the important thing is to find those data sources, and make them available somehow. Figure 5 illustrates a typical data collection and integration scenario.

As Figure 5 shows, the goal of a data collection strategy is to gather data from a variety of sources and aggregate it into a single universal data warehouse, or customer database. This database will drive your personalization efforts on your website by giving you a window into your data so you can answer questions such as the following:

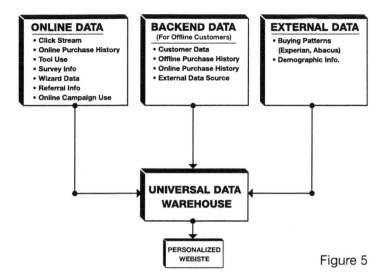

Figure 5

Regarding Online Data:

- How many people do you expect to use your personalized tools and to visit the site?

- What is the conversion ratio of customers who use one of these tools?

- Which campaigns are generating traffic, and which are also generating sales? Which generate traffic but produce few or no sales?

Regarding Backend Data

- What is the purchase history of each customer, both online and offline?

- How does this information correlate with information you've received from an external data source?

- How does buying pattern information provided by commercial services such as Experian or Abacus correlate with customer data?

- How do demographics correspond to tool use and purchase patterns?

Regarding External Data

- How does buying pattern information provided by commercial services such as Experian or Abacus correlate with customer data?

- How do demographics correspond to tool use and purchase patterns?

Chapter 3 Links
Personalizing the Customer Experience

Links pertaining to personalization are included at the end of Chapter 4.

4

Understanding
Personalization Techniques

In this chapter I will discuss:

- Which of the four types of personalization—Basic, Rules-Based, Collaborative Filtering, and Predictive Modeling—are right for your company?

- What are each type's strengths and weaknesses?

- How does personalization work?

- How does basic personalization customize the page for unique customer groups, and how does registration and account information play into it all?

- Rules-based personalization can actually switch customers between different paths-to-purchase.

- What is the role of customer data in personalization?

Levels of Personalization

By now, the need for personalization should be obvious. It is at the heart of Intelligent Selling because it makes the online experience relevant to the individual user, and that is the key to grabbing and keeping the customer's attention and loyalty.

But what kinds of personalization are possible, and what level of response does each generate?

There are four levels of personalization:

- Basic

- Rules-Based

- Collaborative Filtering

- Predictive Modeling

Each successive level requires more in the way of resources and the technologies needed to implement it, but each also adds a an order of magnitude of responsiveness and interactivity.

Chances are, there are some ways that you can personalize your site right now with minimal programming. I won't say minimal effort, as it will still require a lot of careful thought, research, and evaluation of your current data sources. But sometimes the simplest things can have a personalizing effect on your site. The language in your help sections might be targeted better to the people who would use it. Your product categories might benefit from improved messaging and from cross-sells designed to suit your most profitable customer. Start off by reviewing your entire site, beginning with the most-visited pages. Evaluate everything from the personalization perspective, and make a list of the things that would be easiest and most beneficial to personalize. Address those first, and build out from there.

The following is an explanation of the four levels of personalization, and some strengths and weaknesses of the four types, as reported by the Hurwitz Group, Inc.

The First Level: Basic Personalization

Basic personalization is the most fundamental, no-frills type of customization.

Simple programming methods use cookies to store fairly mundane information about a customer, such as their name, product preferences, and the like, on the client's computer. It lets you personalize a site by placing a message like "Welcome back, Barbara!" on a Web page when a customer returns to your site.

These days, very basic personalization is a given on most e-commerce sites. There are three stages to this level of personalization:

a) Hardcoded distinctions aimed at unique groups

b) Registration and account information

c) Name recognition

Hardcoded Customization Aimed at Unique Groups

Even without programming, basic personalization can be done by hand-coding special messages or promotions for unique groups. For example:

If you have an FAQ page about your line of custom-fitted cowboy boots, it might be appropriate to include cross links to your western wear section. This in effect creates a cross-sell opportunity tailored to customers who might need new chaps or a Stetson to go with their new boots.

If you currently are involved in a banner ad campaign with an allied business, link those ads to a home page with product offers and messaging that reflect the content of the ad. Your site is thereby tailored for the customers who click on the ad. You can test and track various offers this way, and start to see which personalization tactics work and which do not.

Hand-coding multiple pages for each message is a crude method, but it can be effective, especially when testing your approach to personalization. The greatest benefit is gained through sufficient analysis of your data to find out exactly what is likely to work.

Registration and Account Information

This level of personalization depends on the customer's willingness to participate. Your generic site and your targeted off-site messaging/marketing must convince the visitor to register before any personalized messaging is possible. The site will know nothing about the customer unless he or she orders something or can be enticed into voluntarily filling out the registration or log-in form.

However, once they have done so, you can store certain rudimentary pieces of information about the customer. This might affect what sub-site or regional service site the customer is sent to, but the greatest payoff comes during the next stage of personalization, which involves building business rules based on the information you have, whatever the source.

What you know at the basic stage is only what your customers tell you. If they fill out the form inaccurately or with deliberate misinformation, you may never know their true interests. However, self-reported information does have the very great advantage in that it is entirely voluntary. You ask — and the user tells you — how they would like to be addressed. They may also tell you whether they are married, how many children they have, and when their birthdays are, depending on what and how you ask them. In many ways, the customers' own self-view can be of greater value than purely quantitative data culled from other sources.

For example, marriage registry data might tell you that Mr. and Mrs. Smith are married. But it will not tell you that they have already separated and both consider themselves single and are only waiting for the divorce papers to be signed.

Alternately, the register might show Mr. Jones as being single, with no record of any Mrs. Jones. However, Mr. Jones and Ms. Adams have been living together as a couple for many years, though unmarried, and for all practical purposes consider themselves husband and wife. They have had two children together and are raising a third child from Ms. Adams' previous marriage. Though official census records may indicate two single people, their own perception is quite different. They see her as Mrs. Jones and him as a father of three, and have registered themselves on your site as such.

People will carefully filter self-reported data to make it most relevant for themselves. Clearly, relying on the customers' own descriptions of themselves will result in a higher degree of accuracy when predicting buying patterns than using official census data would.

Name Recognition

But as helpful as self-reporting registration is, it is of limited utility. Cookies can only store a finite amount of information, and it is all pretty static. The most common use is for simple name recognition.

At the basic level, more information is being gathered than used. The only personalization actions the site is taking is storing the value of a variable, such as "name" and then plugging it in wherever it is programmed to.

Thus on the home page the code will say "Welcome Back, <your name here>" but the HTML will render "Welcome Back George." The only other thing that basic personalization can do with this data is to store it, and make it available to the customer at his request. One instance of this might be checking the mailing address he has on record to make sure it is the most current. There is no denying that the site is more personalized to the user, though in a very simple fashion, but there is very little interaction going on. Having the information there may facilitate sales, but only in a fairly passive way.

Simple personalization like this will work as long as the customer has not deleted the cookie since his last visit, or is not getting to your site from a different computer. Logging in can give the customer access to features such as auto-reorders and reminders that let the customer tell your site when and how they wish to be contacted for the purpose of making a transaction.

Some places to apply basic personalization:

- Home pages.

- Gateway pages (introductory pages for sections of your site).

- Category pages (introductory pages for major product categories).

The Second Level: Rules-Based Personalization

Rules-based personalization is the first level at which an e-merchant actually has the power on-site to switch customers between different paths-to-purchase depending upon the data available.

Capabilities	To What Degree	Comments
Intelligent use of all sources of information	Small	Can make use of only very limited amounts and sources of information.
Degree of individual customer knowledge	Small	Completely reliant on information supplied by customers (self-reported) or off-site data sources.
Ability to respond to behavior in real-time	Non-existent	All it can do is plug in a value or return a stored value on request.
Scalability	High	Since its demands are so small, scalability is not usually a problem.
Ability to predict customers' behaviors	Very small	Self-reporting aspects makes information relevant, but it is strictly limited, and has no predictive powers.
Amount of marketer control	Very small	Marketer can no choice but to create a generic site that plugs in all customer's information similarity.
Technology required	Low	Uses current resources or very simple programming.
Relative cost to implement	Low to medium	Hard-coded personalization is easy but can be time-consuming when attempted on anything but a small scale.

Chart 1

There are two steps to rules-based personalization.

a) Build target customer groups.

b) Apply relationships to form if/then business rules based on the user and the situation.

Building Target Customer Groups

When deciding how to personalize, and at what level, you need to consider what kinds of groups your customers fall into. Dividing the customers of a women's clothing store into groups for high school girls and professional women is one example. Divisions like this can help you make some determinations on interests in style and content, but the resultant categories are still very broad. Within those groups will be a myriad of subtler distinctions. Some groups will substantially overlap. If they overlap significantly in attitude as well as buying habits, it might be just as well to treat them as one larger super-group.

If your research suggests that the buying habits and interests of female doctors and female marketing executives are very much the same, including what sorts of up-sell offers and conversion schemes work on them, it might be more efficient to add the marketers to the doctors group to create a "female doctors and marketing execs" super-group. On the other hand, you won't want to throw away any data you have that helps to distinguish the two groups later; a future analysis may reveal significant differences in the group's response rates to various promotions, promoting you to separate them into two distinct groups, even though both groups typically buy the same items. But at least at this stage of personalization, you need to do some basic research into what your broad groups of customers are.

Apply If/Then Business Rules Based on the User and the Situation

Compile a list of the personalization and campaign rules that are important to your business, and which you would like to implement on the site (chart 2).

Once you know who your best groups of customers are, you need to start applying your marketing plans. By now you should have formed your business goals, and have some ideas about the messages that should reach the different customer populations. Again using women's clothes as an example, you might have determined that women in their early twenties are your most under-represented demographic in the potential customer base, and that there is a large number of them out there with money to spend. Your marketing plan has the goal of gaining these customers and reaping benefits from a long-term association as their professional lives develop and their incomes grow. You have a TV campaign that is bringing them to the site, a free gift plan aimed at them that requires signing up and registering to receive the gift.

Once they are signed up, you know that a certain number of your newly registered customers are 20 - 23 years old. The minute they sign in, and every time their cookie file connects to your store when they return, you can tell that they are members of this group. Your site can then show them a home page kicker (a special kind of ad) aimed at them, offering low-cost, highly attractive items aimed at convincing them to make their first real purchase.

If	Then
Customer has registered but never bought	Offer free shipping for first order
Customer orders same products frequently	Offer "Automatic Reorder" plan at discount
Customer arrives from AOL site	Show special "community gateway"
Customer is over 50	Show "Retired Traveler" gateway
Customer is in high-income bracket	Use "high quality" sort orders

Chart 2

Even though the cookie can store relatively little information, it can still continue to keep track of which group of customers this visitor belongs with, letting you steadily build a healthy and productive merchant-customer relationship that meets your original marketing goals. The guiding principle here was to capture potential customers early and set up a life-time retail relationship with a high ROI. The finite goal was to increase the number of registered young-twenties visitors, and convert as many as possible to first-time buyers. With this modest goal, rules-based personalization was able to succeed.

Here are some places to apply rules-based personalization:

- Specific campaigns.

- Seasonal or product-based promotions.

- Targeted discounts.

- Site messaging.

- Cross-sells.

- Product selection.

- Value-added content such as e-zines or editorials.

Strengths and Weaknesses of Rules-Based Personalization:

Capabilities	To What Degree	Comments
Intelligent use of all sources of information	Medium	Rules must be written for every situation which becomes unwieldy.
Degree of individual customer knowledge	High	Numerous rules must be written to address various behaviors.
Ability to respond to behavior in real-time	Medium	Predetermined rules require monitoring and manual intervention. Ability to create real-time based rules is effective but limited.
Scalability	Low	The process is too unwieldy with potentially tens of thousands of "if-then" rules.
Ability to predict customers' behaviors	Low	Best used when directing customer behavior.
Amount of marketer control	High	But the marketer must account for each possible situation.
Technology required	Medium	Can use existing technology, though some, solutions can be difficult to integrate into existing back-end systems..
Relative cost to implement	Low to medium	Rules must be constantly updated with addition of new prices, product launches and evolutions in customer trends ad behaviors.

Chart 3

The Third Level: Collaborative Filtering

Collaborative filtering is possible when you have a bit more information about your groups, and more than simple if/then triggers that suggest they should be applied.

There are two stages to this level of personalization:

- Use collaborative filtering techniques to automatically determine target customer group from clickstream and other data,

- Apply "customers like you also like…" descriptive rules when the situation seems to warrant it.

Using Collaborative Filtering techniques to Automatically Determine the Customer's Target Customer Group from Clickstream and Other Data
In a previous example, I mentioned two types of professional women: doctors and marketing executives. For this example, we are assuming that early information indicated a high correspondence in the two groups, and that both sets of women tended to select black satin pumps after choosing a beaded black evening gown.

When a new, unregistered customer entered the site and put the beaded black evening gown into her cart, the site was able to entice her to buy black satin pumps just by bringing them to her attention. The purchase of the dress automatically triggered the shoe offer, and the site sorted this visitor into the doctor/marketer group because her behavior was most similar to the behavior of that group. But remember that this doctor/marketer group was originally exclusively doctors; all cross-sells and up-sells are based upon the assumed tastes of doctors. Therefore, the next things this new visitor is offered is a pair of comfortable white shoes and a set of women's golf clubs. Buying the dress automatically generated

Capabilities	To What Degree	Comments
Intelligent use of all sources of information	Low	Treat all customers and all inputs the same.
Degree of individual customer knowledge	Low	Assumes that the best recommendation is from explicit ratings done by people "like you".
Ability to respond to behavior in real-time	Medium	To work at all, must be able to find a way to fit the customer into an existing group.
Scalability	Medium	Loses its validity as the numbers of behaviors, products, and customers grow and as its attempts to find a good fit start to fail.
Ability to predict customers' behaviors	Low	Questions beyond product recommendations (Make an offer or not?) are not applicable.
Amount of marketer control	Low	Marketer has no ability to make a static recommendation.
Technology required	Medium	Can use existing technology. Some solutions can be difficult to integrate into existing back-end systems.
Relative cost to implement	Medium to High	Research must be conducted or bought which reveals appropriate groupings. As relationships proliferate, man-hours needed to monitor and keep consistent with good business practices grows.

Chart 4

the pumps offer, the white shoes offer, and the clubs offer (if dress, then pumps. If dress + pumps, then white shoes. If dress + pumps + white shoes, then clubs). However, if she didn't buy the white shoes, then the rules-based approach would fail. After deeper evaluation of the customer data, the clothing store describes some general characteristics of the doctor group, and another set for the marketing group in order to provide more accurate separation between the two and to take better account of their real-world interests. The accurate picture of the customer develops from click stream data gathered over time.

Apply "Customers like you also like..." Descriptive Rules When the Situation Seems to Warrant it.

In collaborative filtering, the dress-buying woman would be assumed to be in a general group of women, but not necessarily in either the doctor or marketing exec group. However, the group description formed for the doctors also includes golf and comfortable white shoes. The executive group includes a high incidence of red bolero jackets, Burberry raincoats, swimsuits, and terry beach sets. If the customer buys a dress and a swimsuit, she would next be offered a discount on a bolero jacket. If she had put white shoes in her cart next, she might have been offered a 10% discount on golf shoes. If she selected nothing from those two groups, she would remain in the more general group of women who buy evening wear, and would have been offered a more general promotion from the list of popular products.

The Fourth Level: Predictive Modeling

a) Uses probability theory to determine the likelihood of a user taking a certain action.

b) Assigns a score to certain actions or qualities, and offers personalization or marketing campaigns when a user's score in pertinent areas matches that of a target group.

Using Probability Theory to Determine the Likelihood of a User to Take a Certain Action.

Predictive modeling is the prediction of a customer behavior based on analysis of the behavior's relationship with other information in the stored data. By using techniques known as supervised learning, predictive modeling software can be trained on a stored set of data, and used to distill predictions on future behavior. For example, if a department store were to look at its data, it might discover that the customers most likely to become seriously behind on their credit payments are previously good customers who suddenly miss a payment. At least one test market found that this behavior most often occurred with customers in real financial emergencies. A previously unintuitive relationship—that the worst customers started out as the best customers—can be used to recognize patterns and take preventive measures to work with the customer and maintain good relations, which will be rewarded both by cementing customer loyalty and by rescuing an account that might otherwise have ended up as a credit write-off.

Supermarket chains have been testing data correlation for years—collecting data from point of sale terminals and comparing that data with loyalty cards in an attempt to analyze customer buying patterns. One observation found by their data analysis and proven by in-store trials has been that stores can increase the sale of "affinity products" by pairing them in the aisle. Stores also use the data gleaned from these activities to assist in forecasting product sales. Some department stores have responded to these findings by creating store layouts based on each store's local selling pattern.

Strengths and Weaknesses of Predictive Modeling Personalization:

Utility	Degree	Comments
Intelligent use of all sources of information	High	Factors current and past behavior, as well as other information sources in recommendations.
Degree of individual customer knowledge	High	Adapts to the customer's current behavior without explicit ratings.
Ability to respond to behavior in real-time	High	Provides an in-context experience for new and existing customers without manual intervention.
Scalability	High	Because it treats customers as individuals, it automatically accounts for new and potentially divergent customer behaviors.
Ability to predict customers' behaviors	High	Answers customer behavior questions online in real-time.
Amount of marketer control	Medium	Marketer can match a static result to an inferred profile.
Technology required	Medium	Technology available. Example E.phifany, other proprietary systems.
Relative cost to implement	High	Self-adapting saves monitoring costs, and ability to map adaptive behavior models to known profiles speeds integration into ongoing model refinement.

Chart 5

Assigning a Score to Certain Actions or Qualities

Online predictive modeling generally operates by assigning values to certain behaviors or facts, and keeping a running score. If a customer shows signs of matching a certain scoring pattern for a target customer group, then the site can serve up personalization and marketing messaging appropriate to that group.

If, for example, indicators of a target group called "Women's Autumn Fashions" included:

- Putting something in the cart

- Visiting the women's clothing section

- Reading the "Fall Fashions" content

… then a customer who did each of these three things would have gotten another point in a running total as she navigated the site. When her score reached a pre-determined threshold, then she would tentatively be assigned to the women's autumn fashions group, and be shown women's autumn fashions specials, offers, and lifestyle images, until such time as her score in other behaviors began to indicate that assigning her to a different group was more appropriate.

Chapter 4 Links
Understanding Personalization Techniques

In addition to the general links listed at the end of Chapter 2, try these more specialized links.

http://www.clickz.com/res/
Clickz Today
Specifically, search for "personalization."

http://search.darwinmag.com/
Darwin Online Magazine
Specifically, search for "personalization."

http://www.wilsonweb.com/
The Wilson Internet
Specifically, search for "personalization."

http://www.business2.com/webguide/0,1660,41066,FF.html
Business 2.0 Personalization Section
Or, go to the Business 2.0 home page and search for personalization. Many insightful articles.

http://www.personalization.org/
The Personalization Consortium
The Personalization Consortium is an international advocacy group formed to promote the development and use of responsible one-to-one marketing technology and practices on the World Wide Web. The consortium encourages the growth and success of electronic commerce that delivers the benefits of personalized electronic marketing while articulating best practices and technologies that protect the interests of consumers.

http://usableweb.com/topics/001317-0-0.html
Usable Web's search on Usability and Personalization
Usable Web is a collection of links about information architecture, human factors, user interface issues, and usable design specific to the World Wide Web.

http://www.crmguru.com/features/index.html
CRM Guru Online Magazine
Enter "Personalization" in their keyword search form at left to read a series of articles on the interaction of personalization and customer relationship management.

Optimizing Selling Opportunities with Dynamic Merchandising

In this chapter I will discuss:

- Ideally, a website will continually adapt to the customer's interests based upon what is known about him.

- Online merchandising takes many lessons from the off-line world.

- What is the "Optimal Path to Purchase"?

- What are the best practices for merchandising on the various types of website pages?

- What are gateway pages and why are they vital to the merchandising process?

- Merchandising can continue even after a customer has concluded an order. How is this done?

When companies first started going online to market their goods and services, many of them simply posted static renditions of their catalogs on their websites. There was little or no attempt to take advantage of the interactive qualities of the Web. Every page was the same for every viewer, and the art, layout, and merchandising techniques were identical to those used in their catalogs. Unfortunately, this approach proved ineffective. What is even worse is that many online merchants still use this same style even though there is a variety of affordable development tools available to make a far better website.

Intelligent Selling was developed as a means to get away from this kind of ineffective online merchandising. Intelligent Selling takes advantage of Dynamic Merchandising to make every page and every selling opportunity as effective as it can be. A well-designed website uses automated processes to continuously and productively restructure itself to adapt to the individual user's apparent interests. This is the key concept behind Dynamic Merchandising. This is all made possible by today's standard Web technology that enables the easy creation of Web pages on the fly using predefined business rules, data from the merchant's own databases, and in most cases an administration system that allows an authorized user to input new data and define new rules without having to reprogram the website.

The goal is to bring to the website the time-honored merchandising techniques that get people to buy. These techniques were originally developed for use in retail stores, catalogs, and direct marketing. They are executed differently online but they're all based upon the same basic reasons for why people buy.

The Science of Selling

In 1978, Paco Underhill started a lifelong career of studying, from an anthropological standpoint, the psychology of buying and selling. Since that time, he has become the guru of merchandising, helping store owners understand how product placement and store arrangement affect sales. In 1998, he published Why We Buy: The Science of Selling, which revealed many of the psychological influences behind the customer's decision to consider a product, or complete a sale – many of which arc completely separate from things like brand awareness or even bottom-line price issues.

For example, because the majority of humans are right-handed, (and especially in countries where drivers stay to the right of center), shoppers almost always drift to the right as they enter a store. They head off to the right and look toward the right, which is why merchandisers position new products just to the right of known top sellers.

Following this advice, many highly successful websites have made it a practice to put one of the most important parts of a product page – the buy button – directly to the right of the product being sold, rather than burying it at the bottom of the page. This puts it right where it is most likely to be found. Most good websites also place the critical "HELP" link in the uppermost, righthand corner of the page.

Another of Underhill's findings was that people don't read more than three or four words of a sign in a shop window. Web designers are wise to keep headlines and instructions short and to the point.

He found that the amount of time shoppers spend in a store is perhaps the single-most-important factor in determining how much they will buy. Other observations included the fact that male customers move faster through a store's aisles than female customers. Men are target-shoppers and it is hard to get them to look at anything they hadn't intended on buying. Men also don't like asking where things are. If a man can't find the section he's looking for, there is a good chance that he will look around a little, then leave the store without ever asking for help.

How does all this apply to the e-commerce world? In more ways than you might imagine. Merchandising applies knowledge of human nature and human factors to the act of selling. These factors are just as important, if not more so, in online selling. Because customers can only see, not literally feel, touch, or smell the product, good online merchandising must be used to enhance the online shopping experience. To be successful, e-commerce stores need to be aware of human factors and use human predilections to guide the online shopper.

The Science of Selling Online

Messaging and good merchandising are what stimulate online sales. Using the personalization topics mentioned in the last chapter will help make the messaging even more targeted and more stimulating to individual site visitors. And clearly, part of the goal of messaging is to keep customers in your store, make them want to stay with you, keep them shopping, and ultimately, to complete the sale.

Some of the issues I will bring up in this chapter verge on what is called "usability." Usability refers simply to how intuitive, understandable, and pleasant your site is to use. Good usability is an integral part of good merchandising in the online world, so there is a lot of overlap between these two topics.

If the site is well-structured, the route from the customer's entrance into the site to the act of completing a sale should be clear, easy to follow, and easy to complete. Along that path, the user either continues down the road, following the choices you provide, or they leave. In e-commerce design that route is called the optimal path to purchase.

The fact that customers cannot pick up or touch items on the Web is a limiting factor. But good websites will use other methods of stimulating a customer. And many of these methods are not available to conventional stores. Above all, the Web is dynamic. No brick-and-mortar business can afford to re-structure the floor plan, personalize the product displays, and re-prioritize the shelf placements for each individual shopper that enters... and yet, that is precisely what can be done on the Web.

As Dr. Underhill describes it, a successful merchandising strategy is one that allows the guest to become a sensual shopper, experiencing the selling environment through all of the senses—sight, hearing, smell, touch and taste. How items are presented, and in what context, can affect shoppers at the point of sale much more strongly than brand, or even price.

The Web—in potential—is the ultimate merchandising opportunity. The creators or architects of a website actually have much more power over the user's experience than they give themselves credit for—or than they take advantage of. By carefully designing, the Web architect can control what the user thinks, sees, feels and reads, based on the merchandising and the messaging that is built into the site.

Important merchandising topics include:

- How you can use dynamic merchandising to guide the customer through the optimal path to purchase.

- How to stimulate sales through messaging, site design, and carefully crafted merchandising.

- How to effectively use multiple categorization techniques to give customers the maximum access to your product selection.

- And finally, how to use the personalization techniques we discussed in the last chapter to tailor the shopping experience to each customer.

Implementing Dynamic Messaging

As I cover dynamic messaging, I will primarily be discussing ways in which site and product presentation can be optimized. But keep in mind throughout that messaging and personalization go hand-in-hand. The primary thing that personalization and customization accomplish is allowing your site to choose the best merchandising to offer a customer.

It is a circularly dependent process. On the one hand, you need to know the customer to develop the merchandising, and on the other, you need to have some merchandising plans in mind to know how to segment the customer base. Start by doing the research into what the customers want, and proceed from there; as you test the success of various campaigns, you will continually refine the process.

But even if you have very little personalization or even none at all, there is still is logic in how you see, plan, and execute messaging on a site. Most website architects do not think about their design in terms of messaging because they are not thinking in terms of merchandising. Most just think in terms of attractively filling space. And it's not at all about filling space. It's about what you show the user, how you display your products to the user, and how that presentation has an incredible and dramatic impact on sales.

Some time ago, my company rebuilt the website for a popular direct marketing company. We improved many aspects of their infrastructure and gave their site a more professional, modern look. We had a home page with some lifestyle shots, some kickers (integrated ads), etc. And the company saw a 30% decrease in sales.

The main difference was that the messaging had been changed. It was less targeted, and complicated the previously simple purchasing path

So the site looked better, the site functioned a lot better, the purchasing mechanics were a lot better, yet sales decreased 30%. The power of your merchandising choices can be incredible. Remember that on the Web you are not limited to the physical space of a store, how it is shaped, or where it is located. Every choice you make is deliberate. You control what the customer sees, and what you do will strongly affect how they feel and what they think.

And so, when we made a change to the site, we were targeting the wrong problems. The client's customers were very focused; they had seen all the products in a TV commercial, and they already knew that they wanted to buy. The new site wasn't prioritized for that. The problem was that the customer came to the site and had to search around for the products. On the old site, all the products were listed right on the home page. Not very elegant, but it worked.

In the new site, we tucked the products in a pull down. Nobody saw the pull down so they didn't see the product and they left. Our experience with this site taught us some important lessons in customized usability, navigation, matching a site to their customer base, and messaging.

In order to serve that customer population, the home page was re-focused, the products put back into prominence, and all the messaging re-adjusted to facilitate quick access to the products. Your site can't meet its goals if the customer doesn't quickly and easily see how to meet his.

The main way to make sure that the Web shopper accomplishes his goal – to buy – is to carefully construct a merchandising plan. This involves working out your optimal path to purchase, as well as several supplementary paths, and integrates your personalization and promotion plans.

The Optimal Path to Purchase

In simple terms, the optimal path to purchase just means "what is the easiest, quickest way for customers to find products, look for products, and buy products?" A path to purchase is like a storyboard, an imaginary script in which the average customer enters your virtual store, takes products off the shelf, and checks out. The entire site map, even when simplified (figure 1), will be a complex, interwoven set of pages. Some pages are hard-coded, and some are dynamically generated from your database and are much too complex for the average user to mentally map as he surfs your site. The optimal path is a standardized path that should work on a metaphorical level throughout the site. Consistent treatment of navigational elements, gateway, index, and product pages should keep the mechanics of buying consistent throughout the store. To use a visit to the grocery store as an example, the selection and checkout process is pretty much the same whether a customer goes to the dairy section or the cereal aisle. Your site needs to have a purchase loop that is similarly easy to figure out and participate in.

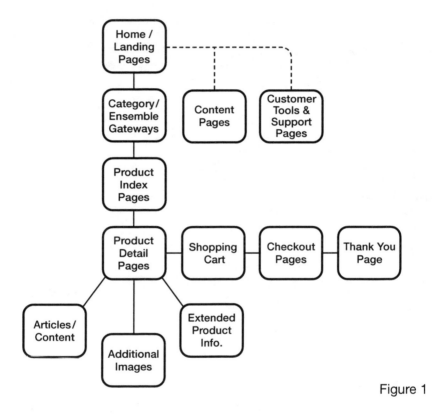

Figure 1

The product page is the heart of any e-commerce site. Ideally, the customer should need to click on no more than three buttons to drill down to a product page, and then, if they decide to buy, the rest of the optimal path is a horizontal path through the checkout process. At each stage, there will be optional paths that may take the customer out to content, tools, or other products, but the main thrust should be to encourage customers to follow the optimal path. Options which take the customer off the optimal path should also lead the customer back to it.

In the physical world, there are merchandising principles which affect the best store layout for maximum effectiveness, and this is no less true on the Web. Following Underhill's finding that an overwhelming storefront can drive away or confuse new visitors, Amazon.com applied that principle to its homepage in 2000, and removed a lot of visual clutter. Similar to his real-world advice which avoids putting major promotions and information in the entry-ways of stores, Underhill's book prescribes a calmer home page and landing page environments to help the consumers orient themselves upon arrival. Simpler, streamlined design and a clear route to the final steps of the buying process allowed Amazon to increase sales, invite customers deeper into the site without giving up, and retain more first-time visitors long enough to buy.

When mapping out the buying paths, try to think like a customer. To the new arrival, everything on your page will be unfamiliar, and only the parts of it that fit onto the browser's screen will be visible.

Monitor size is one limiting factor; but even that does not necessarily dictate browser window size. Many people maintain many overlapping program windows, and only a small proportion of their screen real estate may be dedicated to your site.

Key messaging, important functional elements, and everything important to moving around in the site must ALL be visible as near to the top as possible, to ensure being within the viewable area of a customer's browser window. Studies have shown that if customers are intrigued enough by what they see at the top, they will scroll down or page horizontally through at least one screen. But your only chance to convince them that it is worthwhile is in that initial, first impression.

Start with your Merchandising Plan
You should develop a merchandising plan in conjunction with your personalization plan, your content plan, and all other site plans.

Before starting to implement your merchandising, you need to have worked out the messages that you want your merchandising to support. Determine which headlines for products or services will stimulate click-through. Determine which promotions or products will stimulate the customer to start buying, or to browse deeper into your site. Later analysis of performance data may cause you to amend these decisions, but you will need to start someplace; use whatever current data or research you already have as a starting place.

Content is covered in-depth in Chapter 10. But for now, we will examine how content can be used to support your merchandising and your campaigns. Start planning ways to integrate content with the products, and to create actual sales opportunities through your content. Some examples of content/merchandising cooperation include:

- Detailed product information

- How-to information

- Tips and tricks

- News/articles/editorials

- FAQ

You will probably want your content to have some subtle spin that will contribute to your merchandising strategies, and at this stage, you should have your merchandising experts work out how your content will be presented on your site.

It's also important to define responsibilities for future development once the initial launch is completed. An editorial process for creating and updating content on the site must be put in place. Arrive at a balance between content and commerce that supports the site's attitudes, branding, and commerce goals, while keeping in mind at all times that you will need to be sensitive to the customer's goals as well. Chances are they want some impartial information when they read your content, and too much merchandising spin will taint your content's credibility.

Your planning should include various scenarios, based upon the kinds of promotions you anticipate and the complexity of your product line. Your site should be structured to accommodate a number of paths to purchase.

Many customers will not know precisely the name or location of the product they're looking for, and even successfully targeted visitors may have occasion to look for additional items while on your site. So the generalized, optimal path to purchase provides for searching, information gathering, and various opportunities for all kinds of merchandising, all without interrupting the basic "visit, find, buy" loop.

I say "loop" because ideally, even the final thank you page may not be the end of the process. Think back to our metaphorical grocery store: the impulse racks at the checkout counter might just entice the customer into buying one more thing. Exit page merchandising can be constructed to add promotional, up-sell, or cross-sell items, sometimes without even requiring a return to the primary shopping section of your site.

Putting It Together: Dynamic Merchandising & Messaging Along the Optimal Path to Purchase

Because most of your selling happens on the primary pages of your optimal path to purchase, these pages are where your most effective and significant merchandising opportunities occur.

Approximately 50% of the users who visit a new site never go beyond the home page, or whatever page they landed on when they first entered the site. This number will vary widely, depending on your marketing and advertising strategies. Some of those who come and go are not a good fit for your store, and may never have become customers in any event. But if you are losing a large number of first-time visitors who should have been your best customers, chances are that the home page is disappointing, rather than welcoming, to those who arrive.

To increase your click-through rate, your site must offer instant gratification in terms of comprehension and clarity, and must do everything possible to fit the messaging to the visitor as quickly as possible. If a customer is encouraged and stimulated to click into the site at least one step further, the chances improve dramatically that they will stay long enough to at least become familiar with your site. And when that happens, chances also improve greatly that they will buy soon.

Your first merchandising task is just to optimize your site's usability; all obstacles should be removed from the selling process. It makes no sense to annoy or frustrate the customer with unnecessary material or procedures, especially while he is in the checkout line.

Another task is to make sure that you are providing the information, features, and service that customers expect, in order to facilitate the sale. For example, according to Forrester research, 44% of customers believe that offering a close-up shot of the product would help convince them to buy. Forrester gives the example of llbean.com which lost one customer to REI because it didn't show a picture of the soles of its hiking boots —simple content that turned out to be crucial to the purchase decision. PricewaterhouseCoopers conducted a study to discover which features are likely to increase online purchasing. The results are shown in chart 1.

Features likely to Increase Online Purchasing

Feature	% of Shoppers Indicating Feature May Increase Purchasing
"Close-up" product images	44%
Product availability	39%
Product comparison guides	34%
Search Function	30%
1-800 Customer Service Number	25%
Consumer Reviews / Evaluations	24%
Catalog Quick Order	24%

Chart 1

Only two thirds of the Web stores Forrester evaluated provided sufficient content for detail-hungry shoppers, while just 40% offered interactive tools or integrated customer service into the site. JCPenney forced customers to select a size range *before* seeing whether items were offered in the colors they want and didn't assure buyers that a product was in stock until halfway through checkout. One third of the sites insisted that users enter a credit card *before* being shown the shipping price—a practice known to stop some buyers cold.

But once your have your mechanics down solid, and good usability practices throughout your shop, it is time to start fine-tuning your online merchandising. At each stage along the path to purchase, you have unique opportunities to message to the user and to engage your merchandising skills. Use all your personalization resources to enhance merchandising as well.

The following are some tips and suggestions for merchandising on key parts of the optimal path to purchase, and a few other important pages.

Splash Page

The splash page (fig. 2) is a welcoming page, a top-level "landing area" which loads quickly, introduces either generic or targeted branding information and sometimes promotional or other merchandising information. It is not necessarily part of the optimal path to purchase. Its primary function is to be a safe, quick-responding first page that immediately alerts the customer that the site is up and running the moment he arrives at his URL.

Splash pages are usually designed to only be seen by people visiting the site for the very first time. When the customer returns, cookies will often re-direct them past the splash page, to a personalized home page, or a tailored landing page of some kind. If the customer chooses to bookmark your site, they will usually bookmark the first functional page, not the splash page. So splash pages are often ignored after the first visit, regardless of how you may have programmed them.

Figure 2

Best Practices

- It's often a good idea to put a link to a product in a major promotion, a top seller, or key promotional item directly on the splash page. The faster the customer clicks past this page and into the site, the more likely he will be to stay and shop. If the customer clicks from the splash page directly to a product page or even to a shopping cart, then so much the better.

- Make it crystal clear where and how to enter the "real" site directly from the splash page. Don't force customers to stall at this page, waiting for a timed relay to forward them. Even if there is information you'd like for them to read on this page first, give them a clear, well marked path forward. If they are in a hurry to begin shopping, don't impede them!

- The splash page should load very quickly: if it doesn't, it's not really a Splash page. More complex pages might more accurately be called "alternate home pages" or "alternate landing pages." If that's what this page truly is, then make sure that it has the full complement of navigational tools and other essentials. But if your site needs a true splash page for some reason, then make it load fast, fast, fast!

Home Page

The home page (fig. 3) is the top level organization page of your site. It is the site's face and main road map. Looking at the home page, the customer should be able to get an idea of where to begin looking for anything he or she might want from the site. The home page establishes the conventions for the universal navigational elements that should be present in recognizable form all throughout the site. The navigation should distinguish between major product divisions, and supplementary links to information, such as company information, content areas, policy notices, etc.

Best Practices

- The links to your products or services should be prominent, easy to interpret, and of a limited number, usually no more than 5-7, with nine at the outside. Don't make the home page too cluttered: leave some white space to direct the eye and suggest the importance of key elements.

- Keep important navigation tools as near the top as possible. Make sure any other vital elements that the customer must see are within the viewable area of the most common browser window size. This is also known as "above the fold".

Merchandising Tips

- Use personalization to customize messaging text, lifestyle images, kickers, sort orders, headlines, and even branding images.

- Leave enough white space to direct the eyes to the prominent headlines, kickers, or message text. One of the worst things you can do is to crowd the home page and overstimulate your customers. They are likely to give up on any attempt to sort the parts that matter to them from those that don't.

- Use size, color, and messaging to emphasize the important features. Customers need "safe landing points" that allow them to find their bearings before they can sort out the information on your pages.

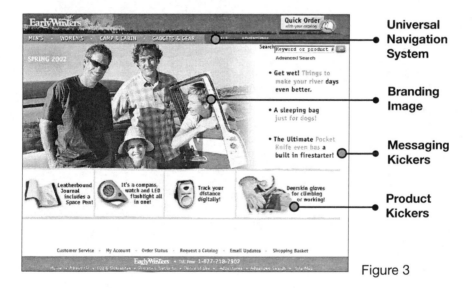

Figure 3

Gateway Page

A gateway page (fig. 4) is an orientation page for customers entering a large department of your online store. Gateway pages serve very much like a home page for a specific section of your store. For example, a department store might have separate sections for clothing, hardware, housewares, electronics, and furniture. An online store would have separate gateway pages for each of these. Each gateway page will have its own navigation tools and navigation scheme based upon the organization of that department.

When robustly designed, a gateway page can stand independent of the home page, functioning as a mini-site in itself. Well-designed universal navigation which is consistent throughout the site adds to the effectiveness of this tactic; every gateway becomes just as effective as the home page, but is targeted more specifically for that subset of your products.

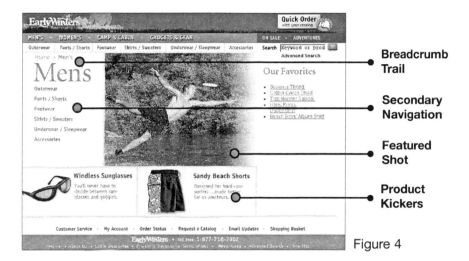

Figure 4

The gateway page serves to transmit the atmosphere the merchant is trying to evoke for that specific area of the site. The gateway page has its own messaging areas, and these will vary from those on the home page. The gateway pages are often used to introduce tools, kickers, and promotions, all of which are liable to be specific to that particular category. This also might be the place to bring in content such as articles and special bargains, and anything else that contributes to satisfying the customers' goals. The gateway page is the staging area for any category-specific elements of the site that can be used to intrigue and interest the user.

Gateway pages are not limited to just the categories visible in the primary navigation. If your categories are limited strictly by product description, you may be missing some good merchandising opportunities. You can create secondary product categories which, though very abstract, greatly appeal to a large number of customers and can stimulate sales in new ways. Such secondary categories will benefit from having a full gateway page of their own too.

For example, if I am selling candles, I might have categories and gateways for tapers, candle holders, aromatherapy candles, water candles, etc. But if a large proportion of my customers buys candles for romantic occasions, it might be worthwhile to construct a gateway dedicated to products from across the board that can help create a romantic mood. Even if a line of candles is primarily classified under aromatherapy, having them displayed with romantic candlesticks and combined in an extravagant way with a number of other candles from all over the site will affect how the customers view those aromatherapy candles. This can stimulate sales to a new group of people.

Alternately, if I wanted to create a sub-gateway for "Relaxation," I would bring in lifestyle imagery to create a mood that supports this idea. Because I am trying to sell by mood, in this case "relaxation", then I want to create relaxation, show relaxation, talk about relaxation, provide product kickers that evoke relaxation, and possibly even create message kickers that take the customer to written content about relaxing.

These sub-gateways are not part of your main product categories. Instead of being accessed through your main navigation bar, these are often given their own separate navigation buttons on your home page, and even on other main gateway pages. The result is a whole new product category and method of selling based upon the products' intended purposes and not their inherent characteristics.

Best Practices

- Your main navigation elements should be identical to those used on higher level pages, so the customer can easily back out of their current location.

- Use clear sub-navigation to keep track of the current location within the category. Many sites use a supplementary navigation bar. Others use a "bread crumb trail" (a small, plain-text, sequential list of the sections of the site a customer went through to get to the current page.)

- Provide a clear listing of subcategories so the customer can always know what else is available.

- Feature products and/or content in prominent places on your gateway pages.

Merchandising Tips

- Beware of making too much content available from your gateway pages. It could distract shoppers from their intended purpose, pulling them off the optimal path to purchase and jeopardizing the sale.

- Use customer favorites or bestseller lists to highlight popular products.

- Use kickers to featured products and/or product groups. This will draw attention to them and make it easier for customers to find these featured items.

- Experiment with ensemble selling on your gateways. Use a product shot that shows related items in use together, and link this to a page where the customer can buy any or all of them.

- Create gateways for not only your primary categories, but also for categories based upon lifestyle, events, and other more subjective characteristics.

Index Page

Index pages (fig. 5) are placed immediately after the gateway pages, and serve to introduce a category's individual products. Index pages can also be used to collect and present products found through the site's search feature. In the example below we see a category index page for Early Winters' men's outerwear. Small images called thumbnails introduce each product and are linked to each product's detailed description page.

Figure 5

   A company with a large selection of products may find that it has dozens of products to show on its category index pages. Thumbnails could be presented on one large scrolling index page or on a number of "horizontal" pages that each show a limited number of products and can be clicked through in succession. The downside to horizontal paging is that customers may only click through a few pages before losing patience or interest. The upside is that each new page has the potential to refresh messaging, or feature a particular product. Also, every page is consistent in size and layout with all the others, helping maintain a uniform look and feel on the site.

You can actually combine your category index page with your category gateway page by replacing some of your merchandising slots on your gateway page with product thumbnails. Though you lose some merchandising opportunities, the advantage of removing one level of hierarchy from your purchase path may be worth it. This kind of combination is probably best done on the sub-category indexes; at that point you would have already had a gateway and a sub-gateway on which to put featured product announcements and other merchandising material. By the time the customer gets to the sub-index, she deserves to stop travelling around your site and see some products.

One exciting use of the index page is to present certain products in a way that highlights or emphasizes them. This is called product dominance. Typical product dominance tactics include using a larger product shot in place of a small thumbnail, adding supplementary images that show off the product's features, and so forth. Dominant products are usually placed to the left of the other products on the page since people read from left to right. Pages that use product dominance should be dynamically created or at the very least be easy to administer, so you can strategically select the dominant product for each page based on your business rules and personalization efforts.

Best Practices

- As suggested in Chapter 6 (Product Categorization), use sort order and dominance to increase the likelihood of placing the desired product on one of the first index list pages.

- Use dominance to point out featured or high-relevance items in the list, and to create visual interest and variety.

- Follow the same rules with sub-categories as you do with main categories. The more your procedures become standardized and consistent, the faster your customers will pick up on it, and the more quickly they will become comfortable with shopping and spending at your site.

- When practical, offer buy buttons or links directly from the category index page. If a customer is already certain that she wants to buy, why make her wait while the product page loads?

- Avoid linking to content from the category index page. On these pages, the customer is scanning quickly for items to catch her attention. Don't slow her down or stop her with unnecessary distractions.

Merchandising Tips

- Help define the way the customer views your product by naming categories, sub categories, and sub-sub-categories in an evocative and helpful way, and then use those names in supplementary links, breadcrumb navigation, and content areas.

- Use some of the same messaging, kickers, and other merchandising on the category index page as you do the gateway. Use this to augment the targeted merchandising assigned to that gateway.

Product Page

Product pages (fig. 6) are the online equivalent of handing the product to the customer so he can examine it more closely. The customer is rewarded with a larger picture of the item and is often provided with links to detailed product information. The page may also include links to pertinent content pages, ensemble pages, accessory products, cross-sells, up-sells, and similar merchandising features.

This is the page on which the "buy" button is most prominently displayed. It is on the product pages where all of a product's features – size, color, accessories, etc. – can be selected. Loyalty tools such as wish lists and gift bookmarks can be

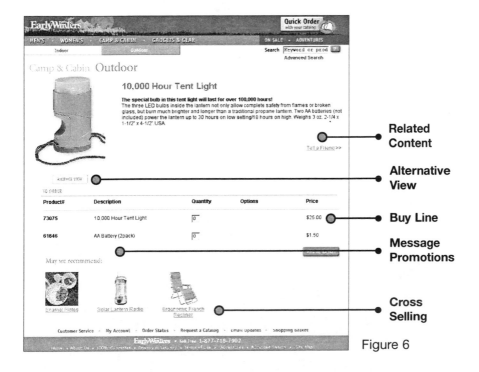

Figure 6

activated from this page. Product pages offer rich and varied merchandising opportunities, and are one of the best places to put customer personalization and segmentation to good use. However, it is important to remember above all that this page should be functional.

This is where the real selling capabilities of your site get tested. The page must load quickly, function flawlessly, and respond instantly when the customer clicks on that buy button. The customer should be immediately rewarded with a clear indication that his purchase is under way, whether you show the updated contents of the cart or you simply serve up a page that announces that the selected product has been added to the cart.

Best Practices

- The buy buttons should be in a consistent, easy-to-locate position throughout all similar pages on the site. They should be "above the fold" – within the viewable area of a standard size browser window—and easy to see and understand how to use.

- When linking from a product page to pages with extended product information or articles, make sure that the target page offers a quick link directly back to the originating product. The product page is usually the decision page; it is where the customer decides to buy or to move on. A balance must be struck between supporting the product with information and the potential for jeopardizing the sale by distracting him.

- The product page is a key element to the buying process, so make sure its underlying architecture is rock solid. The first things that load should be the main product image and the buy button since they are the primary reason for the page's existence. Secondary images can be allowed to load more slowly.

Merchandising Tips:
Use all your arsenal of personalization and segmentation data to choose the right

- cross-sells

- up-sells

- accessories

- articles

- other products

- sizing charts

- gift list

- wish list

- reminders

- reorders

- and any other customizable elements your site may provide.

Content Page

Content pages (fig. 7) offer information about products, including details about their ingredients, materials, and durability. Content can also include articles, survey results, warranty information, customer reviews, and a wide range of other types of information. Finding the right balance between information pages and selling pages is critical for a site. With too little information, customers are less likely to buy. But too much information can distract your customers and add work for your staff without necessarily increasing sales.

Figure 7

Your content should always support the selling process. If your product page includes a link to a related article, include an easy link back to that product page. Some sites may even put a product kicker and buy button on the content page itself.

Best Practices

- Content should reinforce the branding, feel, and messaging of the rest of the site.

- Content must support or be related to products in some way.

- Include links back to products or category pages.

- Make it easy for the customer to find appropriate articles. Consider supplementing your site's search capabilities with content search capabilities.

- Content should be updated on a regular schedule, and customers should be given some idea of when this occurs.

- Maintain an archive of old content, so customers can return and find it.

- Once you have assigned a URL to a content page, do not change it. This way, if a customer has bookmarked it, she can always find it again easily.

- Add only as much content to your site as your staff can keep up-to-date.

Merchandising Tips

- Offer a bookmark function to your registered customers so they can store their link preferences. This will encourage registration.

- Offer kickers and deals related to the content viewed.

- Put buy buttons and product links directly on content pages. But be careful not to include too many product links. Content pages should be there to educate and interest your customers, and too much selling will detract from this and clutter up your page.

Shopping Cart Page

The shopping cart page (fig. 8) provides a summary of the current shopping session and the total cost of the order. It provides an easy way for the customer to keep track of their purchases. Merchandising on the shopping cart pages can be your best chance to communicate up-sells and other special deals. It is also a tactically important place to use personalization to counter the tendency of some customers to abandon their carts and leave the site without completing checkout. If clickstream analysis, segmentation data, or other indicators seem to suggest that the customer may be likely to leave without checking out, special incentives can be offered to entice him. If a customer is close to meeting a volume discount level, this is an appropriate and effective place to communicate it to the buyer. If the customer is $10 away from qualifying for free shipping, this is a great place to tell him that, too, and to serve up kickers for items near $10.00 to help him get up into the discount bracket. However, do remember to keep the main purpose of checkout and basket pages clear and unambiguous. These pages (especially the checkout pages) should be uncluttered, easy to understand, rock-solid in their programming, and quick to load.

Figure 8

Best Practices

- Pages should load quickly.

- Program the site to serve up error messages that appear whenever a customer has filled something out incorrectly or incompletely. Include clear instructions and a back button to make it easy for the customer to correct any mistakes.

- Include a save order button that allows the customer to save his order, leave your site, and return at a later time to pick up where he left off.

- Create a cookie file for each visitor that is updated every time she adds something to her shopping cart. This "persistent cookie basket" will allow her to return to the same shopping cart with the same items in case her browser crashes, her connection is interrupted, or other problems force her to temporarily leave the site.

- Show details like size, color, and any other options for every item in the cart and allow the customer to change these options from within the shopping cart.

- Prominently display your help tools, such as your 800 number, your link to live online chat assistance, and so forth.

- If you provide links on your shopping cart page to product, store policy, or help pages, make sure they are programmed in such a way that the contents of the cart are retained.

- Allow the customer to adjust the quantity of each item right on the cart page, and include the order's running total and a remove button.

Merchandising Tips

- Notify the customer when she approaches a "trigger" total, such as "spend $10 more and get free shipping for your whole order."

- Detect behaviors that may indicate a shopping cart is about to be abandoned, and offer special incentives to convince the customer to complete the sale.

- If errors are detected, offer links to customer service sections, live help, or 800 numbers.

- If the customer abandons the cart and clicks to leave the site, offer to save her current selections so she does not have to hunt them all down and re load her cart when she returns.

Checkout Page

The checkout pages (fig. 9) are a series of pages that guide the shopper through the final steps of the shopping session. During this phase the customer enters the shipping address, indicates shipping preferences, selects gift wrap, and so forth. Checkout pages must be very carefully programmed to handle all inputs correctly and to deal with any errors intelligently and efficiently. Checkout pages should be uncluttered, easy to understand, and quick to load. Many of the same cautions and best practices for the shopping cart apply here too. You should make it possible for a customer to make a purchase without creating a permanent account. Do not create an artificially high minimum order as this will alienate your customers and cost you sales.

Figure 9

One question over which there is still a big debate is whether or not to up-sell during the checkout process. Many analysts recommend against it if it means adding any unnecessary complication. The goal, after all, is to complete the sale and you do not want to jeopardize that. But some e-tailers find it very useful, and in the end, every site will need to carefully weigh the advantages and disadvantages before making a final decision. If the real numbers in your store suggest that it adds to the overall order size and does not prevent customers from successfully completing their sale, then for your site it will be a valuable tool.

Best Practices

- Carefully consider whether or not to up-sell during checkout.

- Allow customers to make purchases without creating a permanent account.

- Make only the bare minimum of personal information absolutely required.

- Whenever possible, use dialog boxes or menus to allow the customer to auto-fill any information that you have already collected, whether from address books, registration, etc.

- Show choice selections for items (for ex. size chosen, color, quantity, fabric, etc.)

- When possible, allow the customer to change choices from within the checkout process

- Design and program checkout pages to load quickly

- Program the site so serve up error messages that appear whenever a customer has filled something out incorrectly or incompletely. Include clear instructions and a back button to make it easy for the customer to correct any mistakes.

- Include a save order button that allows the customer to save his order, leave your site, and return at a later time to pick up where he left off.

- Create a cookie file for each visitor that automatically saves her order. Similar to the "persistent cookie basket" used with the shopping basket, this allows her to return to the same point in the checkout process with the same items in case her browser crashes, her connection is interrupted, or other problems force her to temporarily leave the site.

- Show details like size, color, and any other options for every item and allow the customer to change these options during the checkout process.

- Prominently display your help tools, such as your 800 number, your link to live online chat assistance, and so forth.

- If you provide links to product, store policy, or help pages, make sure they are programmed in such a way that the shopping cart retains whatever contents were in it so the customer can return and easily complete the order.

- Allow the customer to adjust the quantity of each item during checkout, and include the order's running total and a remove button.

Thank You Page

The Thank You page (fig. 10) loads immediately upon the successful completion of an order, and confirms for the customer that her order is being processed. A thank you page is an important part of your site's feedback. For the customer, it is validation that her efforts have been worthwhile and that her order is proceeding as it should. For the online merchant, it is an opportunity to reinforce its relationship with the customer and to increase the odds of generating future sales. At the moment when the customer has completed a transaction, you know as much about that person as you realistically ever could, even if that customer is not establishing a permanent account. At a minimum, you know of at least one product she liked well enough to purchase. That may not be much, but it is a start.

Figure 10

There are a couple of ways to merchandise on the thank you or exit page. One is simply to include a personalized ad or kicker in the page. This would link the customer to a product page, and potentially start the buy cycle all over again. A more streamlined approach is thank you page plus marketing. In this kind of merchandising, the thank you page confirms the transaction, but also includes promotional copy, a product thumbnail or kicker, some instructions, and a purchase link. If the customer clicks the purchase button, then a confirmation dialog box pops up, and if the customer confirms this addition, that item is immediately added to the former order. The customer is presented with a second thank you page confirming the second transaction and giving the new total charge.

There is no need to send the customer back through the checkout process. At that moment you already have all of the information necessary to complete the sale. This allows for true "impulse buy" gratification.

Just make sure your messaging is absolutely clear about what is going on and what they can expect. Do not skip the final confirmation dialog box, or you are liable to get irate customers who felt they were forced to buy because they didn't understand your messaging.

Best Practices

- Write your thank you messages carefully so they support your company's identity and brand.

- Be polite and helpful. Even when using more aggressive sales techniques, make sure the customer's perception of the interaction will stay positive.

- If your site has a post-order tracking section or some other valuable customer service feature, link directly to it from your thank you page. This introduces new customers to this valuable resource and reinforces customer confidence by giving them a window into the fulfillment and shipping process. Sometimes post-order follow-up information is included right in the thank you page.

Merchandising Tips

- Personalize the thank you page with offers calculated to appeal to customers according to their membership in a customer group. This could bring them right back into the site to make another purchase. Such offers should be fairly subtle, so your customers don't feel like they are being dragged back into the store.

- You could provide links to articles and other fun or interesting content. This is an excellent way to reinforce your relationship with your customer.

- If you want to be more aggressive, you can up-sell or cross-sell beyond the thank you page. You could program your site so that when customers click past the thank you page, a new dialog box pops up with some appropriate offer.

Chapter 5 Links
Dynamic Merchandising and Messaging, Part 1

Merchandising and Messaging links are inlcuded at the end of Chapter 6.

6

Online Merchandising Applied

In this chapter I will discuss:

- What are product categories and why are they important on a website?

- What are the three types of product categorization and how are each of them used best?

- Product categories greatly influence the navigation of your website. How will you determine the best category structure?

- How many products can you place on any given page without overwhelming the customer?

- What is sort order and how does it enhance the site's ability to sell?

- What are lifestyle, event-based, and solution-based categorization?

Categories

In a report titled *The Best of Retail Site Design*, Forrester Research found that e-commerce customers typically began their shopping trips by trying to find the most promising product category. Some were thwarted by vaguely worded tabs and toolbars, like the Amazon.com shopper who couldn't figure out if cordless drills were located in the Electronics section or Home Improvement.

Now that I've covered the optimal path to purchase and defined some of the basic tasks of merchandising, I'd like to focus in on product categories. This chapter will cover how the division of your products into various groupings contributes to, and benefits from, your site's merchandising and messaging.

The first thing a human does when faced with a lot of new information is to try to organize it. We divide the information into groups, and give the groups nicknames. As we encounter new things, we drop them into the conceptual buckets we've already set up, unless something just doesn't fit anywhere, at which point we have to create a new bucket.

On a website, those categories usually represent your major navigational tools (fig. 1). To be most effective, those main category structures should be plainly and appropriately presented. By that, I mean they should not be tucked away under a hot button or in a pull-down menu, where you have to click in order to view those categories.

Figure 1

Main category buttons should be plainly visible right on the home page. Do not force the customer to parse the whole page and find hidden navigational elements before they can understand your organizational scheme. Making the main categories obvious and visible means that the first glance from the new visitor rewards him with at least a cursory understanding of your whole site.

That understanding stimulates further exploration. The first click is the hardest sell. Even if the customer chooses to click on a kicker or featured product first, a good navigation scheme means that they will leave the home page already confident that they will be able to negotiate the site.

Using Categories to Shape Perception

By grouping your products or services into a small, manageable number of conceptual buckets, you do part of the mental work for the customer ahead of time. And by doing it well, you also affect what the customers will think of your site from then on.

If you arrange your products into easily usable groupings that make sense, the customer is likely to accept them as they are and not spend any time or energy reorganizing your site within their own mind. By choosing how to define yourself, you are literally exerting some measure of control over how the customer thinks.

There is a danger here however: if the customer already arrives at your site with a clear, well-developed set of pre-conceived conceptual buckets, he may resist adopting yours. If you try to change too radically the way that he already thinks, you may create so much discomfort that he leaves your site for another he feels himself more in tune with. There are ways to gradually introduce new perspectives, but the initial introduction to your site, on the home page, is probably not the place to severely challenge the customer! Therefore, it's important to be aware of how the majority of your customers think about your product line and create your categories accordingly.

But even taking steps to avoid conflict with your customer's previous attitudes and preconceptions, there is still quite a lot of latitude for shading, shaping, and guiding the customer. Choose your categories with care: they will affect everything else on the site from the home page down. They will dictate your navigational scheme, and will affect how you merchandise your site at nearly every following stage.

Product categorization can be done in a number of ways, from the superficial to the very deep. The three types of categorization that I'll be discussing in this chapter are:

- Primary,

- Secondary, and

- Dynamic Product Groups

All types have their uses, and should be used in conjunction to really help customers find what they are looking for. Different methods work for different kinds of shoppers, and by combining all of these techniques with segmenting and personalization, you will maximize your opportunities to reach out to your customers, and you will help yourself by helping them find what they need and want.

Type 1: Primary Categorization

Primary Categorization could also be thought of as your top level organization. Primary categories most closely resemble the major departments in a retail store. This level of category will be the most overt, obvious organizational structure for your site. You should make these categories accessible to your customers at all times by making them a prominent part of your site's universal navigation.

Therefore, it is imperative to put a lot of care into forming these categories. Your site will depend upon them for your navigation, interface, design, and marketing messaging. New customers will scan these headings upon first visiting your site. If a customer can not immediately relate to them, and instantly have some idea how they relate to the products they came to your site for, then you will find a disproportionately high number of new visitors never make it past your home page. In serving the Web surfing population, you must be aware that first impressions are everything; if that first page is not comprehensible within a very few seconds, your potential customer will click away.

Your categories are the first tool most customers look to as they try to figure out your site. Some topics to consider when constructing the top level category structure of your site are:

a) Number of categories

b) Number of thumbnails on index pages

c) Using sub-categories

d) Sort orders and dominance

Number of Categories
Research has shown that humans are most comfortable keeping track of no more than five to seven items at a time, and nine is an upper limit. The user's brain can only digest so many things at one time and if you put too many buttons on the page, the customer won't know where to click Seven to nine is also a practical limit on how many buttons or labels will usually fit across the width of the traditional maximized browser on a common-width monitor.

On your site, clicking on a tab or button in the navigation bar is analogous to going directly to a specific department of a store such as the menswear or the shoe section (fig. 2).

If you follow the 5-7 rule, one category will be about one-fifth to one-seventh of your store. It's a broad category, but it serves to give a shopper a place to start. If your store has many products, each category page will be a gateway or mini-home page, with its own messaging. If your store has few products, clicking on a category may take the shopper directly to a product index page.

Number of Thumbnails on an Index Page
Best practices for index pages indicate that they also present only a manageable amount of information. The index page may show anywhere from four to sixteen items at once, depending on the size of the thumbnail images. (fig. 3) The Men's

Figure 2

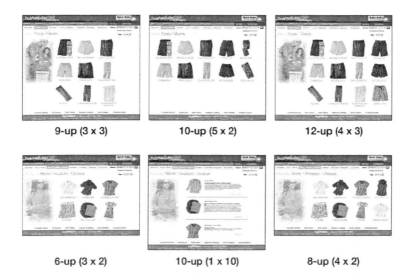

9-up (3 x 3)   10-up (5 x 2)   12-up (4 x 3)

6-up (3 x 2)   10-up (1 x 10)   8-up (4 x 2)

Figure 3

Pants/Shorts index page from Early Winters (fig. 4) shows eight products. Ideally each category will have 12 to 20 items in it. Twenty-five or thirty is acceptable, thirty or above is pretty high and anything more than forty-five or fifty is probably much too high. You should choose an index page arrangement and thumbnail style that shows your products off in their best light, but also keeps the number of index pages to a manageable level.

Figure 4

So, if you in fact do have 10,000 products, then you may need to allow more products per category, or split your categories into subcategories as described in the next section.

There also should not be too few products in any one given category because then there won't be enough of a selection. This makes it difficult to merchandise and can also give your customers the impression that you don't have enough to offer.

Depending on the number of products shown per page, it would take from around 3 to 12 clicks to page entirely through a category's full set of index pages. This upper end is a bit excessive. You will want to divide your products into categories in such a way that your store seems well-stocked, but also so your customer does not have to page endlessly through index page after index page looking for a specific item.

These conceptual constraints are also very practical physical constraints when it comes to designing your pages. Customers tend to ignore items located off the edges of their screen or "below the fold," and pages need to load quickly. Putting too much on any one index page is likely to break either or both of these rules, in addition to overwhelming your customer.

Using Sub-Categories

So, doing the math, if your main site should be divided into no more than 9 categories, and each category should have no more than (and most probably less than) 50 items, what can you do if you have in excess of 450 products?

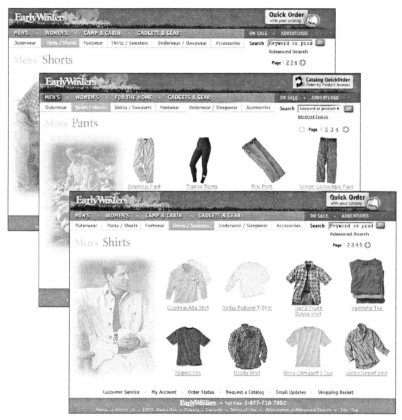

Figure 5

The answer is sub-categories. Subcategories, and even sub-sub-categories have their uses. Each level of categorization allows for more targeted messaging and merchandising on the index or gateway pages for that category; and each selection the customer makes gives you a little more information about the person making these choices. Figure 5 illustrates an instance where a single large category for men's pants and shorts was split into two smaller sub-categories, one for pants and one for shorts.

However, the down-side to multiple categorization levels is that increases the number of clicks the customer must make before he finds the item he is looking for end is able to buy it. In other words, each hierarchical level lengthens your optimal path to purchase. Longer paths tend to be less successful, as each hurdle a customer must jump before finding his goal winnows out a proportion of the less patient. Your web design must constantly perform a balancing act between various limiting factors such as these.

One of the ways to counter the effects of paging through many index pages is to use two merchandising techniques to improve the customer's chances of finding something interesting as early as possible.

Sort Order

The first technique is sort order. Sort order is any method by which you control which products appear first on a page. Sort orders can be used to prioritize anything, from index pages, to kickers, to cross-sells and accessories. Depending on the website development software available to you, you may have only one sort order, a choice of sort orders that must be applied site-wide, or even different sort orders that can be applied to each individual customer based on a personalized factors such as stated preferences, market segment, collaborative filtering, or clickstream data.

Some easy types of sort orders include:

- Alphabetical,

- SKU order, and

- Price.

While many customers find alphabetical good for quick location of items they are familiar with, and price good for the bargain hunter, SKU is rarely useful or even meaningful to anyone but the merchant, and should probably be avoided except in rare cases.

Some more sophisticated sort orders include:

- Best sellers,

- Promotional or marketing campaign items,

- High margin, and

- Seasonal

Finally, if your site uses more advanced kinds of collaborative filtering, clickstream analysis, or can evaluate a logged-in visitor from self-reported tastes and other registration data, you might even be able to offer completely personalized sort orders, based on criteria specific to a particular visitor, at a particular time and date. For example, if a registered customer has provided you with a birth date for his son and during this visit he is searching in your toy section, the site might automatically prioritize the toy list to place toys popular with that child's age group nearest the top. If your products are associated with keywords, you may be able to offer sort lists prioritized for a customer's:

- Favorite color or fabric

- Age group

- Size range

- Brand preference

- Income level

- Or any number of other personalized weightings.

In any of these cases, the main purpose is to make sure that you work as hard as you can to make it as likely as possible that the customer will find at least one product that interests him or her in the first, or at least the second, index page visited.

Dominance

Another technique that can help to ensure that the customer is kept interested and stimulated, and also to increase his chances of finding an interesting product quickly, is dominance. This refers to the practice of setting up a product index page in such a way that one product is featured over the others. The merchant can select the dominant product through any of the methods mentioned above. The dominant product will have a larger thumbnail and sometimes expanded information. By making at least one product appear larger, the customer has something to look at on every page that is more colorful and more detailed. If personalization is employed to make sure that the featured product is also more likely to be of interest to the customer, the product's size helps to bring the customer's attention to it. Used in conjunction with sort order so the dominant product appears first, dominance can be a very effective merchandising technique.

Type 2: Secondary Categories: Lifestyle, Event-Based (Thematic), or Solution-Based Categories

If Primary categorization is analogous to the departments in a store, Secondary categorization is similar to storefront displays, seasonal aisles, in-store showrooms, or the catalog "spread." These categories may also be available to your customers on the universal navigation area of your site, but they should be given a less prominent placement than the Primary categories. In some cases it may be appropriate to place your Secondary categories in a pulldown menu on the universal navigation bar, which keeps them accessible without adding too much visual clutter.

The purpose of Secondary categories is to stimulate the customer by grouping your products differently from the way they are grouped in your Primary, or top level category structure. As discussed earlier in this chapter, your chances of converting a visitor into a buyer are significantly improved if you have categorized your products in a way that is in line with the way he thinks about your product offering. Hopefully, your Primary category structure will serve this purpose for the majority of your customers. But there are always those customers who see things just a bit differently and may not be engaged by your top level category structure. Secondary categories are your way of reaching out to those customers.

Secondary categories can be divided into three main types:

a) Lifestyle

b) Event(or theme)-based

c) Solution-oriented

These categories can be presented through campaign landing pages, a permanent part of the site's universal navigation structure, supplementary gateways, or special pages generated just for an individual user. With the proper software, these secondary category gateways or index pages can be turned on and off as needed, or be integrated into the permanent structure of the site as a whole.

Lifestyle Marketing

Lifestyle marketing establishes an idea or an identity, and groups together products that support that idea or are of interest to that identity. The goal is to organize the products around an idea that draws the customer in and makes them identify with the products. Ideally, several identities will be represented, providing different groups of customers with tailored lifestyle gateways. This can be something as simple as "Teen Girl" versus "Professional Woman". It could be a complex idea such as mothers with preemie babies versus mothers weaning their infants. Sportswear could be grouped into styles appealing to the mature enthusiast (featuring sports such as health-walking and golf) and entirely different gateways for younger populations interested in extreme sports.

The power of the this marketing tool is that it offers the opportunity to present many of the same products appropriately to the right group, but with the proper spin to show its applicability to this one group. A single white blouse, in its entire range of sizes, could be presented one way, with appropriate jeans in the Teen section, and in another way, with a tweed skirt, in the professional women's section. It's just a white blouse, but it can suit many people and so can your marketing.

And here's a point where the Web has every advantage over the brick-and-mortar store. A physical store has limited space. It has to make compromises, and make choices and live with them. In the traditional clothing store, that white blouse might be carried in petite sizes only in the Teen section, and in larger sizes in the Professional Woman corner of the Women's section - if the store even had such a display. But larger teens, and petite women would be forced to go over to the section that didn't otherwise appeal to them, in order to find the product in her size. Once she has left "her" section, the majority of items she is now surrounded with are no longer very appealing, and the chances of coming across more items just by browsing have gone way down.

Stores have to make these kinds of compromises all the time, because they have limited shelf space and very limited display space. But on the Web, your potential display area is nearly infinite, and since none of the items have a physical location on the Web at all, every product can be anywhere and everywhere, all at once, as needed.

In clothing stores as in grocery stores, certain popular items have always been double stocked. The same chips might be placed in the beer section as in the snack aisle. The same brand and make of athletic shoe, but in different colors, might be available in adult and youth departments. But with limited space, only the most popular and/or high margin products can benefit from expanded placement. On the Web, there are no such constraints.

An example of a lifestyle marketing gateway occurs on NormThompson.com. One of its permanent categories is "Travel." Its sub-categories include Women's Travel, Men's Travel, Luggage, and Travel Accessories. Many of the same items available in the Women's Apparel section are also gathered into the women's subsection of the Travel Gateway. In the Travel Gateway will be clothes specifically chosen to be versatile, easy to pack, easy to clean, and resistant to wrinkling. Rather than having to choose which products to either double-stock or leave out of either subsection, both sections can easily include all the products, in all the sizes, which fit into both product groupings.

Thematic or Event-Based Categories

This is a conceptual grouping that assembles products according to the way in which they are commonly used. Groups can be based on an event, such as a holiday. They can also be focused on any common idea, such as a particular room of the house (bedroom vs. kitchen), a particular meal (breakfast vs. dinner), a season (spring vs. fall) or other natural unifying themes.

Let's look a how a brick-and-mortar furniture store might arrange things according to theme. Rather than putting all rugs in one aisle and all tables in another, they might choose to arrange all items by room: one spread for the bedroom and another for the kitchen. Both groups might include rugs and tables, but the kitchen category would have only rugs suitable for the high-traffic and high-soil conditions in the kitchen. The kitchen group would also include all tables appropriate for the kitchen or breakfast nook. In contrast, the bedroom section would include only the softer, more elegant rugs, and night stands, end tables, and vanities.

Many online stores that arrange their products into logical groupings also have a Seasonal category where they display items from any other category when they are appropriate for a seasonal promotion. A clothing store is likely to group a range of varying products. During the spring, a collection of swimsuits, cover-ups, sun hats, light skirts, tote bags, and sandals might all appear together on on one page, even though they could be found separately throughout many different sections of the site. This selection would be replaced in the late summer with a fall line-up of sweaters, wool skirts, knit hats, and so forth.

Several good online marketers of home furnishings use Shop by Room, a feature which gathers together furnishings and accessories appropriate for specific rooms of a house. This emulates the showroom of the furniture store mentioned above.

Other appropriate themes may lead to products being grouped according to special events, such as a Fourth of July barbecue or Super Bowl party.

The merchandising advantages to thematic grouping are considerable:

- Items can be shown in appropriate settings, increasing their appeal.

- Displaying complementary products in close proximity will stimulate customer interest in these products and increase sales.
  items that work well together.

- Customers do not have to sort through pages of un-related products to find items that work well together.

Solution-Based Themes

Some themes grow not from a particular identity or common use, but from a problem that the customer might wish to solve, or a goal he or she is trying to achieve. A drugstore site might offer an Allergy gateway, on which are gathered a variety of items that treat, comfort, prevent, and deal with allergies. Humidifiers, air filters, medication, even pet dander treatments might all be offered on one gateway. On Ouch.com, a health and medical superstore, one of the sub-categories is Pain Management. This section offers a cross-section of products aimed at treating pain, such as massage tools and sleeping pads, and also offers a selection of sub-sub-categories that might be appropriate, such as Magnetic Therapy, Hot Therapy, Cold Therapy, Aroma Therapy, Fracture Care and Casting, and Miscellaneous.

Another example where solution-based categories might be used effectively could be on a site that sells practical household items. The basic categories on the site may be structured around the location of the house where the item would be used (i.e., bedroom, bathroom, kitchen, garage), while secondary categories may be based around household challenges for which customers are seeking solutions: Storage Solutions, Getting Organized, Entertaining with Ease, Cleaning Tips & Tricks, Pest Management, etc.

Type 3: Dynamic Product Groups

In many ways, Dynamic Product Groups are quite similar to Secondary categories in that they stimulate customer interest by providing an alternate way of looking at (and thinking about) your product line. In fact, you may use the very same criteria for creating Dynamic Product Groups that you do for creating Secondary categories (Lifestyle marketing, Event-based, and/or Solution-oriented).

The primary difference between Secondary categories and Dynamic Product Groups is the way that you guide your customers to them. While Secondary categories are typically available from the universal navigation area of the site, customers are directed to Dynamic Product Groups through promotional vehicles such as targeted emails with embedded links, banner ads on affiliate sites, or kickers on your home page and/or category gateway pages.

Dynamic Product Groups are a powerful way to focus your customers' attention on a unique grouping of products that you might not normally display together. While Secondary categories are usually relevant to your customers' shopping experience at any time (and are therefore present in your universal navigation area), Dynamic Product Groups are flexible enough that you may change them monthly, weekly, or even daily! For example, a site may create a "Wild for Red" product group just before Valentine's Day that contains all of the items they sell that are available in red. Or, a housewares site may create a product group around Earth Day that features all of their environmentally-friendly products.

Ensemble Selling

Another term I'd like to introduce before wrapping up this chapter is Ensemble Selling. This refers to the practice of associating products into outfits, or other functional groupings, just as a retail store will dress up a mannequin in carefully selected clothing to show how nicely all works together. These are mini-displays, a chance for you to let your online customer see closely-related items together. Ensembles may share product shots, and may even share product detail pages. Or, ensembles can be gathered together via mini-gateways or campaign pages. Ensembles are a step up from cross-sells and accessory sells; they parallel the attention of an experienced, knowledgeable salesperson, who can suggest items that go well together, help create outfits, and complete the package with the appropriate accessories. Such pages are excellent opportunities to apply personalized merchandising, and really try to give the customer the equivalent of personal attention in your virtual store.

Ensembles can be made up of products from Lifestyle, Event-Based (Thematic), or Solution-Based Categories, or from Dynamic Product Groups. Any set of products that go well together can be turned into an ensemble.

Best Practices for Merchandising Using Categories:

- Give the customer clear, consistent navigation that makes it easy for the customer to keep in mind where on the site hierarchy he or she is, at all times.

- Keep all major navigational elements, important messaging, and buy buttons "above the fold," whenever possible.

- Keep main category navigation to 5-7 "departments," 9 on the outside.

- Divide categories into sub-categories as necessary to keep the number of items in each division to about 12-20, with 50 as an upper limit in most cases.

- Try not to make your hierarchy too deep, as each level added increases the length of your Path to Purchase.

- Choose the number of thumbnails to display on an index page, based on how many products will be in that category. Try to keep the number of pages that a customer will have to "page through" to five or less.

- Use sort order to increase the likelihood that the customer will find something she wants on the first, or possibly second page.

- When appropriate, use dominance to direct attention to a special items on an index page, or to create extra attention and interest in long chains of index pages.

- Use an appropriate mixture of primary and secondary categories, as well as dynamic product groups, that will appeal to as many of your customers as possible.

Chapter 6 Links
Online Merchandising Applied

Merchandising is a very broad topic and you will do well to visit the generalist sites listed for Chapter 2. However, here are a few selected items from some of these sites that might be of use to you.

http://www.wilsonweb.com/
The Wilson Internet
Use the search feature with the words merchandising and messaging

http://search.darwinmag.com/
Darwin Online Magazine
Use the search feature with the words merchandising and messaging

http://www.business2.com/search
Business 2.0
Use this search feature with the word merchandising

http://ecnow.com/Internet_Marketing.htm
ECnow.com
Internet Marketing Techniques

7

Effectively Executing Online Campaigns

In this chapter I will discuss:

- 53% of online buyers visit at least three sites before making a purchase. How are you going to make sure they eventually buy from you?

- Announcing a sale is only one of a wide variety of reasons to conduct a campaign. Some of the best aren't meant to generate short-term sales at all.

- How does personalization fit into an online campaign?

- If you want an effective campaign, know what your goals are up-front. Here are some tips on how to determine them.

- Don't underestimate the potential success of your campaign. Work with your IT department well in advance of the campaign's launch to make sure the systems and bandwidth are in place to handle the load.

- Track, measure, and analyze your results. Here are the key things to watch, and tips on how to interpret them.

Look at Everything as a Campaign

Research by Jupiter Communications indicates that 53% of online buyers visit at least three sites before making a purchase. This shows us two things. First, customers are getting choosy about where they shop and why. Second, simply building a website and expecting it to attract and retain customers is not enough. You have to be proactive about attracting customers to your site.

As in the brick-and-mortar sales world, online businesses benefit from the activity generated by well-constructed sales campaigns. Use your campaigns as a reason to constantly refresh the site, update it, and give it a facelift for new seasons or new holidays. Campaigns keep your site relevant, pertinent, and interesting. The ability of Web tools to collect data about your customers can make your online campaigns far more personalized and effective than is possible for conventional stores.

The online campaign is where your personalization, merchandising, loyalty-building, design, and marketing efforts all come together. In fact, the campaign will touch, in some form, every aspect of your site. Because your site can give you so much measurable data on what customers saw and did before buying, your online campaigns are a unique resource for understanding and satisfying your customers.

The campaign is the living, breathing lifecycle of the e-commerce site. Look at your entire customer communications strategy as a series of campaigns that help you:

- Maintain contact with customers

- Evaluate customer response

- Evaluate sales performance, and

- Provide data for new evaluations

… that lead to the next campaign, starting the process again.

One of your most valuable tools in the online campaign is email. Some comments about the use of email in the campaign are included here, but because email is such a large topic itself, it is treated in far greater detail in a Chapter 13.

Types of Online Campaigns

Because campaigns allow you to apply your business rules, merchandising and personalization to definable and measurable goals, campaigns have an immediate benefit as a driving force in day-to-day site maintenance, affecting images, content, messaging, and kickers. What you learn from a successful campaign can be applied to your site almost immediately. But the long-term effects of a campaign are more profound. Campaigns help with:

- **Customer Acquisition**
  Whether due to an event-based occasion or a special deal, campaigns give you an opportunity to communicate to customers exactly how they can fulfill a need at your site. With a targeted goal and a focused task, a customer's success with a first visit to your site can result in a higher-than average likelihood of conversion to a sale. While having a featured item right on the home page may take up screen real estate that would normally be dedicated to some good broad-based merchandising, having a one-click way to successfully complete that first sale can have a profoundly positive effect in the long run. Once the first sale has been successfully completed, chances are much higher that the customer will return to shop again.

- **Customer Retention**
  When a first visit results in a sale, chances are good that the customer will choose to register. During the subsequent order fulfillment process you will have a number of opportunities to keep in contact with the customer: sending order confirmations, order tracking information, newsletters and the like. Each one of these opportunities gives you yet another chance to message to the customer, show him or her the high quality of your service and the helpful way that you do business, and to reinforce the customer's impression of your site as an establishment worth doing business with. Campaigns can be constructed specifically to enhance customer retention.

- **Customer Loyalty and Satisfaction**
  Some campaigns are specifically intended to increase customer loyalty and satisfaction rather than to sell products. An example might be a campaign built to provide your existing customer base with some special content or a customized discount. Another could be the announcement of "members only" access to a special area of the site: "Because you have been a regular customer we are giving you access to our Preview site where you can view our new fall line."

- **Customer Service Awareness**
  Some campaigns are not designed to push any product in particular or to increase sales directly, but to make your customers aware of the services and facilities you offer. If your site offers webchat with your customer service representatives, phone assistance, bulletin boards, page-pushing

co-browse help, or other special services, you will want your customers to know about it. Ads, contests, and articles on your site may all be part of a campaign to make sure customers know what excellent service you provide.

- **Multi-Channel Promotions**
  A particularly effective type of online campaign is one which promotes your multi-channel capability. In-store advertisements which refer customers to special URLs for a store-related discount, online coupons useful in local stores, discounts online for using a catalog look-up tool, and other types of cross-channel campaigns can help your customers' awareness of the close integration you offer between channels. Studies have shown that customers who use more than one channel tend to buy more, and to buy more often.

- **Event-Related Campaigns**
  Related to the multi-channel campaign is one which uses your online site to promote and improve participation in store-related events. Events can be either online, such as scheduled celebrity chats or a special online gallery exhibition, or off-line such as in-store readings, brand-sponsored concerts and races, and so forth. Use online registration, email notification, calendar notes, event reminders, gateway page ads, and other campaign elements to encourage and reward early sign-up and to increase participation.

- **Improve Sales Conversion**
  Customers reliably have certain needs at certain times of the year. If your site is set up to help the customer meet those needs and save time, more visitors are likely to become buyers. A good example might be the back to-school season. A school supply or office supply site might have lists of the school supplies required by the various state or local school boards. Such a supplier could offer one-click ordering of these collections, organized by school ID district number, to make it easier for students and their parents to get what they need. In addition, the campaign might bring attention to the new school district lookup tool newly available on the site, which lists nearby grade schools by district number, name and address. This kind of convenience will have a positive impact upon sales conversion.

- **Reinforce the Brand**
  The brand reinforcement campaign is aimed at increasing sales indirectly. This sort of campaign may surround a contest, events, special sales, or customer service options, with the aim of supporting the image of your business itself. Success for this campaign would be not in how much product

was moved, but in how many new potential customers became aware of your website, products, and services. A campaign of this sort is an excellent way to inform customers of good inter-channel practices such as cross channel product returns and customer service options.

Useful Components of an Online Marketing Campaign

A major campaign may touch in some fashion nearly everything on your site. The primary tools of a campaign will be those things which directly describe your products, brand, or level of service. But on some level, any part of your site could be useful in making your campaign more effective. Think about how the customer service, content, and navigation elements on your site might contribute to your campaign, especially when running a brand or customer satisfaction campaign.

In most cases, of course, your campaigns will affect product-related content. Here are some of your most powerful online campaign components:

- **Messaging**
  Determine to what level the site's messaging will be affected by the campaign. Messaging integration can be as simple as an advertisement on the home or landing pages, or so complex as to dynamically affect messaging on the whole site.

- **Merchandising**
  Determine to what level your usual merchandising will be affected by the campaign. In many cases, your campaign will take a prominent place, replacing your usual dominant product thumbnails, and affecting sort orders, lifestyle images, cross sells, up-sells, and other parts of your everyday merchandising.

- **Personalization**
  Your personalization capacities should be used to their fullest extent, to support and refine your campaign. Design a version of your campaign for each target group, and decide which sub-section of your campaign-related products should be emphasized for each group. Refine your offers to appeal to the different groups, with targeted campaign messaging for each.

- **Digital Coupons**
  Trackable discount codes, or digital coupons, are an excellent way to deliver a campaign's offer and to track the campaign's effectiveness. Unique codes can be emailed to each target group or applied to differing banner ads. With the right software, unique source codes can be assigned

to every email campaign, allowing you to track both customer and pro-motion accurately without interfering with the customer experience.

- **The Offer**
  Select and present your offer carefully as it is likely to be the heart of your campaign. At its most basic level, the offer is the combination of product and price you are presenting to your customers. Most offers involve a discount or promotion to attract the customer's interest and give him an incentive to buy. Whatever the nature of the offer, chances are that its level of appeal will vary greatly from one group to another, and some groups may have no interest at all. Also, a different approach may be necessary for selling the same item to different groups.

- **Surveys**
  Surveys give your customers the chance to let you know exactly what they want out of your campaign. Surveys are a permission marketing concept, so named because marketing efforts are aimed at those who have given you permission to market to them. A customer who ordinarily does not fill out surveys may well be willing, even eager, to fill out a short one for something of real value to them. So use the answers you receive to enhance your campaigns, to refine customer groups, and to personalize offers to individuals.

- **Site Content**
  Supporting content can be a great way to create interest in your promotion. Both product- and non-product-related content can be affected by your campaign. You can add campaign-related text to your product descriptions, or even special product views. Links may be added from product pages to special campaign content. Articles, essays, editorials, and other content can all provide additional information which either helps to make the promotional items attractive, or helps to complete the sale. Make sure that all related content gives a link or other easy access back to the product page.

- **E-Mail Messages**
  Email messages are an extremely powerful part of any campaign, when handled correctly. Email is one of the best ways to announce campaigns to your Web shoppers, since you can include a link directly to your site, and even to the products themselves. Digital coupons are a key part of such campaigns. Just make sure to follow the rules for effective email campaigns, as related in Chapter 13. Be especially careful to respect the wishes and the privacy of your customers, and email only to opt-in candidates. Highly-targeted emails to opt-in recipients can yield extremely good results.

- **Landing Pages**

  If customers are coming to your site from an email, a banner ad, a link on another site, a published URL, or other guided path related to a campaign, chances are that you will want their first view of your site to be very consistent with the messages in the campaign materials that reached them. For this reason, it may be very effective to construct a number of landing pages, literally pages for campaign respondents to "land on" when entering the site. This page could be a modified home page, a special gateway, an article, or even the product page itself. The type of landing page will depend on your marketing goals, your merchandising methods, and to some degree the design of your site.

Designing Your Online Marketing Campaign

When designing your online marketing campaign, there are a number of steps that are crucial to success. In general, you will want to work out your goals, your offer, how you want to reach your customers, what sort of merchandising you will use and how it will affect your different target groups, and what resources your site will need to successfully run the campaign. Each of these elements is a crucial part of the campaign, and should be worked out as much as possible in advance. You don't want to find out too late from your IT department that an ambitions email campaign will overload your servers, or that your showcased product does not interest your customers.

The process for effective marketing campaign design is:

1. Determine the goals of the campaign.

2. Determine your contact strategy.

3. Integrate your campaign into your overall merchandising plan.

4. Refine the offer.

5. Estimate traffic and hosting requirements.

6. Test the usability of your site and your campaign.

7. Schedule events.

8. Track, measure, and analyze the campaign.

Each step is important in your campaign's success, and you should plan every step in advance of execution. Try to get input from all departments, including your Web hosting or IT managers, as early in the process as possible. Most elements of an online campaign impact each other, and catching mistakes or assumptions as early as possible helps to avoid expensive re-programming, redesign of graphics, and embarrassing mistakes later.

1. Determine the goals of the campaign

The first step is to determine the goals for your campaign. It will be necessary to understand not only your company's goals, but your customers' as well. To be successful a campaign must be worthwhile to both parties. If there is no clear advantage to the customers, they will not have any incentive to participate, and your campaign will fail.

The four basic steps to determining the goals of the campaign are:

a) Determine your customers' goals and objectives

When choosing your campaign goals, you should first be aware of your customers' goals in visiting and using your site. Unless your goals are consistent with what your customers want from you, your campaign ca not succeed. Your most successful campaigns will help you attain your goals while allowing customers to achieve theirs. Some examples of customer goals would be:

- Learn more about products/service.

- Receive special deals.

- Save money.

- Save time.

b) Determine the customer behavior you are trying to create

In order to build an effective campaign, you need to define your goals in terms of measurable objectives and actual customer behaviors. If your goal is increased brand awareness, your only ways to measure this may be surveys, customer interviews, or an increase in first-time customers. If your site sells several brands, you may be able to measure brand awareness partly by sales of one brand of a similar item over another. If the goal is to increase the number of visitors who register, then the behavior you will measure is customers completing their registrations. The more clearly defined your goal is, the easier it will be to understand what customer behaviors indicate success. To understand what customer behavior you hope to see as a result of your campaign, do this exercise:

- Write a description of what you hope will happen when customers are exposed to your campaign, from the customer's point of view. Cover what he customer will think and feel.

- Make a list of the things you hope the customer will do in participating in your campaign (i.e., answer email, visit the site, buy an item, choose to receive a free gift, register, refer a friend, etc.)

- Determine what evidence will indicate that the actions you hope for have occurred.

- Determine ways to measure these actions and incorporate appropriate measures into your campaign design.

- Once you have decided on the behaviors your campaign is addressing, create your target customer groups.

c) **Decide what your goals and objectives are for the campaign.**
   Some examples of your business goals might be:

- Increase conversion rates.

- Improve ROI (return on investment).

- Increase brand awareness.

- Improve customer service.

See the section on "types of campaigns" for more on campaign ideas. A campaign may have more than one goal, and be several types of campaigns at once. Just be sure that the behaviors you want to result from the campaign are clearly described (and measurable) so you will have some way to know if your campaign is a success.

d) **Create a set of guiding principles that measure all actions in the campaign.**
   Your guiding principles will vary widely, depending on your goals, but may involve evaluations such as

- How important are sales numbers versus other longer-term targets such as increased brand awareness or customer loyalty?

- What target segments (if any) are most important to the campaign?

- What measures will you take to ensure customer privacy, and to make customers comfortable with your contact methods?

- Whatever your campaign goals may be, always keep in mind that if they are not ultimately compatible with your customer's, your campaign has very little chance of success.

- Remember that by taking up the customer's time and attention, you have raised the bar in their expectations: it is rarely enough to simply offer items at a normal price or deals that are just business as usual. While the reward does not have to be monetary, make sure that what you offer will be of real value to your customers.

2. Determine Your Contact Strategy

In building your contact strategy, you will need to make decisions about how the campaign will impact two important aspects of your business: the frequency and nature of customer contact.

a) Frequency of Contact

How often do you plan to contact your customers? You will need to answer the following questions:

- How will this campaign integrate with your overall contact plan?

- Should the campaign replace an existing contact tool, such as a newsletter, or should it be integrated into your existing tools?

- Will it be an additional contact? Will this increase the frequency of your contacts beyond what is comfortable for your customers?

b) Type of Contact

You must decide how you should contact your current customers and your potential new customers. Contact strategies can concentrate on one contact method, or on coordinating a number of different methods. Some campaigns will be more appropriate for one channel than for another. It may be wort while to divide your campaign into sub-campaigns, each tuned to the idio-syncrasies, strengths, and weaknesses of each channel, in order to use each to their best advantage. A lot will depend on your campaign and its goals. Some popular, frequently-used contact methods include:

Online contact methods:

- Email

- Advertisements

- Sponsorships

- Viral marketing

Offline contact methods:

- Direct mail

- Print

- TV and radio

- Press releases

- Telemarketing

3. Integrate Your Campaign into Your Overall Merchandising Plan

Your campaigns must be in line strategically with your overall merchandising plan, or you risk diluting your message and confusing your customer. Using the methods described in Chapters 5 and 6, work on ways to integrate your campaign into your merchandising plan.

Your existing site features can be used to support your campaign, and you should decide which of these will play a prominent role. Some of them can be customized to better suit the campaign. All the following can be used to great effect in a campaign:

- Customer surveys

- Decision wizards

- Landing pages

- Post order information

- Quick polls

- Spreads

- Customer feedback

- Cross-selling / up-selling

- Discount / promotion programs

- Membership support

- Favorites lists

- Customer chat

- Gift registry

- Special searching

Make certain the features you incorporate in your campaign help put the right product in front of the right person and show off all your offerings in their best light. Your product kickers and links should be prominent and ought to be placed on your homepage, gateways, and on related content pages.

4. Refine the Offer

At this stage, you will take the "value add" that you have based your campaign on, and build it into the full-fledged campaign offer or promotion. Make sure that the wording communicates the value without misleading, and yet in such a way as to create excitement. In some campaigns you may want to tailor the wording of the offer for each target segment. Sometimes you might even modify the offer slightly to better fit your target.

When determining how the campaign will affect the customer's satisfaction, you need to understand the "value add" for each contact. In other words, what does the customer get out of the deal? Different kinds of offers will have value for different kinds of customers. For bargain shoppers, price is everything. But for your wealthiest or most particular customers, getting something that is available nowhere else or perhaps only to club members may well be more important. If your campaign is aimed at a wide range of your target groups, you might want to have a different offer for each group:

- Monetary/deal – $X off a purchase, 20% off orders over $50.

- Rarity – Items difficult or impossible to find elsewhere.

- Brand exclusive item – Branded products (even t-shirts, bags, or other logo merchandise) not available elsewhere.

- Customer satisfaction – free tech support, free installation, extended money-back guarantees.

- Convenience – Multiple ship-to, gift-wrapping, back-order, reminder, or re-order services.

Consider the following:

- Memberships – Buying clubs, discount clubs, frequent-flyer programs, etc.

- Product and services bundling – Service contract, on-site servicing or installation, home delivery.

- Chain discounts – Percentage off deals that continue as long as orders are made with a certain frequency, or within a certain time period.

Design an offer that will mean something tangible to the customer:

- Offer something of real value. Think in terms of monetary savings (something that will be significant to the target audience), or convenience (time saved, information or knowledge unavailable elsewhere, etc.) Determine the online offer that will yield the desired results. Some more examples include:

  > Free shipping.

  > Volume discounts.

  > Product mix.

  > Free gift.

- Ensure that the value offered is in proportion to the customer's effort necessary to earn the benefit. Make it worth their while to participate, but do not over-reward either.

- Make sure that the value is something that has a real relevance to the audience. For example free daycare while you shop is not very valuable to someone with no children.

Some strategic and tactical tips on designing offers:

- Make certain your site can support the online offer. If you do not have substantial inventory in featured items, your campaign will run aground early.

- Make sure that the number of customers you contact is in line with the amount of traffic your site can support.

- Evaluate your offer against the goals for your campaign and your site. Make sure your offer's graphical design, wording, and product offering fits the overall image of your store and brand.

- Use source codes to track everything. If your site has the right software, it is possible to identify exactly which ad or kicker led the customer to a product. Also track which content customers viewed, which referring sites they came from, and other information that will help indicate the effectiveness of your campaign.

- Create a call to action. Make sure that your messaging is interestingly presented and creates excitement. Involve the customer emotionally and personally, as appropriate to the campaign. Use active language. Rather than saying "Towels are available at 25% off in our Beachfront Specials," use "Get 25% off all Towels. Visit our Beachfront Specials for discounts on everything in the store!"

Once you have decided on your merchandising tactics, selected your contact methods, and refined your offer, you can begin the specific changes to your site's design:

- Changing or adding content.

- Designing new kickers.

- Programming your discounts into your pricing structure.

- Advertising the campaign to your customers.

At this point you are ready to consider the technical requirements for executing your campaign.

5. Estimate Traffic and Hosting Requirements

Once you have the shape of your campaign worked out, you need to start thinking about the technical requirements for supporting your campaign. One common mistake is to underestimate the success of the campaign. If your offer is sufficiently enticing, you could have a high rate of response. If you are not prepared for it, too much success can be worse than too little.

The very worst time for your servers to go down or for site response to be slow is when you have just advertised your site to a huge number of people. If response is greater than expected, peak surfing times can hammer your site as thousands of potential customers try to access your site at once.

Businesses with catalogs have almost certainly experienced the surge at call centers when a new catalog drop starts showing up in mailboxes. Businesses who have used radio or TV ads know to expect heavy phone volume near or immediately after the spot airs.

With a website, downtime can be worse than giving your customers a busy signal. Make sure that your computers are configured to handle the load.

Depending on your campaign, it may be desirable to stagger your advertising, so that the initial impact can be spread out over time. This can mean sending emails out in waves, or mailing catalogs in blocks, so that only a portion of your customers are participating at once. Keep a close eye on your traffic, and have some backup plan for scaling up quickly if necessary. Some hosting contracts give you the option of renting extra machines and mirror servers on an as-needed basis when traffic demands it.

The general points to consider when determining your hosting requirements are:

- **Determine the reach of the campaign.**
  How many customers are expected to respond?

- **Determine the likely conversion ratio.**
  How many customers do you expect will buy as a result of the offer?

- **Estimate the average length of time a user will be on site.**
  What is your average visit time per customer?

- **Determine the number of concurrent users.**
  How many users does your site usually have at any given time, and by how much do you expect that to increase?

- **Evaluate your current hosting environment.**
  How many concurrent users and how much bandwidth is your site capable of now? Will your current servers be enough if response is as predicted? What if response is double your predictions?

- **Determine the needs of your hosting environment at the peak of your campaign.**
  Remember that customers are unlikely to spread their visits out equally throughout the day and week. Be sure to consider what will happen if many of your customers all try to visit your site at once.

- **Manage all customer contacts to optimize the site experience.**
  Solicit and monitor closely all feedback that you get from your site during the campaign. Make sure all channels are informed of the campaign and have them notify you of any pertinent customer comments or behaviors. You should be informed if call centers, catalog departments, or retail locations start hearing things from customers like "I wanted to try the new online sale, but couldn't get through." Give customer service centers the ability to offer the online deal if customers had problems online.

6. Test the Usability of Your Site and Your Campaign

When testing your campaign, start with usability. How understandable is your pitch? How open to interpretation? How easy is it to follow through on the promotion, once the customer comes to your site? Remember that all the theory in the world cannot improve upon an actual test run with a typical customer. Don't make the customer hunt for your special, or be coy with the buy button. Make sure that customers entering the site are able to make an immediate connection with the campaign or promotion, and are left with no question about how to proceed.

Your audience will come to you with a variety of computers, operating systems, browsers, and diverse cultural backgrounds. It may be acceptable to send out a special correction or apology messages to 1% of your customer base in the event of a technologically- or culturally-based error, but it could be ruinous to have to do so for your entire contact list.

Testing can involve showing a mock-up of your site to a test audience and watching their reaction. Observe what they pay attention to, where they look, and ask them what they believe they should do next. Many frustrations can be avoided early on if you catch simple misunderstandings caused by an unclear design or cryptic instructions. Make changes and do your most important tests early, when changes and fixes are relatively cheap and easy to make.

One important way to test your campaign is the limited rollout. Before sending the full campaign out at once, it is wise to present a mini-campaign to just a small representative sample of your customer base. Some errors can only be found by running a live test, and when that happens, you will want it to affect as small a percentage of your customers as possible.

Be sure to monitor customer response carefully. Feedback from your test group may reveal unintended interpretations of your message, problems with the promotion software that only surface with a certain number of concurrent users, and other artifacts of the special interaction between your site's technology and the wide world of customers.

The steps for testing the usability of the campaign are:

- Test each newly added site feature with focus groups.

- Determine the ease of use of the site.

- Roll out the campaign to a test group.

- Measure the campaign's overall effectiveness.

- Test different messages.

- Test different offers.

- Once you have run your test campaign, look for any spikes, patterns, or holes in your data.

- Contact a percentage of the test group, and offer a gift or discount for feedback and suggestions.

- Carefully examine any inquiries the test run may have generated. Make adjustments and test again.

- Make notes on the aspects of the response which caught you by surprise or were otherwise unexpected.

- When you are certain that your message is clear and your hardware and software are up to the task, prepare to go live.

7. Schedule Events

Once you have your goals, outlines, offers, and other campaign elements figured out, work out a timeline for execution of the campaign. Confer with marketing, graphics, Web design, programming, hosting, and fulfillment departments to ensure that the proposed schedule is practical for all departments. One of the easiest mistakes for new designers of online campaigns to make is to send out printed promotional materials only to find out too late that the programming or hosting departments have conflicting priorities that prevent them from making the proposed deadline. Some important scheduling tasks include:

- Set dates for the release of the campaign and for each campaign milestone.

- Coordinate the activities of any supporting events, and clarify the responsibilities of all parties for each deliverable.

- Be sure to leave plenty of lead time for the creation of associated materials. Avoid last-minute printing which is usually more expensive. It is also wise to leave time for a full and careful print review cycle; printing mistakes are not uncommon, and a misprinted Web address or price can devastate a campaign. If dates are in flux, it may be possible to print part of your material early but leave the part of the printing with actual dates, URLs or coupon codes for last.

- Leave as much time as possible in each step for review and error checking. Make sure you have had a chance to correct all interface and user problems long before coordinating messages are committed to print, tape, or film.

Schedule final testing well before the release date of the campaign; tests are run to find errors, and if you do find some, you'll need time to make corrections.

8. Track, Measure, and Analyze Results: Campaign Reporting

Since personalization and campaigns all rely on customer data and feedback, it's important to understand what information you should look for, and how success is measured in practical terms with site analysis tools.

What data you should be looking at:

At a minimum a good website reporting system should tell you the following about each visitor:

- When they came to your site.

- Where they came from on the Web.

- How long they were on your site.

- What they looked at and how long they looked at it.

- The item-to-item sequence of their browsing.

- Whether they looked at any promotional or on-sale items.

- Which items they almost bought but didn't.

A wealth of data can be collected by an e-commerce website, limited more than anything else by its own capacity to store, handle, and process that data. Collecting data does little good if it is not examined and used intelligently. For many sites, using only basic Web reporting tools will be enough of a challenge in the early stages. Collect and evaluate the data that is within your ability to process for now, and work on acquiring the tools for more powerful reporting and analysis later. But a basic traffic report from WebTrends (or one of the other good traffic reporting systems) can yield a wealth of information that merits close study.

In addition, your Web reporting system might also be capable of giving you more detailed customer information like:

- If they were a repeat customer.

- How much they usually spend.

- If they came to your site as a result of an advertising or promotional campaign.

- If they looked at things they don't normally look at or buy.

- If they left to go to an affiliate.

- If they left to follow some cross-selling program or banner ad on your site.

As you can see, even a first-time visit to your site can generate a lot of information. This information can be summarized in a report on customer purchases. Chapter 11 on Data and Analytics covers a number of other kinds of reports and methods of analysis.

You should always keep a close eye on your metrics. Before the campaign, do your best to calculate what the response is likely to be. During the campaign, monitor its progress to spot any problems in execution. Afterwards, analyze your results to see how effective the campaign was. Even an unsuccessful campaign, or one with low sales figures, can result in some very useful data. Use what you learn from this campaign to make the next one even better.

When measuring campaigns, a lot will depend on the campaign's goal. If it was to increase sales, you will want to measure your conversion rate. If your goal was to increase brand awareness, you would measure customer acquisition and site "stickiness" to find out how many new customers visited your site and how long they stayed.

The statistics available to you are determined by the software and reporting tools your site uses. But in general, here are some of the more popular measurements used to measure site effectiveness and to analyze online campaign performance:

Conversion ratio = number of orders ÷ number of visits.

Acquisition cost = advertising and promotion costs ÷ number of visitors

Conversion cost = advertising and promotion costs ÷ number of purchases.

There are also a number of other metrics that can be very useful in assessing your online campaign's effectiveness. Some slightly more advanced formulas that may prove useful are:

Frequency: an estimate of how often a customer visits the site. This can help measure such goals as brand awareness, customer interest and satisfaction, etc.

Frequency = number of visitors ÷ number of unique visitors

Duration: a measure of how long your customers typically stay at your site. A short duration with high sales numbers may mean a highly successful campaign in which customers were able to arrive, find their products, buy them, and leave quickly, satisfied and likely to return. Short duration, few page views, and low sales often means that customers found your home or landing pages confusing or unappealing. Duration can be very useful indicator of what customers are doing on your site, and how they are using it.

Duration = total number of minutes viewing pages ÷ number of visits during the month

Reach: a standard in the television industry, reach refers to the potential to gain the attention of your target audience. For TV, it is defined as the number of people (or households) who have the chance to see an advertisement, given a program's total active viewership. On the Web, a campaign's reach is the number of unique users who visited the site during a particular campaign (or other time period) divided by all the visitors the site has ever had. It measures what proportion of unique visitors were acquired during the campaign.

Reach = number of unique visitors during the campaign ÷ total number of unique visitors ever attracted to the site.

Stickiness: a composite calculation that measures the effectiveness of your content in holding the viewers' attention.

Stickiness = frequency x duration x reach.

RFM (recency, frequency and monetary value)

RFM is a fairly complex statistical measure that is based on the idea that past buying behavior is one of the best indicators of who might buy from you in the future. RFM is plotted on a weighted graph which factors in how recently a customer bought something from you, how often they buy from you in general, and how much they spent the last few times they bought. You will probably need to use campaign software to get this statistic, but in general, the steps are something like this:

1. Create a list of customers, ordered according to how recent their last purchase was, with the most recent at the top. Divide this list into 5 exactly equal segments (quintiles).

2. Choose a measurement of frequency, such as number of purchases made in the last month, or number of items purchased in the last two transactions. Sort the customers in your database from most to least recent, and again divide the database into five equal segments.

3. Divide your list into quintiles by how much each customer has bought from you in the last year.

Customers who are in the first group for all three measures will have the highest RFM scores. Since recency is the most important indicator, it may be weighted when calculating actual RFM values. Each company may come up with its own RFM calculation, and the one illustrated here may not be right for you. But this should give you a general idea of how to calculate RFM scores.

Chapter 7 Links
Effectively Executing Online Campaigns

http://www.business2.com/webguide
Business 20. Web Guide
Click on the Marketing link. Though there is nothing here specifically called "campaigns," there is a wide number of sub-topics, all of which can be applied to online campaigns. Also, use the Business 2.0 search feature with the word campaign.

http://www.wilsonweb.com/wmt5/plan-4p.htm
Wilson Web
This article takes a look at some venerable marketing basics and outlines how they can be applied to marketing online.

http://www.digitrends.net/marketing/13639_16525.html
Digitrends.net
An article on webcasting. Interesting insights that can be applied to future campaigns.

8

Building Online Customer Loyalty

In this chapter I will discuss:

- How do you build customer loyalty online?

- Embrace the concept of Customer Lifetime Value (LTV) as the indicator of where your real profits will come from.

- How to use all your channels in a cross-channel effort to boost loyalty.

- Design your site to keep your most valuable customers happy, and then work on attracting more like them.

- Customer Loyalty Tools: Make the customer's life easier, encourage them to invest their time and energy in your site, and above all offer great service with product selection wizards, reminder tools, re-order scheduling, and interactive help. And that's just the beginning...

- How do you measure customer loyalty?

Defining the Task – What is the Value of Loyalty?

Quite simply, the value of customer loyalty is enormous. It has been known for some time now that successfully increasing or maintaining good customer loyalty translates into better sales. Over the years several studies have indicated that repeat customers tend to spend far more at a website than do first time customers, often by a ratio of two to one.

According to McKinsey & Company, less than 5% of visitors to websites ever complete a transaction. Even more dire, their study found that only about 1.3% of most online shoppers become repeat buyers. But there are ways to brighten this picture. Harris Interactive has found that resolving customer service issues on a first contact more than triples a consumer's likelihood to come back and buy again — i.e. become a loyal customer.

These statistics illustrate in a nutshell the two-way nature of the merchant/customer loyalty relationship. Loyal customers trust the companies they buy from, and they buy more and they buy more often. And good service and value are necessary to inspire that trust and loyalty.

In the now-famous study "E-Loyalty: Your Secret Weapon on the Web," by Frederick Reichheld of Bain & Company, Reichheld announced the now frequently-quoted statistic that it is five to ten times more expensive to gain a new customer than it is to retain an existing customer.

A corollary to this statistic is just as startling. For the most part, new customers are so expensive to attract that they are actually unprofitable, sometimes until after the second sale.

Customer Lifetime Value (LTV) is an essential concept for the Web business to understand and embrace. When online businesses fail, it is because they failed to make money – an obvious conclusion that nevertheless caught many dotcoms napping.

Websites today cannot afford to ignore the purchasing behavior of their customers. Trust and loyalty translate directly to more sales. Customers who buy the most over the long term have a high lifetime value and return the highest profit on acquisition costs , or the investment the company made to gain them as customers in the first place. These customers must be identified and tracked. Once you understand who your most valuable customers are, you will want to:

- Do what you must to retain them.

- Try to figure out which of your other customers might be good candidates to become like your most valuable customers, if offered the right incentive or program, and

- Closely watch your most valuable customers for early warning signs of dissatisfaction or new needs.

Déjà Vu All Over Again

All of a sudden, recounts Steve Waterhouse, president of the Waterhouse Group, a sales training firm, everybody seemed to figure out that the "New Economy" was really just the old economy run by people who didn't know what they were doing.

"And once they realized that profit has something to do with keeping an organization running, we started getting back to fundamentals," says Waterhouse. He notes that the industry's fixation on the top line created enormous month-to-month pressure to book business and ultimately led to sloppy deal-making. But now, that mind-set has been replaced by a clamoring for the "basics of filling the pipeline with good stuff," Waterhouse says.

Weren't the Rules Different Before?

In a powerful growth period for any new industry, there is some logic to the idea that any and all customers are worth almost any price, as early customer base growth is part of what establishes one company in the public mind as the resource for a particular product or service. The first stakeholders in a market do indeed get the advantage of setting standards, defining the metaphors, and determining how that market will be run, but they also get all the headaches, take all the risks, and invest all the resources that go along with it. Even such trend-setters as Amazon and Yahoo are still struggling today to operate in the black.

Few businesses can match the depths of Amazon's pockets. To succeed at this point in e-commerce your site will need to support itself – and furthermore, make a profit.

What Works Today?

In their book The Profit Zone: How Strategic Business Design Will Lead You to Tomorrow's Profits, the authors Slywotzky and Morrison cite examples such as General Motors, IBM, and American Airlines to illustrate their claim that huge market share does not guarantee profitability. The premise of their book is that the design of the business is far more valuable when it comes to generating profit. A company must understand where their real profits are coming from and set up merchandising and processes that support and increase the areas that drive profitability.

Roy Tavenor, head of strategy and design for the TS&B Group in Australia, which sets up and provides consulting for loyalty programs in Asia-Pacific, believes that the programs that work are those that combine techniques for

Marketing Goal	Frequency Strategies	Loyalty Strategies
Increase new customers	Sign-up rewards & sales incentives	I feel welcome
Retain active customers	Points based rewards	I am recognized
Reactivate inactive customers	Points rewards & sales incentives	Come in and see us
Regain lost customers	Re-sign rewards & sales incentives	Come back into the fold

Chart 1. From Adding Value to frequency Programs: Marketers Around the World Are Finding Answers by Roy Tavenor

increasing frequency of purchase, with those that improve loyalty. As he points out, "there are only two ways to increase sales: 1) Get more customers. 2) Get more sales per customer. Every aspect of loyalty and frequency marketing stems from these goals. And once you break these tasks down further, it is clear how frequency and loyalty techniques can be combined for greater effect" (chart 1).

Exactly what is it that brings customers back for more? What causes customer loyalty? The core of inspiring loyalty is in understanding your customers and what they need and want from you as a retailer or service provider. To make loyalty work as a way to increase your success, you need to achieve three things in designing your company policies and business plans. You need to:

1. Understand LTV and customer retention

2. Understand the value of customer service in its broadest sense

3. Take a holistic approach to integrating customer loyalty with your entire business.

1. Understanding Customer Retention and Customer Lifetime Value (LTV)

At this point in its development, the Web commerce environment closely resembles the established retail market. As in traditional retail, the cost of acquiring one new customer can often be more than the profit on the sale itself. Therefore, profitability relies upon the first sales experience being enough to bring the customer back to buy again, without incurring further acquisition costs.

As mentioned, a high LTV (Customer Lifetime Value) relies on repeat sales. You can also reasonably hope that the customer will recommend you to friends and family, and bring in even more customers over the course of time. Customers who return once may allow you to break even – the truly profitable customers are those who return again and again and again.

As in traditional brick and mortar establishments, it is important to know who your most valuable customers are. The main job of customer loyalty programs, therefore, is to gain your customers' trust and retain those who buy, especially those who buy most. Your incentive programs should be chosen to increase not only your sales numbers, but sales totals... for the business as a whole, not just for your Web channel.

Brand name drives loyalty in a very big way. While some brands have an image or history that is so compelling that it creates loyalty on name alone, for most retailers it is best to assume that customers will stay loyal for precisely as long as their loyalty to you gives them more benefits than leaving for your competitor would. These customers want convenience and your website can provide it.

Key business behaviors that help create convenience and retain customers are:

- **Saving them time in a way that the competition can't.**
  In some cases, this may simply be because you maintain records of the customer's past orders and history that the competition does not have access to. Features like quick re-order lists, shopping lists based upon previous purchases, or customer-created lists such as registries, favorites, and wish lists all save the customer time. And once these lists are created, your customer has some degree of effort invested in your company. But if you have this information and never utilize it, then you lose any advantage it might have offered and you increase the risk of losing customers to your competitors.

- **Offering the customer convenience in a way that competitors can't.**
  In some cases, this may simply be because you maintain records of the Other information investments include account information which makes payment and check-out faster and easier, address books based on customer entries or on former shipping addresses that make shipping easier to set up, and other conveniences like calendars and reminders. Once a customer has invested the time and effort to build up resources with you, then moving to another site becomes less and less attractive, even for minor monetary savings.

- **Meeting the needs customers didn't even know they had.**
  If you can think of innovative ways to bundle your products, provide services, or suggest new uses for your products, customers will start coming to you for ideas. If you have design suggestions, fashion tips, travel hints or

other valuable data that you can offer right at the moment that you suspect that they need it, you can establish your site as a place to browse for new ideas that make life easier. For example, if you run a travel clothing site and cart analysis shows that a new swimming suit, beach shoes, and towel are in someone's cart, you might offer her an online weather service that for casts the projected temperatures for trip or vacation dates. You might also offer a product kicker for a hat or high SPF lotion, and perhaps an article about good resorts to visit. When customers know you try to anticipate their needs, they are more likely to come to you more often, just to see what suggestions you will offer.

- **Becoming a Valuable Resource to your customers.**
  In many cases, customers don't know that they want your products until you show them why they do. But because customers have so little time to research new hobbies and follow fashions and discover the latest fads for themselves, they are often appreciative of the hints and information you provide. If it is good information, they will come back for more. Martha Stewart has made a career of offering decorating, baking, and home styling tips because many people want to add a touch of gracious living and hand-made uniqueness to their lives. Burpee creates clubs and writes articles about their products, introducing customers to new plants, flowers and accessories.Sites that offer education, tools, training, and tips become a valuable resource that attracts frequent returns and, research shows, they tend to increase sales.

2. Customer Service Means Serving the Customer

Good service is much more than simply dealing with complaints, returns and dissatisfaction after the fact. True customer service involves:

- Anticipation of the customer's needs

- Preventing as many mistakes as possible in the first place, and

- Streamlining all your business processes so that retail tasks (especially buying, returning, and reordering products) are as convenient and pleasant for the customer as possible.

Loyalty programs alone are only a patch on a bigger problem – and often an ineffective one at that. Jupiter Media Metrix found that 75% of online consumers who participate in loyalty programs say the loyalty programs are not what motivates them to make online purchases. The study found that what was really important to customers was functionality. Only 22% of those surveyed said loyalty programs served as an incentive to buy online (Chart 2).

Influences for Online Purchases, 2000

Efficient return policy	40%
Good customer service	37%
Vast product selection	37%
Loyalty program	22%

chart 2

Your site design, site content, tools and services should all be geared toward convincing the customer that he really is getting the best possible service by dealing with you online.

Do everything you can to simulate the services of a dedicated salesperson, advisor, or service rep through the tools and functions on your site. Then work to exceed those services.

Online banks are succeeding by offering online the kind of detailed, up-to-the-minute account monitoring, payment, transfer, and financial application forms that were once available only by waiting in line at the bank. And unlike a bank branch, website services are open 24 hours a day. About the only thing that a customer cannot do from home is actually withdraw cash. The reduced requirement for tellers saves the bank money, while at the same time, many people who bank online feel that they are actually getting better service than they would have gotten by going in person to the branch office.

Often, the online experience can offer service and convenience that would be difficult to match offline. One example is the business-to-business vendor who sets up a purchasing system that makes it easier for the customers to place orders and easier for the vendor to process them.

Imagine a Large Technology Company (called LTC) that builds electronic devices. It no longer finds it practical or cost-effective to maintain large inventories of components and parts on-site. LTC management decides it must set up some kind of just-in-time delivery and stocking procedure with its suppliers.

LTC looks for and finds a supplier with a big advantage: they offer online ordering and a lot of related online tools that make LTC's plans possible. The vendor's web site allows LTC's approved engineers to log on, select the parts they need, and place an order. Extended product descriptions and technical specifications are available online, making it easy to identify the correct items. A shared shopping cart collects all individual orders from each department or even from the entire company, making orders easier to track and reducing the record-keeping load. Shopping carts can be saved to make future orders easier and faster to place.

In order to comply with LTC's purchasing policies, the purchasing department is notified whenever an order is placed, and a purchasing agent can review all orders online before processing them. Such a system could also send notification to senior engineers who may share responsibility for approving purchases.

If there are problems with the order, either the purchasing agent or the senior engineer can split the order into two orders, one which is approved and another which is awaiting further authorization or changes. A purchase order is generated, the order is automatically placed with the vendor, and the vendor sends a confirmation. LTC's inventory, accounting, and cost center management databases are automatically updated to show what has been ordered.

In this example, the vendor's online tools become integrated into the way LTC does business. This kind of integration and service takes a lot of work to set up and train all participants in, but the value to both the vendor and the business customer is quite high. Once a common history of sales patterns, orders, resources used, and other data is built up, it is likely to remain advantageous for LTC to stay with this vendor. And, once the integration has been set up, it is very much in the vendor's interests to continually update the reference material, expand inventory to meet the LTC's needs, and to make sure that their customer is satisfied in other ways.

This is the sort of business relationship that both causes and inspires loyalty from both sides. The best business relationships are always those which are mutually beneficial.

Loyalty like this can also grow in a business-to-consumer relationship, if the merchant offers highly useful tools, features, and service.

3. Take a Holistic Approach to Customer Loyalty

To really make loyalty work in your business, it needs to be completely integrated into the way you do business every day. To fully develop your company's potential to inspire loyalty in your customers, you need to:

- Offer the right tools to attract all users, but especially your most significant target groups.

- Develop intelligent personalization for your most significant target groups.

- Develop marketing programs that help build loyalty.

- Listen and respond to all your customers, paying special attention to your customers with high LTV.

Remember that everything you do is a part of your customer service, part of your merchandising, and also part of your loyalty plan. Every piece depends on every other piece.

Start with the customer, and figure out what she needs and wants. Then look at your business and see what you need and want from your customers. Finally, find a way for you to give the customer what she needs while still getting what you need out of the transaction.

If you do things in that order, then you will build your business around the customer, and around satisfying the customer, in a way that will create loyalty. Loyalty breeds success, and your business will survive so you can learn more about the customer and refine your service even further. A positive reinforcement cycle of mutual success and increased familiarity will build a consumer relationship that will not only be strong, but also increasingly difficult for any competitor to break.

Furthermore, tell your customers that you're interested in building a relationship. When you ask customers for information, tell them why, explain how the information will help you help them, and sketch out the ways you hope to improve your service in the future. Provide methods of feedback on your site that let your customers tell you directly what they want: email, surveys, polls, rating forms – all have their place in your process of self-evaluation and the search for new ideas and improvements.

But remember, that to really work, your commitment to serving your customers and meeting their needs must be real. Once you get feedback, listen to it and use it. Lip service to the ideals of service and good customer relationships will not create the services, build the shared knowledge, or provide the advantages that create loyalty. To gain your customer's loyalty, the processes that cause loyalty need to be built into your business from the inside out. You'll have to get it right to make it work.

Keys to Success in Customer Loyalty: Where do Loyal Customers Come From?

Granted that loyal customers are good to have...but where do they come from? Good advertising and graphics, catchy jingles and billboards will only get you so far. If these make the customer aware that you exist, then they've done their job. But loyalty hasn't even begun there yet.

Loyalty isn't an issue of what your customers can do for you, but of what you can do for your customers:

- First, you must offer something that the customer needs, or at least wants.

- Second, you must offer it in the way or form that the customer wants to receive it.

Loyalty is a behavior that customers exhibit when you have met those two requirements, and only if you are better at it than your competition. While the emotions may play some role, the longest-lived customer/brand relationships are built primarily upon pragmatic foundations. Loyalty must not only be earned, but re-earned over and over again.

Your first task is to make sure that your business model supports the idea of customers returning to you again and again. Certain kinds of businesses can have trouble with this. If a business makes something that people only use once or twice in a lifetime, then opportunities to get repeat business are slim. If all Sears sold were Maytag washers and dryers, then most likely their sales would suffer; most people only buy a few sets of these appliances in a lifetime. But Sears is a department store that sells a huge variety of items. By selling a solid, reliable washer/dryer set, they set up a relationship with the customer which often leads to a life-long pattern of buying many small appliances and other home items. And customers that start with small items later go on to buy the big-ticket items.

Businesses that expect to deal with a customer once and possibly not again for several years, such as real estate agents and car salesmen, often have to use other models. But most e-commerce sites are dependent on loyal, returning customers. So be sure to build into your plan an idea of what the second and third sale will be.

Tips for Success in Building Loyalty:

- **Figure** out which customers you want to be loyal.

- **Design** your site around your valued customers using features and functions calculated to please.

- **Tailor** site usability to both reward and foster loyalty. Your features and ease of use are critical here.

- **Listen** to customer suggestions, requests, and complaints. Respond to feed back.

- **Build** tools to make customers' lives easier.

- **Ask** them for a relationship with you. Show them your commitment to building that relationship and making it mutually beneficial.

Mistakes in Building Online Customer Loyalty

If you fail to serve the customer, you will lose a sale and possibly others which might have followed, which is serious enough. But if you fail to manage your customer relationships intelligently, you will lose their trust and destroy your business relationship. This is even more serious.

Here is a list of a few of the more common mistakes that have a negative impact on customer loyalty.

1. **Channel misalignment**

    Misalignment occurs when customers expect one thing but get something else. Customers get disappointed and lose respect for your business when online discounts are not honored offline, when return policies in one channel are different in another, when retail store staff is unaware of products offered on your website... Any one of these sorts of disjoints between what you do and what you say (or what the customer thought you said) can damage the most crucial part of your loyalty-building toolkit – trust. Chapter 8 covers multi-channel integration in far more detail.

2. **Poor website design**

    The desire to build brand identity can get out of control and lead to overblown graphics and inefficient navigation. Resist all temptations to elevate form over function. Yes, bandwidths are continually expanding and looks are important in the merchandising world, meaning that you just might be able to get away with a busier page now than you could a couple years ago. But in the unique environment of the Web, quick is still more successful than beautiful. And of course, quick AND beautiful are better still. A good Web designer who understands and can work within the limitations imposed by the Web will save you large amounts of money over the long term, and directly improve your ability to satisfy customers and win their loyalty.

3. **Lack of helpful tools**

    In a search to pare your site down to its fastest and most efficient there is always the danger of throwing the baby out with the bath water. If you have tools that customers expect to find, that they need, or that they simply like to use, you probably better keep them, even if they seldom if ever lead directly to sales conversions. Chances are, if it is truly a helpful tool or service, your competitors will offer it if you do not.

4. **Poor customer service**

    This nearly goes without saying, but nevertheless I will mention it, for one simple reason. In spite of all the research and studies that point out exactly how crucial good customer service is to maintaining a good customer relationship, an amazing number of Web-based or partially-Web-based businesses simply fail to provide adequate, let alone exemplary, customer service. Too many multi-channel businesses treat their Web division as a poor relation, giving it only sporadic and sometimes inconsistent support from customer service representatives. Emails get answered slowly or never, and customers' requests for assistance by phone may wait days. Solving this problem relies upon a company's management supporting a comprehensive customer service approach. Every aspect of the Web presence must be involved, from your site's features to the manner in which your customer service representatives answer the phone. Customer service reps must be well-trained in every aspect of the website and other channels, so they can help customers use the site's features, explain store policies clearly and accurately, track orders, and so forth.

5. **Over-taxed technology and sites going down**
   Again, this is one of the basics, but it is worth mentioning. In the effort to add personalization, analysis capabilities, customer convenience tools, and to track customer behavior and store customer data, you could suddenly find that your site's technology can't keep up with demand. Unless you increase computing and storage capacity along with functionality, you could find yourself getting worse site performance at the very times you need it at its best – during campaigns and other peak times. Consult with your IT department before you get too far with plans for site upgrades or campaigns. Chapter 7 (campaigns) has more information on matching your technology to your needs. Remember that the very worst time for your site to go down is when you've just told a million people to come visit you.

6. **Lack of privacy policies**
   Again, the issue is trust. If you do not have a privacy policy – or if you do not communicate it to the customer—they will have no choice but to assume the worst even if you do not share it with third parties. Personal data issues can be a can of worms on many levels. Not only can they cause problems with the customers directly, but some businesses have found it to be slippery slope legally. Just recently WebMD got into legal battles with Quintiles Transnational Corporation, a company with whom they had originally contracted to provide non-specific customer data. However, WebMD later determined that releasing "non-personally identifiable customer data" wasn't enough to protect their customers' privacy. WebMD stopped providing the data to Quintiles, and Quintiles then sued. Because the laws on privacy vary to some degree from state to state, and national laws are even now being written, anything related to the concept of selling customer data exposes you to

risk. Your customers will want to know exactly what your intentions are, and how you are able to back up those intentions with your site's security and encryption capabilities. So adopt a privacy policy, adhere to it, and post it in an easy-to-find spot on your site. As this example shows, the flip side of proactive, relationship-building information gathering is invasion of privacy. Where should you draw the line? The customer must be the final arbiter of when enough is too much. Have empathetic opt-out policies and a fall-back plan for customers who want more anonymity.

For every innovation in technology that makes your life as a retailer and merchandiser easier, there is also a potential down-side that you must be aware of. Pay close attention to the cautions given elsewhere in this book. Failure to deliver on any of the points of Intelligent Selling can disappoint your customers. If you disappoint your customers, what you are not doing is building loyalty. A good proportion of loyalty-building is simply paying attention to the basics.

Things You Can Do to Build Loyalty on Your Site

Loyalty tools come in a variety of types: some are designed to foster loyalty by offering tools or services that save the customer time and/or make some task easier. Others strengthen the customer relationship by improving business-to-customer communication or by providing avenues to solve customer problems. Whatever the method, the goal is the same: find ways to better satisfy the customer. Some examples of some time-saving, loyalty-building, customer-centric tools and features are:

Tools that Make the Customer's Life Easier

- **Advanced Search.**
  When available, advanced searches that allow Boolean operators and multiple keywords can be a powerful way to allow experienced users to find what they want more quickly. For some users, this can be a powerful incentive to use your site rather than a competitor's.

- **E-Mail Confirmation Messaging.**
  Send your customers transaction receipts via email detailing what they bought, the total cost, and shipping information. Give them personalized thank-you gifts in the form of coupons, gifts, or simply access to a special "members only" part of the site. These emails can also offer suggestions for related products that may hold some appeal, notify the customer of upcoming events at a nearby store, or provide links to content such as new articles and features. If you have a "points" program, you can automatically send emails to announce when a customer has reached her certain point levels

- **Multiple Ship To.**
A multiple ship-to feature is surprisingly rare, considering how basic a
service it really is. This simply allows customers to fill a cart once and pay
for it once, and to designate different parts of the order to go to different
locations. Multiple ship-to is especially useful during holiday periods and
other gift-giving occasions because the customer does not have to make
separate purchases for each recipient. This is particularly valuable if you
offer cart total discounts because the customer will have one large
valuable cart rather than several small ones that may never reach the point
at which they earn a reward. It's easy to see why customers would be more
loyal to a site which offered this option.

- **Product/Gift Selection Wizards.**
Selection wizards usually take the form of a questionnaire that helps narrow the selection according to the customer's input. The wizard asks the
shopper a series of questions, usually multiple choice, about the visitor's
needs, interests, demographics, budget, and also about the detailed characteristics of the product desired. In the end, the site serves up a selection
of products that fit the stated parameters. You can give each wizard its
own unique spin. Some are formatted as gift selection tools, with questions about the recipient's interests, age, gender, and so forth. Others are
designed to make it easy for the site visitor to find something for
himself.

Tools that Provide a Unique or Valuable Service or Information

- **Gift or Wedding Wish Lists and other Registries.**
Wish lists and registries allow a customer to build and keep a private list
of products available from your site. Customers can grant access to others
so they can view their list, making it easier for friends and relatives to find
and buy items. This also helps bring new potential customers to the site.

- **B-to-B Tools.**
Purchase order management, shared shopping carts that can be
assigned to specific departments, catalogs created specifically for business
customers... any number of tools are possible. Designing and building just
the right ones for your most valuable customers can be tricky, but usually
well worth the effort.

- **Site Tools or Links to Off-site Tools.**
Examples include mortgage calculators, calorie counters, weather reports,

etc. Even if you can't provide such things on your site, finding one available through a third party and then providing a link to it can be just as good. Tools like this strengthen a customer's view of your site as a useful place to start a browsing session.

- **Reminder Tools/Reorder Scheduling.**
  Reminder tools and other features such as reorder scheduling are a powerful way to allow customers to ask for the merchandising messages they want. Quite simply, you send the customer an email on a schedule he sets up, to remind him to re-order a certain product. This gives the customer control over when your business can contact him, making your merchandising messaging welcome and more effective too.

- **Address Book.**
  An address book can be a powerful feature when combined with other site features such as stored shipping addresses, multiple ship-tos, reminders, wish lists, tell a friend, etc. But even alone it can increase the value of your site, making it more likely that the customer will return rather than shop elsewhere.

Tools that Encourage Customers to "Invest" Loyalty in Your Site

- **Purchase Lists**.
  Purchase lists maintain a record of everything a customer has bought. Each item shows up once on the list as it would on a grocery shopping list, along with a note on total quantity and when it was most recently purchased. This makes it easy to find a particular product and re-order it. Purchase lists contrast with order lists, which are historical records of each order placed. On an order list, the same item will show up repeatedly, depending on when and how often it was ordered. A purchase list might be convertible to an auto reorder form, a wish list, or a tell a friend list. This feature creates loyalty in several ways, but is especially useful because it grows and becomes more comprehensive with each order. As you learn what products are valuable to this customer you can offer him targeted sales and merchandising that encourage him to stay on your site longer and expand his purchases. Once the relationship is set up, leaving for another vendor would require him to start fresh. As long as relations between you remain positive, he is unlikely to invest the same effort needlessly all over again somewhere else. Purchase lists are particularly valuable in B-to-B relationships.

- **Re-Order List.**
  Many customers order the same or similar things frequently. Helping a customer keep track of what was ordered in the past helps reinforce repeat buying, and allows a business to offer targeted incentives for repeat business.

- **Private Bookmarks or Saved Lists of Site Contents/Products**. When a site is large and complex and full of varied and rich content, it is to a business' benefit to allow customers to keep track of their favorite items. This increases the customer's ability to find products and content for future browsing and buying, involves the customer in the site, and increases the likelihood of repeat or future sales.

Tools that Enhance Your Level of Customer Service

- **Post Order Information.**
  This service allows customers to pull up their order information, and check its status as it moves through the fulfillment and shipping process. It is also possible allow the customer to track the progress of the package from the factory to their door. This information can be useful for reference if returns become necessary, or if the customer later wishes to re-order the same items or to recommend identical products to a friend.

- **Buttons for Interactive Help Options.**
  Examples include webchat, voice-over Internet protocol (VoIP), call-back, co-browsing, and page push. When interactive help options are available, access to them should be placed throughout the site for ready use wherever a customer may be likely to need it. It is especially important to provide access at points of highest interest and at difficult spots such as checkout, navigation, and customer service.

- **Tell Me More.**
  Even when a site offers a great deal of online information about its products, it is impossible to anticipate all needs and questions. Often it is useful to put a button prominently on a product or service page to make t easy for a customer to submit a question.

- **Shopping Buddy.**
  There are a number of ways to implement a shopping buddy. In general, this feature helps guide customers to appropriate products when they themselves aren't sure what to get, such as when they are shopping for a gift. Shopping buddies are often designed to simulate a helpful salesclerk.

- **World-Class Customer Service Section.**
  A well-constructed customer service section is a must in the process of building loyalty. A good customer service section gives customers the tools they need, and also demonstrates your commitment to good relations and good service.

Site Features that Reinforce and Enhance the Relationship

- **Customer Feedback.**
  there are a number of ways to collect customer feed-back, depending on exactly what sort of information you hope to collect and what trends you hope to reveal. Survey forms, polls, essay feedback boxes...all have their place. The important thing is that it be a method the customer is comfortable with and that it not take up too much time.

- **Mail to a Friend.**
  The mail to a friend feature is another way to allow customers to share information with each other. This helps bring highly targeted visitors to your site.

- **Thank You Page Messaging**
  Messaging on this page offers some of the same options as follow-up email messaging. Put personalized messaging on this page to offer incentives to return: digital coupon codes, free gifts, or simply access to a special "members only" part of the site. Thank you page messaging can also offer suggestions for related products, notify the customer of upcoming events at a nearby store, or provide links to content such as new articles and features. The conclusion of a transaction is an excellent time to send the customer off into the content areas of your site.

- **Personal Account Management.** Setting up a personal account encourages customers to register and give you at least a little personal information that will help you more accurately evaluate and serve their needs. The account management section lets the customer change opt-in/opt-out choices and set up or change other customer service parameters such as reminder services and other loyalty tools. Knowing that features can be turned off easily when desired makes a customer more likely to feel comfortable signing up in the first place.

- **Links for Your Job Center and its Application/Resume Submission Tools.**
  Sometimes a site's most ardent customers can also become its most loyal

employees. An employee who shops with a company makes a particularly convincing salesman.

Customer Programs for Building Loyalty

Anything that strengthens the customer/merchant bond can potentially help create loyalty. The more that customers begin to feel that you know who they are and what they want, and the more that you are actually able to meet those needs, the more your customers will prefer you over your competition. Here are some examples of programs that increase loyalty and improve the customer relationship:

- **Membership**
  Many of your best customers will not be those who are excessively bargain conscious. Incentives that merely offer a few percentage points off the purchase price have a low drawing power for these customers. Customers like this may be more strongly attracted to special treatment: expressions of appreciation for their business, being included in a special group or club, or being given access to privileged information or services. For an airline, it costs almost nothing to let first-class customers board first, but early boarding and first exit rights are a powerful part of the draw of first class travel. Hallmark has a membership club which rewards those who are "their nicest customers" — those most likely to send cards and gifts to other people. The members then earn points that let them earn gifts, making it a guilt-free way for them to buy things for themselves. A different perk in the Hallmark Gold Crown program is aimed at those members who are collectors. For them, Hallmark offers special news about upcoming collectible figurines and ornaments. Because they closely track customers' spending habits, they have a very good idea exactly what subset of their news and incentives will interest a particular customer. Such programs cost little but can greatly increase the customer's personal and emotional investment and generate a high return in customer lifetime value.

- **Build a community environment**
  Motherwear.com's primary offering is clothing for nursing mothers. But the site offers much more than clothing and baby supplies. It offers online chat, discussion boards, articles, and a host of other community-building features. When a new mother comes to Motherwear, she has just had an amazing experience and has a monumental, and perhaps a bit scary, task ahead of her. If it's true that it takes a village to raise a child, it's also true that in today's modern cities, small nuclear families often aren't sure exactly where to find that village. The Internet provides a way for a large number of far-flung people with the same interests to meet in a fairly private, anonymous

environment to share ideas, ask questions, and find resources. And when new mothers spend a fair amount of time reading and contributing to the Motherwear web-site, it's only natural that when it's time to buy something, they will try Motherwear first.

- **Preview Sites**
  Show off your new goods with a preview site. For customers that anticipate your new seasonal fashions, want a first chance to order limited-edition releases, or simply like being "in the know," a preview site can create a lot of good feeling. Such sites also help create a feeling of excitement for your new products. Giving your best buyers a chance to buy things a bit before their friends can adds a touch of exclusivity at no real cost to you. Further, pre-sales with a target group can give you early indications of the popularity and demand to expect from your new line.

- **Newsletters and Other Content**
  Newsletters and other content such as editorials, how-tos, guest speakers, and so forth, all create loyalty by establishing your site as the place to come for valuable and interesting information. When content has a good tie-in to your products, it can even help sales. If content is too self-serving, your audience will see through it and it will lose its punch, so it is important to offer real news and items of real interest. But there is still a lot of latitude for promoting your business. A clothing store could offer seasonal articles about new fabrics and materials that would be appropriate for the upcoming season. Since these articles could discuss old stand-bys -- like wool or Gore-Tex -- and also the latest high-tech rain repelling materials, these articles will appeal to a wide variety of customers. The fact that the company also sells garments made of these fabrics is seen as a convenience to the customer. When content and merchandising team-up like this, it is a great boon to the customer and serves to positively reinforce the customer's impression of both the content and retail sides of the site.

- **Shopping Rewards**
  Credit cards, airlines and car rentals have all joined together to help encourage each others' customers to buy and spend more, increasing total amounts spent while theoretically getting a better value for their money. Grocery stores offer their customers discounts in return for allowing them to track what, how often, and when a family buys different items. Some shopping programs are based on increasing total amount spent and frequency of purchasing, and others are based on giving rewards in return for the privilege of collecting shopping pattern data. In either case, shopping pr

grams can increase loyalty if they are part of an overall loyalty program. Many loyalty programs try to rely exclusively on discounted pricing. This does not always work, and some merchants have had problems attaining any actual increase in loyalty. Where this does not work, using points or shopping rewards as an element of a customer relationship is often very effective. The Hallmark Gold Crown club is, again, a good example of such a plan. It is the customer's total sales and frequent shopping that qualify them for a reward or special privilege, but the rewards themselves are highly individualized, targeted, and only partly monetary.

Shopping reward programs which offer something unique, particularly interesting, or personally appropriate do work well to help encourage loyalty. Programs based on strict monetary rewards, however, are usually perceived by the customer simply as hoops to jump through to qualify for the "real" price. This sort of reward program seldom actually convinces the customer to be more loyal to one store over another, since the customer is likely to be simultaneously participating in a number of programs with different merchants just to get the lowest prices possible. It is best to combine elements of the shopping reward concept with other loyalty tactics for best effect.

- **Multi-Channel Integration**
  There is a much more complete discussion of the advantages of multi-channel integration in the multi-channel chapter, but it is worth taking a moment here to discuss the effects of good integration on your relationship with your customer. When your loyalty programs are instituted in a consistent way across all your channels, they become much more effective. The more ways you allow your customers to contact you when they feel like buying, to communicate with you when there is a problem, and participate when you are offering a loyalty incentive of some kind, the more successful those efforts will be.

  Integration offers a number of positive advantages. You can bring your website into your retail locations with in-store kiosks; customers at your store can look up online gift registries when shopping for baby, wedding, or birthday gifts. As for merchandise return and exchange, let your local stores handle returns for things purchased online so your clerks have a chance to satisfy the customer by helping them find a replacement item rather than merely refunding their cash.
  But the biggest argument for integration is to avoid the negatives. When your stores, website, and catalog offer different or conflicting return policies, product offerings, and incentive programs, your brand and your customer

loyalty suffer. Integrating your programs helps you to increase your customers' trust in you as a partner they want to do business with.

- **Specials and discounts**
  Specials and discounts can help increase loyalty, although, like the shopping rewards programs, they are most effective when used in co junction with other, more personal and less purely price-based programs. When competing strictly on price, you will always be at a disadvantage compared to retailers with lower overhead or those willing to live with smaller margins. But when paired with other incentives, a lowered price can be very effective. If the aim is not to directly increase the bottom line, but instead to increased purchase frequency or to reactivate the interest of inactive customers, then the lure of a special discount can be exactly right. Even if you make no profit on the sale, if it revitalizes the buying habits of an old customer, it will be well worth it.

- **Ease of return/retail**
  Anything you can do to make your customer's life easier will help to foster loyalty. Studies have shown that even if it is the wrong size, the wrong color, or a disappointment in any other way, many customers never bother to return items they ordered by mail order or on the web. While at first it may sound good to not have to deal with a return, the catch is that such customers also rarely return. In such a case, saving the profit on that one item has most likely cost your business far more than it was worth in terms of future value from that customer.

  One of the reasons many customers don't bother with returns is simply that making returns can be much more trouble than most customers have time for. One way you can save that customer is to offer streamlined return services. Some companies include a pre-addressed, pre-paid label in the shipment for the customer to use in the event of a return. Others provide an online tool that allows customers to print such a label themselves. In either case, the customer can drop the package with his nearest carrier or post office for a fast, painless return. Other companies use third-party services such as Return.com which has online tools and resources that accomplish the same thing. Retailers with a brick-and-mortar presence may allow walk-in returns. However you do it, the easier and more convenient you make it for your customer to make the return, the more likely they are to do so, and stay loyal to you as a result.

- **Fast delivery times**
  Many customers order through the Internet assuming that it will be faster

and more efficient than local and store-based special orders. Many have been disappointed to discover that the company's online fulfillment shop is slower than phone or local orders! With the pace of life accelerating all the time, the faster you can turn around your fulfillment processes, the more satisfied your customers will be. Offer a variety of shipping options, including overnight and the less expensive but still speedy two- and three-day rates. Make sure your warehouse is set up to act on those orders immediately. Remember that to the customer, the clock starts the moment they place the order, and if it does not arrive on the day they he expected it you will have an unhappy customer. You will certainly have to charge more for shipping, and also add a dollar or so for handling, but customers will expect that. Just don't dis- appoint them by failing do deliver on what they pay for.

Furthermore, offer your best customers and frequent buyers shipping related upgrades as perks. Customers who would scoff at a $5 or $10 discount nevertheless appreciate things like an automatic upgrade to 2-day delivery.

- **Money-back guarantee**
  As with mail order and telephone sales, selling online requires a much higher degree of trust than does shopping in a walk-in store. Customers are not able to touch, examine, feel, or try on the items they are ordering. For this reason, a money-back guarantee is an essential element of online customer relationship building. For most customers, if you do not have a money back guarantee, you will never have the chance to develop a relationship because they will never buy anything from you in the first place. Loyalty comes from gaining customer trust and in making them feel comfortable shopping with you. A money-back guarantee is almost as crucial as a privacy policy and a secure shopping cart.

- **Personalization**
  Personalization can be used to enhance all your other programs. Personalization builds loyalty by using customer information to make informed choices about what the customer will like best, and then slanting as much of the site as possible towards those preferences. For example, Amazon.com keeps and continually updates exhaustive data on each registered customer, and on every customer who completes a sale. Every time the customer makes a search, the search engines update the database of user preferences by tracking which of the search results a user actually clicks on. After collecting this data for a while, the search engine learns

what kinds of links the user prefers and it assigns such links a higher placement in later search results. Once the site begins to learn about a customer, each new visit is that much more likely to contain the kickers, cross-sells, discounts and recommendations that the customer will like.

In short, the job of personalization is to shorten the distance between the customer and the merchant, and to help the e-retailer form as clear a picture as possible of the customer and what will increase his loyalty.

How to Use Personalization to Increase Your Customers' Loyalty

Survey your customers to find out what they want

Onc of the best ways to find out what customers want is simply to ask them. Start with unrestricted, open-ended forms and ask for input. Look for patterns and recurring themes.

Next, organize your responses according to your target groups, and then examine the responses again. Are there any new patterns? Pay particularly close attention to two groups: 1) the customers with highest LTV, and 2) the "near miss" group. A near miss group is the target group which is demographically most similar to your best customers, and yet which doesn't seem to be buying much from you. If you do not currently have such a group defined, then you should definitely do so.

This is the group which is most likely to hold potential for joining the high LTV group, if you can discover what they want. You may just find out through a well-designed survey. In fact, you may discover that an unusually high proportion of this group responds to your survey. If you did not have a near miss target group defined before the survey, you might even want to use the survey to help identify the characteristics of this new group.

These are, after all, customers which frequently visit your site. Or customers who are willing to fill out surveys. There must be some reason that they found your site in the first place. They may be staying and returning for some content, tool, or service that you offer. But there is at least a chance that there IS something they want to buy from you and that they eventually will, if you can identify it and offer it in the correct way. Chances are good that the customer will tell you what it is, if given the opportunity.

Make your first surveys simple and to the point, and fairly short:

1. Why do you come to this site?

2. What is your favorite part of the site?

3. What do you buy most often here?

4. What products/services that are not available on this site do you think should be sold here? If they were, is this where you would buy them?

5. What do you like best about the site, and what do you like least, and why?

6. If you could change one thing about the site, what would be?

Target the Customers You Want to be Loyal

Once you have gathered the information from your customers, and re-divided or assigned your target groups as necessary, it's time to start testing the waters a little. Devise a few small promotions intended to increase sales, and aim them at each of your customer groups. See what effect the campaign has on each group and to what degree.

Concentrate on the high-LTV and the near-miss groups. Find out which products seem to matter to them most. Offer the same item to subsets of the group using different kinds of promotions, and see which have the highest conversion rate. Try percent-off, flat rate off, free item, bundles, upsells, and digital coupon codes, and compare the results within the group.

Measuring The Effectiveness of Loyalty Programs

In winding up this chapter, I'd just like to take a few moments to discuss measuring and tracking. In Chapter 11 (Data and Analytics) and in Chapter 7 (Campaigns) you will find quite a bit about measuring the effectiveness of your campaigns, and in tracking your results. But in brief, the things that you will want to measure and evaluate are the following:

- **Frequency of Purchase**
  Loyal customers buy more often. An example of a frequency-based loyalty program would be an automatic re-order discount. Another might be a post-order email incentive - in this program, the merchant includes a message in the email receipt for a finished order. The wording might be something like "Thank you for your order from XYZ corporation. As an appreciation gift, here is a coupon code for 10% off your next order!" Depending on what you consider to be a good frequency, the expiration date of the offer could be as short as two weeks, or it could be good for a year.

- **Repeat vs. one time customer**
  This is an extreme case of the first example. After the first purchase, the

biggest hurdle is getting a customer to go from the first sale to the second. After that, going from the second to the third is much easier. With each completed sale, two good things are happening: a) the customer is becoming more familiar and (one hopes) comfortable with the way your site works and b) you gain more information on what that customer likes and what content and advertising she will respond to. Loyalty programs aimed at getting the customer over that hardest hurdle, from one-time-buyer to repeat customer are things like "free gift with your next purchase" or loss leaders with a high drawing power. Basically, in these loyalty incentives you are in some sense paying the customer to learn your site. It is worth some investment on your part to offer a reward to the customer for climbing over that threshold — after which doing business with you will be more convenient for the customer than it would be with other businesses.

- **Average order size**
  Once a customer has started to get into the habit of ordering from you frequently, the next way to increase the customer's value is to find a way to encourage him to increase the order size. Loyalty programs with this aim find additional products that customers actually need that the site can offer, and they find a way to make the customer's life more convenient, pleasant, or rewarding if he buys those things from you rather than from someone else. This allows you to give the customer a good reason to increase his order size (the value to you) while at the same time improving his own life (the value to him). An example might be a pet store site which has a good customer who frequently orders toys for her pets, but spends relatively little. Through a customer poll, the site may discover that the customer pays a fairly high price for premium pet food from a local store, in a brand that the site carries. With the shipping cost of the food, the food is actually a bit more expensive from the site than it would be in the local pet shop. By offering free shipping for a 6-month reorder commitment, the site might be able to convert the customer to buying the food from the site rather than from the competitor's store. Even if the price ended up the same, the customer would then gain the convenience of having the food delivered regularly, rather than having to make time to shop for it. Piggy back incentives could encourage other orders by making shipping of other items such as toys also free, if ordered in time to be delivered with the food.

- **Lifetime Customer Value**
  Always keep an eye on the LTV. Know which target segments are giving you the highest LTV, and develop loyalty programs to retain your most valuable customers, and to turn other customers into valuable customers.

This measurement is essentially a running total of the profit a customer has gained you, minus any expenses she may have cost you. After the initial acquisition, a customer's LTV is likely to be not only zero, but negative: acquisition often costs more than the profit (if any) of the first sale. Also, keep track of support costs; customers who make frequent returns and need a lot of customer support may actually turn out to have a small over all gain, even if their purchase total is high. Measure all the relevant elements when measuring customer value.

- **RFM**
  RFM (recency, frequency, monetary) is discussed in more detail in Chapter 7 (Campaigns), but here I'll just make this note: be sure to measure it! This is a composite measure that helps to quantify exactly who your customers with the highest lifetime value really are. The basic theory is that you should focus on retaining those customers who bought the most recently, who buy most often, and who over time have spent the most money. When designing your most attractive, top-tier incentive and loyalty programs, these are the customers that you are designing for. Make sure that you understand what is a worthwhile incentive to such customers, how you can make their lives easier, and what things they really want from you.

- **Conversion rates**
  Measuring conversion rates basically means keeping track of where, how, and by whom your sales are being made. You will want to know what co tent contributes most to making sales, what kinds of cross-sells, up-sells, kicker ads, promotions, etc. are more efficient and effective in actually convincing customers to buy. Conversion simply means, did the customer actually put something in the cart? And if he did, was the sale completed?

- **Membership and Loyalty points program usage**
  When designing a membership program, two things are very important: 1) does it actually offer something that people want enough to use and 2) is it actually attracting and retaining the customers that it was designed for? Measure conversion rates, program usage, actual participation in membership programs, and survey members to discover actual satisfaction levels. If you find that some of your target group is not responding as hoped, or is actually not able to participate as expected, be ready to tweak and refine the program. Be always mindful of fairness issues, however; once you start a club with rules and instructions for gaining incentives, substantially changing the rules without warning will cause a lot of bad feeling – exactly the opposite of your goal. While it is important to keep an eye on the bottom

line, it is also better, especially when starting up a new program, to err on the side of generosity when it comes to qualifying members for perks and incentives that do not cost much in actual hard costs. A little good will goes a long way.

Chapter 8
Building Online Customer Loyalty

http://ebusiness.mit.edu/research/papers.html
eBusiness@MIT
Exhaustive list of published papers and research provided by the MIT Sloan School of Management.

http://www.crmguru.com/features/index.html
CRM Guru Online Magazine
Enter "loyalty" in their keyword search form at left to read a series of articles on the interaction of customer loyalty and customer relationship management.

http://retailindustry.about.com/cs/loyaltycrm/
About.com's section on Loyalty and Customer Service
Contains articles, essays, and tips.

http://www.emarketer.com/
eMarketer : The World's Leading Provider of eBusiness Statistics
Excellent source for the latest statistics and trend reporting, aggregated from some of the major research sources. Featured reports and other useful data.

http://www.colloquy.com/
COLLOQUY: The Voice Of The Loyalty Marketing Industry Since 1990
Published by Frequency Marketing, Inc., COLLOQUY is dedicated to the dissemination of information and analysis related to frequency-marketing strategies and programs of all types, worldwide.

http://www.ecrmguide.com/
The eCRM Guide
"The Definitive Source for Customer Relationship Management Technology" Articles, news and more on the wide-ranging topic of Customer Loyalty. Use the word loyalty with their search tool.

http://www.e-loyaltyresource.com/reports/
The e-Loyalty Resource
How-to articles on e-loyalty from Ellen Reid Smith, author of e-Loyalty, and by some of the industry's best e-loyalty marketers.

9

Intelligent Customer Service

In this chapter I will discuss:

- Competition among e-commerce sites means that only those that differentiate themselves through exemplary customer service will be truly successful. Price alone will not be enough.

- According to a study published by the International Customer Service Association [ICSA], only 36% of online customers were satisfied with their online transactions and interactions.

- What are the six most common complaints of online customers, and how can you address them?

- Create a privacy policy that puts the interests of the customer first. Post it in an easily-accessible spot on your site.

- If your company sells through a catalog or retail locations as well as online, boost your customers' trust in you by accepting refunds and exchanges through any channel, regardless of how the original purchase was made.

- Treat email inquiries with the same respect as you would a phone call. If your staff can't answer them immediately, use an autoresponder to at least send a confirmation that the customer's inquiry is being addressed.

Customer Service is the Key to Online Differentiation

With forecasters predicting that the online business-to-consumer market will reach 205 billion by 2003 [IDC], one might be tempted to suppose that online commerce is working as it should. After all, there are already customers making purchases, and some sites are making money. Why interfere with something that is working?

The answer is that for many sites, the current state of online customer service is not working.

The economics of today's Internet market teach a harsh lesson. Once profit margins on product sales have been shaved to within a penny of profitability by global competition, factors other than price provide the only real differentiation. The sites which will stand out are those which really offer something special in terms of convenience and personal relevance. I've already spoken about ways to make a site more personally relevant and convenient to the customer. But another key factor is service.

With every competitor in the world literally one click away, customer service is one area where your online business both can and must make its reputation in the e-commerce marketplace. In order to compete in the area of good customer service, an online store will need to carefully monitor its customers' perceptions of how it does business. Good site design must be given the highest priority, with an eye to designing for the customer's convenience, not the store's.

While it is unlikely that an e-commerce site can duplicate the service of the local corner store where every customer is personally known, a new approach that recaptures some of that old-style one-on-one treatment is now emerging to regain the interest and the confidence of dissatisfied online customers.

Online Customer Service: Problems and Solutions

According to a study published late in 1999 by the International Customer Service Association [ICSA], of the nearly 10,000 online customers surveyed, only 36% were satisfied with their online transactions and interactions.

In the majority of cases, for online shopping to be worth the inconveniences (waiting for delivery, cost of delivery, loss of the personal shopping experience) either the advantages must be correspondingly high (such as super low price) or the perceived inconveniences of online shopping must be erased. And customers' dissatisfaction with the service they are receiving must be addressed.

The bottom line is that, in order for online shopping to reach the next level of growth, it must become not only as satisfying as shopping in physical stores, but more so.

Customer Perceptions of the Online Commerce Experience

Online customers generally have six basic complaints about online shopping experiences. Many of even the largest and seemingly well-designed sites can be perceived as:

1. **Unfriendly** – Customers do not feel welcome.

2. **Unresponsive** – Customers feel ignored.

3. **Unintuitive** – Customers cannot easily figure out how to use the site or how to find what they want.

4. **Untrustworthy** – Customers are not sure who they're doing business with.

5. **Unreliable** – Customers are inconvenienced by slow or buggy sites.

6. **Uninformative** – Customers cannot find the information they need.

Every one of these problems can occur in even the most well-meaning and carefully-planned website. But however inadvertent, the policies and practices that cause these negative perceptions are an ongoing problem and will continue to drive away (or simply fail to retain) the very customers that are most profitable.

The Need for Intelligent Customer Service

To counteract the public's negative perceptions of online customer service, your Web business will need to be aware of these perceptions, and take active steps to answer customer concerns and counter them with customer-centric and customer-friendly policies and practices. Gaining and retaining online customers through the use of intuitive, customer-centric design, appropriate customer service practices and customer loyalty tools is the heart of intelligent customer service.

To design a site that shows an understanding of the needs of your customers, and that accurately meets and exceeds the online customer's expectations, it is helpful to examine the negative perceptions that exist. Knowing the causes of these perceptions is a first step to avoiding them. The following guidelines are useful when designing sites for intelligent online customer service, dedicated to the satisfaction of the online consumer.

1. Problem: Unfriendly

The perception: Customers do not feel welcome at the site, or feel that the business does not show respect for their time or personal preferences.

The thought: "They really don't seem to care if I want to shop here or not."

As unbelievable as it might seem, many online businesses take a hostile or antagonistic stance, thinly veiled by a surface politeness. While it is unlikely that unfriendliness was their intention, this perception by the customer is not unfounded. Online businesses often retain many of the habits of the old "conquer and overpower" or "marketing is war" ideologies of the mass marketing customer model era.

These practices include:

Outright spamming (sending unwanted emails to the customer).

Deceptive "opt-out" rather than "opt-in" messaging practices.

Failure to respond to emails and other efforts at communication.

Excessive legalese.

"Bouncer" entryways (programming that prevents a customer from entering the site, even to see product offerings, unless the customer has first provided mandatory and often highly personal data).

Solution: Sensitivity to customer concerns, rights, and preferences

If your business adopts an autocratic attitude, no matter how well disguised by pleasant language, the customer is going to notice, if only subconsciously.

If site visitors are treated in an impersonal or antagonistic manner, they are unlikely to become a customer, or to return to the site at all. And yet many online sites do just that, treating their online clientele with a lack of consideration that customers can only interpret as disdain. Although starting with the best of intentions, businesses can nevertheless set up their sites in a way that completely ignores what the customer needs, wants, or finds convenient. Often the problem is only one of ignorance; if a business had known that its customers found its navigation hard to use, or its products hard to find, most businesses would have made some effort to improve things. But that is the heart of the matter; if you don't know, it can only be because you didn't ask.

It is your job to make sure that you are satisfying your customers. If you don't do so, you run the risk of giving your customers the impression not that you didn't know, but that you didn't care.

Some Examples of Friendly vs. Unfriendly Practices

- Your privacy policy must be designed for the benefit of the customer, it must be easy to find, and it must be easy to understand. It is the opinion of many consultants that no privacy policy should need to be more than one page long. Extensive legalese to express the simple facts of what a business plans to do with customer information gives the distinct impression that the policy is there more to hide what the site is up to than reveal it. Online resources are available to help you plan your customer service section, and one even has a tool for helping you build a simple, easy-to-understand, and appropriate privacy policy. Check out http://www.the-dma.org/ for a look at this and other useful topics. Not all legal situations are equivalent or easily dealt with, and site requirements will vary. But keep in mind that if a policy is too long, counterintuitive, or complicated, then your customers will probably not read it.

- To be successful, the overall tone of a website should be welcoming. The quicker and easier it is for a customer to find products and proceed directly to checkout, the higher the site's success rate. Except in rare cases, a site should never interrupt the customer with registration and signup forms at the beginning of a visit. Long forms requiring the user to reveal detailed and highly personal information before using the site are likely to be ignored until the customer is convinced that it will be worth the trouble.

- Avoid duplication whenever possible. If a customer has entered an address once, it should auto-fill in other locations. Streamlining the information-gathering process reduces customer frustration and improves compliance rates.

- Another example of necessary attitude adjustment is the "opt-in/opt-out" defaults for site-generated e-mail. The default for such e-mail choices should always be "off." A customer should be given the opportunity to choose whether or not he receives any e-mail not directly related to a transaction or individual request. Tricking a customer into submitting a form with a default marked "on" does not fool the customer into thinking that he or she actually did want the service.

- Random unwanted e-mails are difficult if not impossible to trace to the source, but your unwillingly-subscribed customer will know exactly whom to blame when your deluge of e-mail begins. The "default-on" trick is not the only way to get customers to accept communications from an online store. Successful companies use intelligent customer service models, loyalty-building tools, and customer-centric marketing instead of business-centric practices. Find ways to be friendly, considerate, and helpful, and your customers will be glad to hear from you. Tools that save the customer time, such as wish lists, reminder tools, gift registries, and automatic reorder schedulers are examples of Intelligent Selling methods that allow customers to tell a business how they most prefer to be contacted.

Guidelines for Site Friendliness:

- Treat customers in a manner that makes them feel respected, valued and known. One-to-one marketing must be matched by one-to-one customer service to be effective. Online companies should try to accomplish, at the minimum, the following behaviors:

- Maintain a friendly tone throughout all contacts. Whether asking for past-due payments or issuing an invitation to take part in a discounted buying promotion, all communications with the customer should be professional but friendly.

- Give the customer as many choices as possible to participate in online features and communications, but avoid making any but the most necessary mandatory. Customers are much more likely to participate in the first place if they know that they can opt-out at any time.

- Let customers know early and often that their privacy is respected and protected. Display icons for programs that the site may be participating in that show an awareness of customer concerns, such as Verisign, BizRate, the Better Business Bureau, or any other appropriate organization that shows the site's reliability and responsibility to customers.

- Keep track of customer contacts. To the customer, a site is one company, not a collection of departments. A customer expects that the customer service rep she spoke to yesterday will know today what she called about, and also what promises might have been made in sales or in the tech support office. Presenting a consistent and informed face to the customer reinforces the impression that the company knows its customers and that the customer's business is important and valued.

- Actively solicit customer feedback. It is important to do more than simply be willing to accept feedback when it is offered. Feedback forms in the customer service section of a website indicate up front that a company is interested in customer satisfaction. Even more effective can be post-sales surveys sent to customers after their purchase has arrived, offering coupons or other incentives in return for detailed information on their shopping experience.

2. Problem: Unresponsive

The perception: Customers feel ignored. Calls go unanswered, emails get late replies or none at all.

The thought: "They don't think I'm important enough to reply to. My little account isn't worth their time. Either that or they not competent enough to set up a working system to handle my simple inquiry."

Sadly, it is true that customers are often ignored. Even when good customer service policies are in place and intelligent practices have been written for the website, a site's customer service is only as good as its actual practices. A surprising number of even the largest and most well-known Global2000 sites (the world's 2000 best Internet-based sites) do not answer their e-mail in a timely manner. According to a Rubric, Inc. study in July, 1999 an astonishing 40% of e-mail questions went unanswered... including those from sites that promised a reply within two days.

Compare this to call centers and direct customer service practices. According to a 2000 poll, the average hold time for approximately 52% of support organizations was less than one minute. It's been calculated that in 1998 businesses lost $1.6 billion by neglecting their online customer service operations. The amount doubled in 1999, reaching approximately 3.2 billion in losses (Datamonitor).

Across all industries, online customers' expectations are rising. This is particularly true among the most affluent and valuable customers; in other words, among the customers businesses most want to attract and retain.

Solution: Robust customer service tools, adequate staffing, quick reply times.

Some Examples of Responsive Web Practices:

- Customers are demanding more personal service. When they contact a company with whom they have a relationship, they want the customer service representative (CSR) to know who they are and to understand their needs. They also want a consistent level of response. Whether contacting the billing, tech support or sales departments, customers expect them all to be in communication with each other.

- Staffing should also be adequate to respond in a timely manner. Customers will not tolerate waiting 48 hours for a response to an e-mail inquiry. Call center response times for an efficient call-in center are between one and five minutes. E-mail customer service should be as responsive and efficient as other customer service venues. Customers in general expect, at the least, an acknowledgement of receipt of their e-mail within an hour, and an appropriate, specific reply within a day.

- One of the first mistakes to avoid is simply underestimating the power and significance of e-mail as a customer service tool. All e-mail should be answered, and should be considered as important as a customer phone call. Not answering an e-mail is tantamount to hanging up on a customer. An unfortunate number of sites provide an e-mail address for contact, but never assign adequate staff to collect, answer, and integrate the e-mail into other parts of the customer service center.

- Ideally, e-mail inquiries should be handled as quickly and carefully as phoned-in requests for service. Some CRM software solutions even provide methods to enter e-mails into the same communications systems that sort, assign, and track calls and chats. Even though the customer sees only a single e-mail address for your company, there should be some method for distributing the e-mails to the CSR team once they are received. An early mistake was to send e-mails to the webmaster, who might know a lot about the site, but not necessarily have information on purchases, inventory or other customer service issues. In fact, it is a good idea to provide a number of e-mail addresses on the site: one for technical support issues, one for feedback about the website, one for sales inquiries, and so on.

  When set up and handled correctly, with frequent updates based on customer feedback and input from knowledgeable CSRs, automated systems can often handle a large amount of a site's e-mail volume, wit out sacrificing the quality of one-to-one customer relationships.

- For companies whose only sales channel is their website, it is important to mention that e-mail alone may not be enough. In an emergency or other urgent situation, responsiveness may mean offering a phone number and live customer service as well as e-mail-only customer service. A phone number, Web chat, call-back button, or some other method of immediate response should be offered prominently throughout the site, whenever possible. It cannot be overstated that in the new era of online commerce, online stores must try to be more responsive than brick-and-mortar stores; they cannot afford to be less so.

Guidelines for Site Responsiveness:

Make every effort to integrate all aspects of customer contact methodologies. Keep records of customer contacts, history, and interactions. Best practices include:

- Differentiate between different e-mails on the site for different purposes to increase efficiency in sorting and assigning e-mails to those who will handle them.

- Maintain adequate staff to handle the volume of e-mail being received.

- Use appropriate software to route, track and assign e-mails to the best possible expert.

- Keep a record of e-mail interactions, and integrate it with other customer interaction records.

- Use auto-responders when possible to let customers know that their e-mail has been received, especially during off-hours, weekends or holidays. The message should give the customer an accurate idea of when to expect a response.

- If the volume of e-mail a site is receiving reaches the level where the| number of customer service reps can no longer handle it all in a timely manner, it may be time to consider implementing an e-mail management software package. EGain, Kana, Cisco, Clarify and Siebel are just some of the companies that offer e-mail management systems with some integration into the overall CRM software environment.

Costs and implementations vary, and will depend on the needs of the company, but all should offer at least the following basic advantages:

1. Analyze incoming e-mail.

2. Determine whether messages are hostile or friendly.

3. Send back an automated response to straightforward questions, or at least an acknowledgement of receipt of the customer's e-mail.

4. Route more complicated messages to the appropriate expert.

5. Generate automatic emails for specific events, such as order notification, delivery delays, backorder announcements, and other standard events.

6. Track emails and "trouble tickets" in a centralized manner, integrated with records of other customer contacts. These should include pertinent sales calls, phone calls, IVR messages (interactive voice response phone systems), out-calls, mail, billing, and any other related contacts.

7. Automated answers should also offer direct links to other places to get information on a self-serve basis. Examples include technologies such as IVR, FAQs, telephone call centers, fax-back systems, or other options, in case the automated answer is not enough, or the projected answer time for a detailed e-mail response is not soon enough for the customer.

3. Problem: Unintuitive

The perception: Customers feel frustrated, confused, possibly even angry when they cannot navigate easily through your site or find the products they want. Some will dismiss the site as badly done, others may feel that they themselves are to blame. Either way, they will not feel that this is a place they can get what they need. Most will be gone within the first eight seconds.

The thought: "These people are nuts. It's impossible to find anything! Back to the search engine to find another store."

Bad interface design can be the death of an otherwise excellent online store. Even where the business model is robust and the fulfillment centers are poised and waiting, a site that is confusing, poorly merchandised, hard to use, or simply annoying will never reach its true potential. It may even be doomed.

Bad design has little or nothing to do with art. Although overblown and slow-loading graphics will hamper any site, the real culprit in a failing Web design is poor organization. One mistake many companies make is to organize a site for their own convenience and not the customer's.

Solution: Careful organization, well-planned merchandising, usability studies, and accessible help tools.

Good design starts all the way down at ground level. The first question a site designer should answer is, "How should the site be organized, and how do we best present our products?" Remember that product categorization must be based upon your customers' perceptions. Organizing your website according to the company's departments makes no sense if these divisions don't mean something to the prospective buyer.

Good customer service begins long before the customer has visited the site. If a site has been designed correctly and intuitively, a customer may never need help in the first place. Good site design is the purest form of good customer service.

Two areas on which customers place the most importance are navigation and checkout. A site that succeeds in these two areas will attract customers, and will gain a lot of tolerance for other small frustrations that may occur.

Navigation

Every site should have some sort of universal navigation. At any time, it should be possible for a customer to see exactly where he or she is within the site, and be able to instantly jump to any other major section.

The site should be organized in a way that is most meaningful to your customers, and not in the way that is most convenient for your business. For example, a grocery store might get billed in one way for all daily-delivered items such as pastries, milk and eggs, and in another way for frozen foods. Bulk goods may have a completely different distributor and billing scheme. If the store's own convenience were paramount, it might have placed items into categories according to billing or delivery method. But this would be confusing and inconvenient for the customers, since they tend to think in terms of similar products. They expect to see milk, eggs, and cheese in a dairy section, and pastries in the bakery. Grocery stores are usually arranged so that customers find items where they expect them to be.

Organization of products or content in a way that makes sense to the customer is essential, and it is worth doing a certain amount of usability testing to find out ahead of time how customers visualize your site's products. There is no better method than to simply ask a representative sample of real users how they would find it most convenient to locate items.

Cross-post items whenever confusion may occur, and give customers a search function to use if the site's categories fail to help them find the desired product. Above all, provide multiple paths to common items, and where possible provide search functions, decision wizards, well-defined categories and helpful FAQ content to allow the site to answer as many questions as possible with a minimum of searching. For more on organizing your site, see Chapter 6, Product Categorization.

Checkout

According to studies done by GreaterGood, Inc., 43% of purchase attempts fail. These failures may have represented $14 billion in lost sales worldwide in the 1999 season alone.

Over 40% of failed purchase attempts were due to difficulties in checkout. This figure represents GreaterGood's observational lab study of online shoppers attempting to buy a specific item. The research determined that over 40% of the time the reason that the customer failed to complete the sale was some problem with the checkout cart process that was so serious they could not make it work even after multiple tries.

Make sure that your site's software is rock-solid, and that its interface is as streamlined and intuitive as possible. Test every feature with real users before release. And for those customers who are still in need of help, provide chat buttons, call-back request forms, chatbots, and even 800 numbers to assure customers that if, at any time, the site cannot answer their needs, the company is willing to provide the extra help necessary to complete the sale.

Some Examples of Intuitive Web Practices:

- Within the checkout and customer service sections, the artistic design, functionality, navigation, tone, and presentation should be either consistent with or complementary to the rest of the site. They should carry branding and policy messages that are consistent with those of the business as a whole.

- Whenever possible, companies should make a study of their prospective customers to discover how they view the products, before ever beginning to design their online presence and its merchandising themes.

- Ideally, a visit to a site should be as efficient as possible. A customer should be able to:

  1. Enter a site,

  2. Find any desired products,

  3. Get any information on the products that may be needed,

  4. Be automatically informed of related issues,

  5. Be offered related items or useful upgrades as appropriate,

  6. Proceed to checkout easily,

  7. Finalize the sale,

8. Automatically be informed when the item was shipped and when it should arrive,

9. Be informed how to track the package, and

10. Look up a record of the order on-site,

...all without delay, confusion, or frustration.

Guidelines for an Intuitive Site:

Navigation, especially path-to-purchase design, should be as clear and straightforward as possible. Organization of the site should be designed to reflect customer needs and expectations. Some best practices include:

- Organize the site with clear, logical areas of content and products, including clear links to customer service and product information. Build customer service sections with as much care as the rest of the site, with consistent design and navigational graphics. Test the customer service section for usability as thoroughly as you test the rest of the site, and poll customers to find out if they were able to find help when they needed it.

- Avoid cute or hip metaphorical division names; don't make the customer hunt for what she or he is looking for. A new visitor should be able to tell where to find anything at a glance. Drill-down schemes should be logical but as short as possible.

- Use universal navigation bars that allow the customer to move instantly between sections of the site in one click.

- Use a design scheme that informs the customer where he or she is at any given point.

- Place help buttons and links prominently and put specialized ones exactly where problems commonly occur. Examples are 800 numbers, co-browse help, or Web chat buttons right in the checkout section. Customers should always know that help is never far away, and that the company is interested in giving the support necessary to complete the sale.

- Put information links on items in the checkout so customers can get last minute questions answered without losing the shopping cart, or having to start over.

- Inform customers of special quantity discounts or shipping advantages as early as possible. For example, the customer may be more likely to complete the sale or even increase it if they know in advance that buying only $10 more product may save them $15 in shipping costs or give them an automatic shipping upgrade.

4. Problem: Untrustworthy

The perception: Customers aren't sure who they're doing business with. They are unsure whether they will be able to talk to a "real human" if there is a problem with products or billing.

The thought: "Who are these people? Why are they hiding behind that PO box? Do they even have a phone number? What do I do if I have problems? Who do I talk to if I have a complaint?"

More and more new e-commerce sites are not created by new companies, but by traditional companies entering the Web commerce space. As a result, the quality of the average website is rising. The faceless, unbranded, anonymous discount site offering only the most rudimentary of customer services is fast dying out. But the memory of these early, second-rate sites lingers with many online customers, and the perception remains with many shoppers that all e-commerce is risky.

While the no-frills, no-service, discount-reliant Web stores may never disappear completely, too many people have been disappointed and/or outright cheated for most users to be comfortable with them. The first and biggest mistake such sites make is a lack of any identity or contact information at all. It was once an all-too-common event that a website would lack all traces of the true owner, a physical address, or other "real world" contact points. All but the most naïve user shuns such sites now.

Solution: Be Accessible, Guarantee Satisfaction, Provide Service

Newer websites have benefited from the comfort shoppers feel with known brands, retail identities, and vigorously-promoted customer-protection policies such as free returns, money-back guarantees and transaction protection from credit card agencies.

To compete with the entry into the market of more traditional businesses with known names and more customer-centric business practices, some online-only businesses have adopted better business practices. Ironically, some now have better customer service online than the new brick-and-mortar business websites that have recently arrived.

Some Examples of Trustworthy Online Business Behaviors:

- To best compete online, and to enhance their customer base at their physical stores as well, it is imperative that more traditional businesses leverage their identity and services already present in the physical store. For Web only businesses to compete, they will need to match or surpass traditional businesses' services and methods. As competition in Web commerce grows more and more fierce, the only true remedy is effective customer service. Any online sales presence should have a robust, well-integrated customer service section.

- In addition, websites should take care to integrate their online brands and corporate personality to give customers strong confidence in both the product and the institution they are considering buying from. When customers are left feeling confused, lost and unconfident, they are unlikely to commit themselves to making an online purchase.

The primary concern when establishing upper level strategic planning for the development of a website and a customer service department should be to ensure that these elements integrate seamlessly into the business as a whole. All channels of a business should support one another, and ultimately present a consistent, unified, well-branded face to the world.

- The website must integrate with the business. This is not as much of a problem for Web-only e-commerce sites, but fewer and fewer businesses are truly Web-only. Even sites that have no brick-and-mortar store may have other faces showing to the world than what is only on the Internet, at one domain name. Some businesses may have print catalogs, kiosks, or even a boutique presence within other websites. They may also have an advertising presence in banner ads, TV ads, radio and print ads, movie trailers, and any number of other media.

- Enterprise-level sites rarely make a mistake like presenting a refined, upper crust identity in a Wall Street Journal promotion and then launching a web-site that looks more appropriate for Nickelodeon. But it is a subtler and more difficult task to make sure that the brick-and-mortar site and the online site not only have the same branded identity, but also the same business and customer relationship tone.

It is self-defeating and customer-alienating to have customer service policies that vary from one branch of the business to another. Whichever venue's service is the lesser will contaminate the satisfaction and customer trust levels of the other.

Customer groups are not segregated; the populations intermingle. The customer who buys in a store one day may be even more likely to visit that store's website the next, especially if using online customer service will save a trip out into the cold. In fact, such an event is a strong mark of success. It is worth going the whole distance in business-wide consistency, even to the point of allowing mail-in RMAs (returned merchandise authorizations) for in-store purchases such as would be used for an online purchase. After all, customers may have bought at a store far from home, and have no physical store nearby.

Guidelines for Gaining Online Customer Trust:

Be accessible and accountable, and offer guarantees of satisfaction. Wherever possible, integrate online and offline policies and procedures across all channels. In general, an online business should make every effort to show its commitment to quality, service, responsiveness and trustworthiness. Best practices include:

- Post information on warranties, return policies, technical support and other information prominently and post links to this information throughout the website. Placement is particularly important at points where customers are most likely to need help and reassurance (checkout, registration, product information pages, etc.)

- Any online business should offer multiple ways to be contacted, including email, fax, mail, phone, and possibly technologies such as Web chat and call-back buttons.

- Make the customer service section and its features easy to find and use.

- Clearly post links to important policies (privacy policies, security policies, etc.)

- Back up all claims with consistent fulfillment.

- Participate in customer review programs, site verification and security services and other confidence-establishing programs. Some examples include registration with the online Better Business Bureau, BizRate and VeriSign.

- Establish and maintain the site's security certificate and keep it updated.

5. Problem: Unreliable

The perception: The site is slow or buggy. It could be your hardware or your software, or just a design that is overloaded with large slow-loading graphics. The problem could occur constantly, only during peak surfing times, or just when new catalogs or web-related campaigns have been released. Regardless, this presents the danger of getting a reputation for poor site performance.

The thought: "Why is this taking so long? Where's everything I had in my cart? Do I have to start all over again? Aaargh!"

There are several kinds of unreliability, and all are bad for business. One commonly reported frustration in years past was hardware unreliability. When traffic exceeded expectations, hard-hit websites became slow, crashed, or otherwise failed the prospective buyers. Countless sales were lost, and with them, the customers. Without proper planning, too many orders can be as bad as too few.

In recent years, improved technology and site hardware has often answered traffic and website stability concerns, though this will be a continuing challenge as Internet popularity grows. But even as the technical issues come under control, during the 1999 holiday shopping season customers discovered a second, worse kind of unreliability.

Endangered by their own success, a number of online toy stores became swamped and missed their promised delivery dates. These stores not only got a lot of very bad national press, but in some cases were sued by embarrassed and dismayed families. Even if customers are not afraid that their money will be stolen, they are still not likely to order from a company that cannot guarantee delivery by important dates, such as Valentine's Day or Christmas.

Solution: Robust fulfillment strategies; real-time integration of backend and inventory systems

The only way to reliably avoid these problems is to deeply integrate backend fulfillment and inventory systems with the website itself. If warehouses are out of stock, the online customer needs to know immediately, and be offered an informed choice on whether to backorder, choose another item, or look somewhere else. A refund will not satisfy the customers you left with empty boxes and broken promises on birthdays or holidays.

In 2000, Jupiter Communications reported that 44% of 27 major e-commerce sites it surveyed had yet to complete real-time integration of Web and call center operations. In addition, 46% had no real-time inventory management. Sites that can offer these services and make good on guaranteed delivery dates will have a powerful advantage in the most popular shopping times of the year.

Some Suggestions for Building Reliability into Your Website:

- Make your hosting plans robust, and plan for success. All your hosting platforms should be scalable, and you should have emergency plans for backing up your site data and for responding to unusually high peaks in your site traffic. Make sure that your machines never have to operate at above 90% capacity; have mirror sites and distributed servers for processor-hungry functions whenever possible. If your resources are limited, stagger the release of your campaign or catalog materials.

- Intelligent customer service provides accountability and credibility and creates customer comfort. When customers know that they will be well informed about inventory, delivery and return issues, their fears about site reliability will be relieved. It is up to the website designers to make that information clearly available and accessible to the prospective customer.

- Business management software and online systems must work in support of each other, and messaging systems must be put in place to communicate clearly and frequently to the customer about any concerns they may have. What a site may lose in sales by admitting lack of stock is negligible compared to the rewards brought by customer confidence and loyalty.

- A good example of a highly useful, but not too technically-demanding tool is integrated shipping tracking. A number of shippers, including DHL (www.dhl.com), UPS (www.ups.com) and FedEx (www.fedex.com) allow online tracking of packages en route and have B2B services that integrate with an online business for the customer's benefit.

Guidelines for the Reliable Site:

Wherever possible, integrate online and offline policies and procedures. An online business should make every effort to demonstrate and communicate its commitment to quality, service, responsiveness and accountability. Best practices include:

- Notify customers immediately of any problems or delays in their order, and offer recompense for unexpected delays with offers such as free shipping, discounts on the next order, or other incentives.

- Integrate backend inventory data as much as possible to avoid disappointing your customers by allowing them to place orders that cannot be filled. Make sure that the site "knows" when items are back-ordered, and if possible offer alternates. Some sites are programmed to remove product listings once inventory levels drop below a pre-set level. At the least, let customers know when they can expect delivery of back-ordered items, whether the rest of the order will be delayed, and if it will incur additional shipping charges for separate delivery.

- The best sites not only inform customers, but allow them to choose which is preferred: lower delivery cost or immediate delivery of the available portion of the order. Goodwill and customer loyalty can be increased by offering frequent buyers perks such as no extra cost on shipment of back-ordered items.

- Offer post-order e-mail notification and online order history, and whenever possible integrate with shipping sites to provide package tracking. FedEx, USPS and UPS all offer automated functions to allow your site to keep customers informed of the progress of their delivery.

6. Problem: Uninformative

The perception: Customers cannot find the information they need. They are left with questions and the site does not provide the answers.

The thought: "This site isn't very helpful. I need to know which model/what materials/what ingredients this product has; where can I get more information? What are the privacy policies? I want to know if it's safe to sign up for this newsletter before I agree. Who is this company? I want to know more about them before I buy."

One of the problems with many sites and their customer service sections is that they simply do not offer the information the customer is looking for. The Internet is an information-rich environment, and customers usually expect to find even better information about products online than they would in a walk-in store. While offering a large amount of content may take some planning and effort, such a project is usually well worth the investment.

Even though the expected content may be there, it may be inefficiently organized, hard to read, or difficult to search. The customer service section of a website should look as though as much time and creative effort were spent on it as on the more obviously revenue-generating parts of the site. Site visitors should not be left with the impression that the customer service section is an afterthought or is less important than other sections.

Solution: Careful planning and design of services, content, and infrastructure

Bare-bones sites give the customer little reason to return and they do little or nothing to increase customer loyalty. As mentioned above, price alone is a meager incentive for customer loyalty. A well-designed customer service site will offer many sources of information, many contact points, and a variety of tools to engage and interest the customer.

Some suggestions for building a helpful website:

- Even if customers do not buy online, they may use the site to get information on products and services. The more useful a site is to a prospective customer, the more often he will return, and each return increases a site's opportunities to convert the visitor into a buyer.

- As much as possible, full specifications, warranty and guarantee info, technical support information, online manuals, FAQs and other information should all be available to the customer online.

- In addition to information about products, a customer will expect to find information about the store itself, its policies, identity, and online services.

Guidelines for Building an Appropriate Customer Service Section:

Depending on the individual store's products, resources, and clientele, any customer service section should at the very least include the following:

- **Contact information.**

- **Guarantee policy.**

- **Shipping policies.**

- **Refund policy.**

- **Security policy/protection.** Links/logos for Verisign, SecureLink, Better Business Bureau, etc.

- **Privacy policy.** This should be at the most one page long. At the time of this book's publication, the DMA offers a free online tool to help you build your privacy policy. Check the list of links at the end of this chapter.

- **FAQs.** Frequently Asked Questions and Answers

In addition, it is strongly recommended that the customer service section also include as many as possible from this list:

- **"About Us" information.** A short history of the company, store or fulfillment locations, e-mail addresses and phone numbers, etc.

- **"How to Use this Site" instructions.** Few sites remember to include this section, but it is always appreciated. Don't take for granted what the customer knows; if a customer needs more information, make sure it is available.

- **Guided tour.** This can be as simple as a text page with screenshots, or as fancy as a multimedia movie that demonstrates site features. This is especially useful if your site has any complicated features.

- **Site map/search tools.** A site map is a tree-like structure showing where pages are and what content is found on them. If a site's navigation is well planned and easy to use, this may not be necessary for most users. For some customers, especially those with visual or other handicaps, this feature can be extremely valuable. A search function is especially useful to all users, and is often the very first method new visitors use to find what they are looking for. If the search function does not return an expected result, a customer will often assume that the item is not available, so it is important to make any search function as robust as possible.

- **Instructions for advanced tools.** It is useful to have separate instructions for a site's fancier features, so that they are immediately available to the experienced user without their having to sort through the beginning user's instructions on basic site use. Advanced features are more likely to be confusing, and even knowledgeable users may need instructions to get the full use of them.

The Visualize website (fig. 1) has an exemplary customer service section. Finding the right information is easy with a wide selection of well-organized links to the required and recommended items in the previous lists, as well as several from the following collection of more advanced customer loyalty and marketing tools:

- **Advanced search.** Advanced searches that allow boolean operators and multiple keywords can be a powerful way to allow the experienced user to find features and products on a website more quickly. For some users, this can be a powerful incentive.

Figure 1

- **Shopping buddy.** There are a number of ways to implement the "shopping buddy" but in general, this is a feature that helps guide customers to a product when customers themselves don't know what they are looking for. These are often designed to simulate a helpful salesclerk.

- **Product/gift selection wizards.** Selection wizards are similar to a shopping buddy, but are usually a form or questionnaire that helps to narrow the selection according to the customer's input.

- **Added-value content.** Some sites offer additional features not directly related to the products for sale there. For example, a site selling diet foods may offer a body fat calculator or other features that bring the customer back to the site, increasing the chance to offer merchandising messages and other offers.

- **Address book.** An address book can be a powerful feature when combined with other site features (such as shipping addresses, multiple ship-tos, reminders, wish lists, alert a friend, etc.) Even alone it can offer the customer a valuable service that, again, brings the customer back to the site more frequently.

- **Job center/application/resume submission links.** Sometimes a site's most ardent customers can also become its most loyal employees. An employee who himself shops with a company makes a particularly convincing salesman.

- **Reminder tools/reorder scheduling.** Reminder tools and other features such as reorder scheduling are a powerful way to allow customers to ask for the merchandising messages they want. These tools allow customers to let a business know when they would not only allow contact, but welcome it.

- **Order histories/order progress check/repeat order** (related to reorder tools). Many customers order the same or similar thing frequently. Helping a customer keep track of what was ordered in the past helps reinforce repeat buying, and allows a business to offer targeted incentives for repeat business.

- **Private bookmarks of site contents/pages/products.** When a site is large and complex and full of varied and rich content, it is to a business' benefit to allow customers to keep track of and easily find their favorite items. This increases the customer's ability to find products and content for future browsing and buying, involves the customer in the site, and increases the likelihood of repeat or future sales.

- **Personal account management** (opt in/out, loyalty tool settings/modifiers/updaters). Setting up a personal account encourages customers to register and fill in at least some personal information that will help a site more accurately evaluate and serve customers' needs. And knowing that features can be turned off easily when desired makes a customer more likely to feel comfortable signing up in the first place.

- **Site tools, or links to tools.** Examples include mortgage calculators, calorie counters, etc. if your site does not have things like this, it may be useful to provide links to a third party site that offers them. This increases the customer's view of your site as a useful place to start a browsing session, and increases the likelihood of return visits.

- **Gift/wedding/wish list/etc. registries.** Wish lists and registries are similar to product bookmarks, in that they allow a customer to keep a private list of products available on a site. In addition, the customer can grant someone else permission to view their list, making it easier for friends and relatives to shop for them. This brings new customers to the site who are highly likely to buy.

- **Mail to a friend.** Mail to a friend features are another way to allow customers to share information about products with another, and again help to bring highly targeted visitors to a site.

- **Tell me more.** Even when a site offers a great deal of information about its products online, it is impossible to anticipate all needs and questions. Often it is useful to put a button prominently on a product or service page, to facilitate questions from a customer. Such buttons can pre-fill some form fields, or offer other ways to track sales campaigns and customer demographics. A wise site designer will value any request from a customer that allows the online business to create a good customer relationship and increase chances of conversion to a sale.

- **Buttons for interactive help options.** Examples include webchat, VoIP, call-back, co-browsing, and page push. When interactive help options are available, access to them should be easily found and placed throughout the site, wherever a customer may be most likely to need it. It is especially important to include this at points of highest interest and greatest difficulty such as checkout areas, navigation (finding things) and customer service (getting help).

- **Instructions on use of interactive aids.** When the above-mentioned advanced features are available, it is wise to include a section with specific instructions on their use and answers to frequently-asked questions about them. Customer testing is a very good way to get some clear ideas of customer concerns before posting new features.

Figure 2 shows the shipping page of the Visualize customer service section. Note the universal customer service navigation panel on the left, which allows the customer to travel easily from one section to the next. The shipping information is complete and logically organized, and the customer service toll-free number is at the top of the page in plain sight.

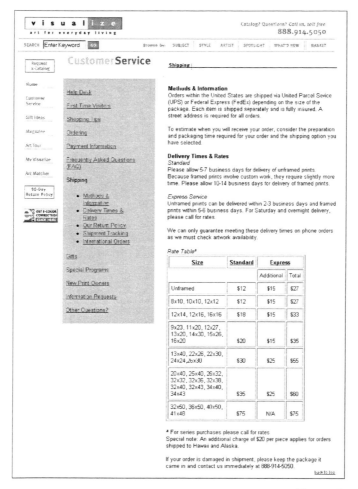

Figure 2

Customer Success is E-commerce Success

The business that recognizes the Web customer's new-found freedom, accepts it, and uses it to build a happy, satisfied customer base will be the business that succeeds. In order to compete in the online market, an online store will need to carefully monitor its customers' perceptions of how it does business.

Good site design must be given the highest priority, with an eye to designing for the customer's convenience, not the store's. Using all the tools of intelligent customer service, the successful online store will be friendly, responsive, intuitive, trustworthy, reliable, and informative. Its site will be so well organized and well developed that most customers find their information easily, never needing customer service at all; and those who do need help will be able to find and receive that help in a quick and timely manner.

A site that is easy and pleasant to use will create a large base of satisfied and loyal customers with a high retention rate and a correspondingly high Customer Lifetime Value (LTV) as they return to the site to buy again and again.

Richard George, a marketing professor at Saint Joseph's University in Philadelphia has done a study that reveals the value of keeping the customer satisfied. "If your business has a 70 percent customer-retention rate, every revenue dollar today will be worth $4 in ten years," he says. "And an 80 percent retention rate will increase today's revenue dollar to $6 in ten years."

It is difficult to know exactly where the Web will be in 10 years. But it is clear that sites that gain customer loyalty now will be exactly the sites that — 10 years from now — will be reaping the benefits of whatever the Internet of the future will have to offer.

Chapter 9 Links
Intelligent Customer Service

http://www.the-dma.org/library/privacy/creating.shtml
DMA: How to Construct Your Privacy Policy Privacy Policy
Includes a link to the DMA's Privacy Policy Generator.

http://www.cio.com/research/crm/
CIO Magazine site – research center for CRM
Articles, research, and opinion on a range of topics related to customer service relations and customer satisfaction.

http://www.benchmarkingreports.com/
Best Practices, LLC
Best Practices, LLC is the premier provider of best practice and benchmarking information. Their Best Practices Benchmarking™ reports will provide you with fast and effective access and intelligence to world-class excellence. Although their reports are not free, some very interesting information is provided in the "Study Snapshot" and "Key Findings" description of each report. A trial membership is also available.

http://www.ecrmguide.com/
The eCRM Guide
"The Definitive Source for Customer Relationship Management Technology." Articles, news and more on the wide-ranging topic of customer relationship management.

http://retailindustry.about.com/cs/loyaltycrm/
About.com's section on Loyalty and Customer Service
Contains useful articles, informative essays and tips.

http://www.bbb.com/
Better Business Bureau
Online dispute resolution tips. Be sure to check your business's rating with this public agency and take steps to address any problems.

http://www.bizrate.com
BizRate.com
Independent business-rating and post-sale survey company. Be sure to check your business's rating with this public agency and take steps to address any problems.

Using Content to Increase Sales

In this chapter I will discuss:

- Well-planned content induces customers to stay on a website longer, and the longer they stay, the more likely they are to buy.

- A January 2001 survey by PricewaterhouseCoopers indicated that product related content such as close-up product images and in-depth descriptions was the single greatest inducement to buy.

- Direct content and indirect content: What is the difference and how can they both be used to improve the customer experience and boost sales?

- Be warned: too much content or improper placement of links to content can distract the customer, draw them away from the path-to-purchase, and endanger the sale.

- Some thoughts on what content to personalize and how to go about doing it.

- Content is there to help you sell; develop a content management plan to keep it fresh.

The point of Content – Creating a Balance to Increase Sales

As I've mentioned at several points now, the purpose of an e-commerce site is to sell. Everything that you do on your website should be ultimately designed to increase those sales.

Some time ago, Meta Group predicted that the "ability to effectively manage business-critical content will become a recognized differentiator for eBusiness by 2002." I have found this to be true, primarily because the content a site offers has a direct correlation to how effective it is in convincing a visitor to complete a sale.

A January 2001 survey by PricewaterhouseCoopers indicated that product-related content such as close-up product images and in-depth descriptions was the single greatest inducement to buy, being rated as "likely to increase online purchases" by nearly half of those surveyed. Indirect content such as customer reviews and evaluations was also one of the top influencers, being listed as a strong inducement to buy by approximately a quarter of the survey's respondents. Many customers use the Web as a research tool, specifically to find out about products before making a purchase. Price comparisons, feature details, color/style choices, tech specs, consumer reports, and other information can all be found on the Web for most products.

The Value of Content

Content makes your site attractive by informing, educating, amusing, and/or impressing your audience. Frequent updates to your content give your customers a reason to return again and again. Providing the information and features that are valuable to your customers entices them to stay on your site longer. Studies have shown that the longer customers stay on your site, the more likely they are to buy – as long as buying is well integrated into the site.

Other influencing factors are the personal relevance of the content, and the interest you generate in your products through suggestions about new ways to use the products and through lifestyle images demonstrating the products in stylish or innovative environments. Anything is useful if it helps make the customer want the products.

Increased sales, improved branding, lower product returns, and elevated customer satisfaction are all achieved by putting the right content on your site, in the right places, and updating it frequently.

Types of Content: Direct and Indirect

In the Intelligent Selling model, content is chosen with one deliberate goal in mind: increase your bottom line. However, the return on investment for content is not always a simplistic one-to-one relationship.

Site content comes in two major types: direct and indirect. The purpose of both kinds is to increase sales, but not all content refers to a specific product or will have an easily measured impact on sales. Content that refers to a particular product directly is called direct content. Direct content includes such elements as:

- **Additional images**
  Photos taken from different angles, lifestyle images that show the product in use, zoomed images, virtual models, alternate style choices, color or fabric swatches, grouped or "display case" images.

- **Product FAQs**
  Frequently asked questions about specific products and their uses.

- **Product demos**
  Photographs, video, or animations of products being used or displayed.

- **Fit and care instructions**
  Examples include size charts, washing instructions, measurement guides, size conversion charts, assembly instructions, replacement and repair manuals.

- **Detailed Product information**
  Specifications, extended text, expanded or personalized merchandising messages, cultural notes, appropriate age ranges and skill levels, fashion and flair uses.

- **Product background info**
  Manufacturing, place of origin, environmental friendliness, artist bios, style notes.

- **Legal information**
  Warranty, guarantee, liability, shipping restrictions, minimum age requirements, terms of use agreements, contract terms, etc.

At other times you will design your site to increase sales indirectly, by providing research and education opportunities and by improving the online experience and consequently the customer's satisfaction.

Content of this type may relate to:

- groups of products

- the uses of a class of products

- your business and its brand and services as a whole

- things of interest to the customer that may have only a tenuous connection to your products, but nevertheless increase sales by increasing customer interest in your site. This leads to more frequent visits, and ultimately increased sales.

Indirect content supports your sales by making your site more attractive and satisfying to the customer. It increases your site's "stickiness." Research has shown that sites that establish themselves as a resource — with content and services that save the customer time and provide facilities for product research or education and ideas – attract customers and induce them to stay longer, return more often, and buy more.

Examples of effective indirect content are:

- **Education**
  Comparison charts, on-line classes, reference tools, color charts, etc.

- **How-to information**
  Instructions, recipes, patterns, assembly instructions, manuals, schematics, blueprints, demos.

- **E-zines (online magazines)**
  Articles, editorials, research papers or notes, background, histories, stories, spreads, letters to the editor, advice columns, features, news, case histories, celebrity endorsements, etc.

- **Customer stories & testimonials**
  Customer reviews, testimonials, customer ratings, customer polls & surveys, discussion boards, man-on-the-street interviews, in-store demo videos, and more.

- **Events**
  Online chats with celebrity guests, online virtual or in-store readings, appearances, and performances, community room chat boards, local support group parties or in-store demos.

Content in the Decision-to-Buy Cycle

It's important to understand the real role content plays in the context of your website. Wherever they are visiting a website, the customer is part of a constant decision loop.

For most customers, a site visit will go something like this (fig. 1):

1. Initial need or interest brings the customer to the site

2. The customer selects a link to content or a gateway that seems to match her interests or is most likely to fulfill her need.

3. The customer reads or inspects the content.

4. The customer makes a decision: Am I read to buy yet? If she is, she proceeds to product pages, buy buttons, and shopping cart.

5. If not, she burrows deeper into the content, and the cycle starts over.

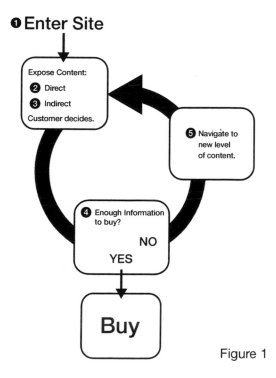

Figure 1

For this reason, content should start fairly general and gradually get more and more detailed. The exception would be for quick interest or feature items that should be placed along the way as a part of personalization or messaging campaigns. But in general, the rule of thumb should be the deeper into the site, the greater the level of detail.

The customer should be exposed to a variety of levels of content right from the home page. If the customer already knows that he or she wants to buy, then it should be possible to go directly to product gateways (via universal navigation) or possibly directly to specific product pages via kickers, catalog codes, or other direct links. However, for customers who do not yet have enough information, clear links to the site's content should be available.

A Properly Built Content Section

The Visualize website provides an excellent example of a well-designed content section. It contains all the best elements and presents them in balance with each other so that no single feature overpowers any of the others. They all support the Visualize goal of helping customers find artwork they like. Every company will

Figure 2

have different needs in a content section, but they would do well to follow the careful thinking, planning, and design exhibited here.

This good use of content starts on the home page (fig. 2). At the very first glance, the design itself invites the user to begin browsing. Some of the main navigation links are for the major content sections on the site, including a guided tour of the site and their popular online magazine or e-zine "Off the Wall." Their secondary navigation bar on the left includes links to information about framing and a glossary of art terms. Most noticeable is a large kicker image for the "Off the Wall" magazine in the main part of the page. This is all interspersed with various tools and product kickers that let customers select artwork in a number of different ways, yet all elements are carefully organized to harmonize with each other in a pleasant, artistic shopping environment.

Let's take a look at their "Off the Wall" magazine (fig. 3). This is available through a couple of links on the home page and also from every other page on the site. As with any magazine it has its main features and these are prominently placed in the middle of the page. Secondary features are placed to the sides and below. All features are carefully designed to catch the visitor's eye through interesting imagery and to address the interests of art afficionados. They include advice and how-to articles, a recurring item called "Museum of the Month," and

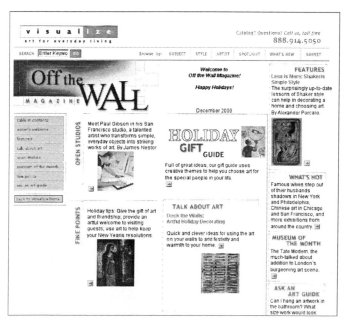

Figure 3

their largest regular feature called "Open Studios," which spotlights the artists whose work is available for sale on the Visualize site.

The "Open Studios" section (fig. 4) reads just like an article in any fine art magazine. It is written and designed to appeal to the widest possible audience and includes plenty of direct quotes from the artists, the insights of the author and critics, and (most importantly to the merchandising on the site) there are several images of the artists and their work which, when clicked, link to enlarged images for easier viewing. All artwork is linked directly to product pages, so readers have an easy way of making a purchase if they find something they like. Yet this section is not all about selling. Rather, it serves as a place to gain insight into artists and their work and provides the visitor the courtesy of an easy and low-key route to make a purchase.

Figure 4

However, the "Open Studios" section – originally intended as indirect content — can serve as direct product sales support as well. When a customer finds a product through another search method, and if that product or its artist has been featured in the "Off the Wall" e-zine, a link to the e-zine content is placed on the product page to make it easy to get more in-depth information (fig. 5). This all illustrates the important concept of integrating content into product pages, and products into content pages.

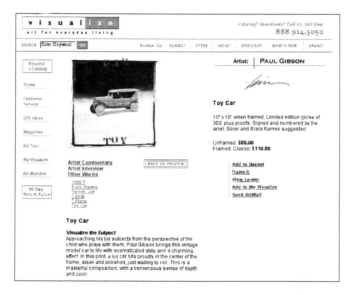

Figure 5

Even the title of the section, "Off the Wall," is perfect for its purpose. It not only evokes the idea that the featured artists and artwork are out of the ordinary, but also the whole concept of taking the artwork in your hands, examining it closely, and finding out the real story behind it.

What Content to Use, and When to Use it

The key to keeping content in balance with the goal of selling your product is to constantly ask yourself what your content does for the customer. Does it increase product awareness, customer satisfaction, or save customers time in ways that bring attention to the products and/or business? If you cannot answer yes to at least one of these questions, then your content could be out of balance with your site.

Again, the key is balance. Products and content should have a reciprocal relationship. If you link a product to supporting content in hopes of increasing sales, you should also link your product back to related products (fig. 6)

Figure 6

Remember, the content is there to help you sell. If an article or how-to section raises interest in your products, make it as easy as possible to let that article support sales; link it directly back to the pages for related products, product groups, or cross-sell items. If appropriate, put a buy button right on the content page.

Some content will not refer to any specific product. In that case, provide easy links back to the referring page, or to an appropriate product gateway.

Appropriate Levels of Content for Your Business

The kind and amount of content on your site will vary, depending upon the nature of your site and the resources you have available. Keep the volume of your content at a level where your company can maintain it and keep it fresh. It is better to provide a manageable amount of content and handle it well than to disappoint your customers when you can't keep up with an overly-ambitious content program.

Businesses with a fairly straightforward type of product will often not need much more content than what is directly associated with their products. An apparel shop selling professional clothing will want to provide plenty of product information on fit and care, materials, wearability, and perhaps even fashion, but chances are good that customers will not feel the need for an online discussion forum or possibly even customer ratings. A list of frequently asked questions (FAQ) about wash and wear requirements, and perhaps even some travel tips, is likely to cover the vast majority of customer needs and interest.

But other sites will have more of a community focus. In Chapter 8, Customer Loyalty, I referred to a hypothetical large technology company called LTC. To keep LTC's engineers happy, their vendor may well need to provide in-depth product specifications, blueprints, a table of cross references for part numbers, up-close product photos from different angles, white papers, articles, product reviews, a discussion forum, cost calculators, hazard warnings, and any number of other reference materials.

Personalizing Content

If your site has personalization capabilities, be sure to use those capabilities to let your customers customize their site experience.

For customers who are already very familiar with your products or for other reasons do not need extended information to help the decision-making process, it may make sense to let them opt for streamlined product pages and fast-loading gateways with a minimum of extraneous text and graphics. While you will not want to compromise your messaging opportunities, it is still possible to minimize product information and other aspects of your site for customers who prefer it.

Although new customers may need and appreciate prominent placement of decision wizard tools, step-by-step instructions and extended buying tips, more experienced customers may find such things unnecessary, distracting, or even irritating. Allow your customers to give you their preferences and create a tailored website experience.

It is usually best not to completely remove links to extended content. The time may come when the customer does need the special information or help, and will expect to be able to find it – but these links can be made much smaller and more unobtrusive.

Another way to personalize content is to provide tools such as special bookmarking features, which give customers an incentive to register with a personal account.

Community services such as message boards, advice columns and shared customer ratings establish a relationship that brings the customer back more frequently. It may be very useful to allow customers to determine which of these message boards or forums should be presented most prominently.

In fact, nearly all of the personalization techniques discussed earlier can be of some benefit when applied to content.

Best Practices for Content

- Find out what content would actually be useful and interesting to your customers. Use polls, customer surveys, and analysis of site traffic patterns to find out.

- Your merchandising staff should control your website content, just as they control your ad copy and website architecture.

- Your product copy will benefit from skilled copywriters. It should at least be reviewed by those who handle your product merchandising.

- If your site has an e-zine (online magazine) your writers should be skilled in creating interesting articles. If your content is not appealing, it is a waste of time and effort to provide it.

- If you do not have the time or resources to create content, contract with a content provider.

- If any one piece of content is more than about 150 words long, provide a brief synopsis of the piece on your initial page with a "more" button at the bottom, and put the rest on a subsequent page. If your customers are interested they will drill down to find it.

- Integrate your content with products in such a way as to increase interest in sales. Don't let content bury sales information

- Make content easy to find by putting links to it in your navigation scheme, but put it at a lower level than your products.

- If your site doesn't have a real need for content, spend your time and money on other facilities that are of use to your customers.

- When possible, create a partnership with a content provider to obtain a deeper selection of content than you could create alone.

- Periodically ask your customers what they think of your content to make sure that what you offer matters to them.

- Analyze site traffic to see how often content is viewed, and to evaluate its impact on sales.

Tips on Managing Content: Keeping it Fresh

A well-structured end-to-end content management capability is not easy to achieve. There are numerous challenges businesses need to overcome as they develop their capabilities. A survey by Forrester Research found the following major challenges:

- Not enough resources.

- Updating content/keeping it timely.

- Getting content from other parts of the organization.

- Workflow/version control.

- Broken links.

- Managing content for multiple browsers.

- Moving from static to dynamic.

- Synchronizing multiple sites.

The most important advice that I can give is to carefully plan the resources your content will require. All too often the Web Manager is left with the overwhelming job of not only overseeing site programming and hosting, but also for managing and updating the content. Content generation, maintenance, proofing, and styling should be done by someone other than your Webmaster, though your content creators will work closely with your Web staff.

Not all content has to be created in-house. Many companies partner with a content provider to set up a mutually beneficial relationship that provides a showcase for the content provider's material and adds value to the e-commerce site. Suppose there were an art school that, as a community service, offered free online tutorials in drawing and painting. The artwork provider Visualize could contract with this art school to make their tutorials available through the Visualize site, providing an interesting and compelling reason for art lovers to visit again and again. Both organizations would benefit; the Visualize site would provide important promotion for the art school's programs, and Visualize would gain more customers as visitors who initially came just for the tutorials eventually explore the rest of the Visualize site.

Tips for Offsite Content: Leading Them In and Bringing Them Back
Similarly, you can create content which does not show up on your website.

- **Place your articles on other sites.**
  If your staff has the expertise to write articles and other content, it is possible to find other sites that would welcome your content as a way to make their own site more interesting. Synergistic partnerships – between a pet store

and a humane society or between an art school and an art dealer, for example – can be very rewarding for both parties. The art school mentioned above may be very interested in articles and biographical sketches about specific artists.

- **Create content that reaches customers through e-zines and newsletters**
  If you offer an opt-in newsletter or e-zine, you have an excellent opportunity to use content to remind customers of your products and why they should return to your site.

- **Use viral marketing to let your content spread interest**
  Tell a friend, wish lists, article bookmarks, and many other site tools can generate emails that allow your customers to tell each other about your products. When these emails are about products for which you have related content, adding a link to the content can be a good way to bring customers and new visitors to your site.

- **Lead customers back to your site through links in e-mails and on carefully chosen site pages**
  There are many cases where customers want communication from you. Order confirmations, responses to complaints or queries, order reminders, and even thank you pages in the shopping cart all offer an opportunity to provide a simple description of useful content and a link back to your site.

  Even complaints can give you the opportunity to offer the customer links to helpful pages in your customer service sections and also a link to your customer review and feedback pages. The more reasons and opportunities your customers have to visit your site, the more chances you have to sell.

Chapter 10 Links
Using Content to Increase Sales

http://www.clickz.com/design/cont_dev/
Content Development
If content is king, Susan Solomon wonders: "Then why is website content so thoroughly mediocre?" Also check this site for info on the "Creative Message" and "Writing Online."

http://ipw.internet.com/site_management/publishing/index.html
Internet Product Watch's section on Content Publishing
Links to tools for creating, managing, and updating dynamic content for your website

http://usableweb.com/topics/000414-0-0.html
Usable Web's area on Content
Usable Web is a collection of links about information architecture, human factors, user interface issues, and usable design specific to the World Wide Web.

http://www.clickz.com/design
Clickz Today
Comprehensive list of articles and whitepapers, on the topics of design, content, and creativity.

http://html.about.com/cs/content/
About.com's section on Content
Contains useful articles, informative essays and tips.

http://www.adbility.com/show.asp?cat_id=344
Adbility's section on Instant Content
A place to find syndicated content.

http://www.infoworld.com/news/contentmgmt.html
Infoworld's section on Content and Content Management
Articles, essays, tips and interviews, all on the related subjects of site content, and content management methods and systems.

http://usability.gov/methods/collecting_writing.html
Usability.gov section on Collecting, Writing, and Revising Content
Advice on finding and posting information that users want and need.

http://iqpc.nac.net/
The Content Management Network
News, forums, conferences, and white papers.

http://www.content-wire.com/Home/
Content Wire
Content Wire is a website dedicated to all areas of content management. It provides articles, commentary, a newsletter, and an interesting section on content lifecycle.

http://www.contentmanagementfocus.com/
CM Focus magazine website
"The essential publication for the content management professional."

11

Making Your Site Work Smarter

In this chapter I will discuss:

- How to use data to discover your most valuable customers, personalize your site for them, and refine your product offering.

- What kind of statistics you can gather from your website and what they might mean.

- Analysis of website traffic or "hits" is useful for some things, but is only the most basic kind of e-commerce reporting.

- How do I analyze a sales report?

- How can I use website data to evaluate the behavior of my customers?

- Campaign reports can tell you how effective your marketing efforts are, and which techniques and approaches work best together.

Measurement and Analysis for a Better Website

Measurement is a key component to managing your site intelligently. Unless you know what is working, you won't know what to keep and what to throw away. Monitoring sales figures, product sales trends, page views, and other data are crucial tools in the on-going task of monitoring your site's performance.

Your site reports will help you make a number of very important decisions about what products to keep, which to discard or price and bundle differently, which to include in sales incentives and for which target group that incentive will be most powerful. Every month, you should be pulling your sales figures and analyzing those numbers to guide you in constantly evaluating your site's content, its merchandising, its tools, and product selection. In addition, you should be looking for evidence to help you accomplish several important goals:

- **Discover Your Most Valuable Customers**—Remember that some customers are more profitable than others. This may be the result of the regularity and size of their orders, their purchase profiles, their payment history, their low ratio support costs to profit, or any other way of calculating value that makes sense to your business.

  If you know which customers are most beneficial to retain, you can direct your strongest merchandising and loyalty efforts to this group. Less profitable customers can be offered lower or no loyalty programs.

  If sales to profitable customers decline, analysis of your campaigns may help identify why you have lost them. And, in case your competitors have pulled them away from you, you can also respond promptly by offering special terms to tempt them back.

- **Personalization**—Every customer of a standard walk-in store sees the same physical premises, is limited to the same on-site range of products, is offered the same prices and has pretty much the same experience of the store as any other customer.

  You can do better on a Web-based store site. If the customer is registered or has a cookie, your site can remember who the user is, and can offer a different product range, prices, messaging, special offers, and even customized site navigation. By storing shipping and accounting information, the site can make the whole buying process go quicker and easier.

  Part of this desirable personalization can be carried out automatically, based on previous choices and behavior of the customer, so the site can learn from previous visits. But the personalization can extend to automatically serving up brief reports to remind visitors of what they have purchased previously or what special discounts are available to them based on their loyalty or interests. This could extend to showing how an extra purchase could move the buyer to a higher discount rank.

- **Product Refinement**—Every product offered on your site carries a certain overhead in terms of inventory management, data storage for information, and product images, and expands the results of searches and category index pages. If you are offering a product that no one is buying, maintaining it on your website might be costing you more than selling it is gaining you. For some stores, offering a wide variety is important, but others may want to concentrate only on their best sellers.

Even more important is gaining a true understanding of the appeal of your products to your customers. If you can correlate demographic information, target groupings, and product sales, you can discover which products are most likely to appeal to your best target groups, and which might increase the interest of groups whose performance is below par. When deciding which lines to expand and which to reduce, which categories to retire, combine, or create, and which items to sell only seasonally, you need to have a clear picture of the actual sales performance of your products.

The Data to Gather

There are eight main data types you should be gathering for your site. These are:

1. Traffic Statistics

2. Sales Reporting

3. Customer Reporting

4. Product Reporting

5. Campaign and Promotion Reporting

6. Content Reporting

7. Site-Gathered Data Reporting

8. Path-to-Purchase (Clickstream) Reporting

Each kind of report will give you part of the story; none will be adequate on its own. There is a considerable overlap, as some of these reports use the same data viewed from a different angle: but all are useful in understanding what trends and behaviors are developing within your customer groups.

1. Traffic Statistics

You use a traffic report when you need rudimentary, base-level information on your site. Generate traffic reports when you need to look at server loads, how traffic comes in, what time of the day it comes in, how it affects your overall concurrent usage (charts 1 and 2), and so forth.

What are Traffic Statistics?

This is the most basic form of Web reporting, often referred to as hit reporting. A hit is the retrieval of any item from a Web server, like a page or a graphic. For example, when a visitor reaches a Web page with four graphics, they generate five hits, one for the page and four for the graphics. Every one of those hits is recorded on your server in the log files for your site. Traffic analysis typically involves analyzing these log files to create a variety of reports.

Most e-commerce sites spend far too much time on traffic analysis. Audit trails, server and network load analysis, and identifying major trends in overall site activity are important up to a point. Beyond that, your focus should be on analysis and reporting activities that help you convert visitors into buyers, attract new customers, maintain repeat customers, identify key customer and market segments, and strengthen and expand existing customer loyalty. In the majority of situations this is accomplished best with a reporting and analysis system that is fully integrated with the rest of your e-commerce site, and one that keeps traffic analysis in its proper perspective.

What do Traffic Statistics Tell You?

These reports can tell you how many visitors, views, and hits took place on your site over various time periods, like in the hours and days after running an email campaign or a television commercial. Along with counting visitors to your site, traffic reports based on analysis of Web server log files can yield a variety of other traffic information but in essence they are all fairly high-level trend reports and that is probably their greatest value.

Reports can include the following:

- *Where*, on the Web, your visitors came from.

- *What* they looked at on your site.

- *What* they downloaded.

- *How long* they stayed.

- *What* website they came from.

- *What* key words they entered into a search engine to find you.

Chart 1 is an example of one kind of traffic report. Chart 2 is a closeup of Chart 1.

Most Requested pages

Most Requested Pages					
	Pages	Views	% of Total Views	User Sessions	Avg. Time Viewed
1	http://ultimatesoundarchive.com/default.cfm	1,684	20.77	1,312	00:01:05
2	http://ultimatesoundarchive.com/srchpost.cfm	508	6.26	367	00:00:39
3	http://ultimatesoundarchive.com/sa/pricing.cfm	441	5.44	413	00:00:33
4	http://ultimatesoundarchive.com/search.cfm	440	5.42	396	00:00:27
5	http://ultimatesoundarchive.com/soundlist.cfm	323	3.98	191	00:00:41
6	http://ultimatesoundarchive.com/sa/srchpost.cfm	294	3.62	120	00:01:24
7	http://ultimatesoundarchive.com/examples.cfm	253	3.12	222	00:01:17
8	http://ultimatesoundarchive.com/cat.cfm	201	2.48	188	00:00:37
9	http://ultimatesoundarchive.com/sa/freeinfo.cfm	196	2.41	185	00:01:21
10	http://ultimatesoundarchive.com/sa/search.cfm	178	2.19	129	00:00:28
	Sub Total for the Pages Views Above	4,518	55.75	N/A	N/A
	Total for the Log File	8,104	100.00	N/A	N/A

Least Requested pages

Least Requested Pages				
	Pages	Views	% of Total Views	User Sessions
1	http://ultimatesoundarchive.com/sa/sounds artist.cfm?artist id=192	1	0.01	1
2	http://ultimatesoundarchive.com/sa/sounds.cfm?sound group id=1178	1	0.01	1
3	http://ultimatesoundarchive.com/sa/sounds.cfm?sound group id=1803	1	0.01	1
4	http://ultimatesoundarchive.com/sa/sounds.cfm?sound group id=1179	1	0.01	1
5	http://ultimatesoundarchive.com/sa/sounds.cfm?sound group id=433	1	0.01	1
6	http://ultimatesoundarchive.com/sa/sounds.cfm?sound group id=435	1	0.01	1
7	http://ultimatesoundarchive.com/sa/sounds.cfm?sound group id=455	1	0.01	1
8	http://ultimatesoundarchive.com/sa/sounds.cfm?sound group id=780	1	0.01	1
9	http://ultimatesoundarchive.com/sa/sounds.cfm?sound group id=451	1	0.01	1
10	http://ultimatesoundarchive.com/sa/sounds.cfm?sound group id=453	1	0.01	1

Chart 1

Most Requested Pages	
	Pages
1	http://ultimatesoundarchive.com/default.cfm
2	http://ultimatesoundarchive.com/srchpost.cfm
3	http://ultimatesoundarchive.com/sa/pricing.cfm
4	http://ultimatesoundarchive.com/search.cfm
5	http://ultimatesoundarchive.com/soundlist.cfm
6	http://ultimatesoundarchive.com/sa/srchpost.cfm
7	http://ultimatesoundarchive.com/examples.cfm
8	http://ultimatesoundarchive.com/cat.cfm
9	http://ultimatesoundarchive.com/sa/freeinfo.cfm
10	http://ultimatesoundarchive.com/sa/search.cfm
	Sub Total for the Pages Views Above
	Total for the Log File

Chart 2

Traffic analysis can be used to determine the loads on your servers and networks at peak periods, and to evaluate site, server, and network scalability. While traffic analysis from log files may be widely used, they have some serious shortcomings.

The log files themselves can be extremely large, frequently exceeding giga-bytes per day for large, popular sites. In order to gain any useful information from them, they must be parsed and analyzed. If they are analyzed on your Web server, that process can, in some cases, slow your site significantly or even bring down the server.

In most cases, log files are periodically transferred from the Web server and then analyzed on a separate system with specialized software packages that process and write the log files into a separate data analysis system for analysis and reporting.

In addition, the data in log files may not tell you exactly who each visitor is or where each visitor came from due to the dynamic IP addressing schemes at large ISPs and Internet portals. It is quite easy to get 100,000 hits from AOL vis-itors, all showing the same IP address in Virginia. Beyond this, hits themselves are a misleading indicator. For example, one person coming to your site who looks at 10 Web pages, each of which contains 5 images and then buys nothing would gen-erate a total of 50 hits in the log file. A different person might come to the site, look at one page, buy $1,000 worth of one item, and generate fewer than 10 hits.

Finally, log file analysis and traffic reports based on them suffer from another critical deficiency: they don't tell you much about who actually buys things on your site.

2. Sales Reporting

Sales reports are an important tool to evaluate the efficiency of both your inventory and your campaigns overall. You use sales reporting because you need to evaluate short- and long-term trends for products individually and by department.

What are Sales Reports?

Sales reports are any statistics that tell you how specific products or groups of products have sold. They may also bring to light some information surrounding those sales and the factors that contributed to a customer's decision to buy. Sales reports will also be combined into other sorts of reports, but even in their simplest form, they reveal important information that will affect your inventory, marketing, and pricing decisions.

What do Sales Reports Tell You?

These reports can tell you how many of each product was bought, what campaigns were most effective in selling them, which products were most likely to be abandoned in the cart, seasonal attractiveness of certain products, and which target groups bought the most of certain items.

In order to do sales reports you need to be able to keep statistics on what products sell, how they sell, and to whom. Some examples of sales reports are:

- **Sales by customer group.** How many of each product were sold to each target group. This information can be especially useful when designing your personalized marketing plans.

- **Sales conversion reporting.** Conversion statistics by product. When evaluating conversion figures, it will often be useful to see which items in particular are "converting" most successfully. Use other information to help pinpoint whether successes are the result of a better ad, higher customer demand, a promotion, or other factors.

- **Abandoned cart reporting.** How many of each product were abandoned in the cart. When customers put something in the cart, but then do not complete the sale, this can be an indication of some problem, especially if it is happening more frequently for some products than for others.

- **Average order size reporting.** The average size of orders containing the product. This can affect what sort of promotions the product should be included in (chart 3).

Sales - Average Order Size Report
Filter = Time
From 11/1/2000 to 11/6/2000

Daily	Orders	Sales	Average Order Size
11/1/00	1,000	$25,000	$25.00
11/2/00	1,100	$26,400	$24.00
11/3/00	900	$30,600	$34.00
11/4/00	1,500	$66,000	$44.00
11/5/00	1,400	$75,600	$54.00
11/6/00	1,100	$41,800	$38.00
Total	**7,000**	**$268,400**	**$37.91**

Chart 3

- **Sales Summaries.** These are overall reports which show information such as average numbers of items per order, average sales per visit, the abandoned cart rates, average order size, etc., all in summary form.

- **Sales trends.** Trend reports show how certain product groups are doing over time, in terms of number of sales and amount of those sales. These can be very useful in getting an idea of how sales may be improving or declining in response to various promotions and customer tastes in general.

Why are Sales Reports Important?

Sales reports let you know when products should be dropped from your site, which products would be most effective as part of a campaign, which might be good incentives as gifts, and what products should be moved higher or lower in sort orders. It may also tell you which products are generating high interest and might be good candidates for an email newsletter article, a gateway kicker, or other promotion.

Your Web sales reporting system should have one overriding goal: to tell you what is driving sales on your website. A great deal of Web sales reporting does not go much beyond showing sales volume per day or average sales per visitor. These can be thought of as cash register reports. These kinds of reports include:

- Sales details, in dollars and units, by product and product group(s) over time periods of interest. This information can be very useful, though limited. Use them to get a general idea of the performance of specific items and groups of items. Specific items that are performing very badly should probably be dropped from inventory entirely. Some items, however, will have a seasonal component, so be sure to look at year-long patterns as well as short term data. Product information will be much more useful later, when combined with other data such as performance by customer group, for example.

- Sales averages by size, products, and product groups over various periods of time. Again, this information is fairly one-dimensional, though it can give valuable information on inventory needs and stocking requirements.

- Abandoned cart reports that show the proportion of users who left your site with unpurchased items in their online shopping carts.

- Sales summaries which show overall numbers. These reports help monitor fluctuations over time of your site as a whole. Snapshot views of sales can help you to evaluate the overall effects of sales campaigns, seasonal fluctuations, or other broad-scale tendencies. Overall sales are good to monitor in conjunction with other reports: if your overall sales totals suffer during a campaign even if traffic is up and kickers are converting well, then it is possible that your campaign is detrimental rather than positive. Of course, your campaign goal may be something other than overall sales, but it is still crucial to be aware of the effects your campaign is having on sales.

Truly effective sales reporting for the Web must go beyond these traditional types of reports. Higher level reports take advantage of all the customer and sales data collected on your website, as well as information available from relevant external data sources such as survey and demographic data relevant to your business, customer groups and market segmentation.

The reports should focus on customer views from a variety of perspectives or dimensions rather than just cash register views. These dimensions can include sales categories such as lifestyle events like vacations or holidays, as well as grouped or segmented buying trends for new and existing customers that will allow you to create highly personalized reports.

Some examples of useful higher-level sales reports include:

- Sales trend reports that tell you how products are performing over time. This information can tell you which products should be stocked, presented, or featured only seasonally, and which products might be best to discontinue altogether. When a lot of activity is occurring in an individual category, and little is happening in others, it may indicate that a category should be expanded, split into several sub-categories or even be recreated as new top level categories.

- Conversion reports that map viewers (browsers) to actual sales—see the section on conversion reporting later in this chapter. Conversion reports are especially important when you want to know which of your marketing efforts are most effective for which products.

- Market and customer group segmentation reports based on your own sales data as well as external data sources that can give you ideas for targeting new customer groups in the future.

- Sales conversion ratios by products or product groups. These reveal the conversion statistics for products, or product groups. A conversion ratio is the number of sales per view.

- Other sales and site reports that show you how well your search tools, coupons, reminder services, gift registries and other specialized site tools are working.

3. Customer Reporting

Customer reports are a necessary tool to evaluate the efficiency of your customer segmentation and your marketing. You use customer reporting because you need to evaluate short and long-term behaviors of your customers.

What are Customer Reports?

Customer reports help you look at the behavior of your customers according to a variety of demographic information. This information can be invaluable in evaluating your target groupings, in designing promotions, mapping out personalization plans, and creating site content. Because lifetime value is such an important indicator of long-term retail viability, it is crucial to know which customers are proving to be the most valuable over time. Some customer reports reveal which customers are returning to buy again, and what sort of products they are buying. Others break down customer buying patterns according to geography, age, gender, or other factors. All of this information can be cross-referenced to provide valuable insights.

What do Customer Reports Tell You?

Customer reports give a lot of information which, properly analyzed, reveal a lot about what is important to your customers. They also give hints on how to better serve them by offering promotions, package deals and other incentives that are relevant to them. Some examples of customer reports include:

- **Summary**
  Summaries can tell you how many new customers and returning customers you have gained, broken down through a variety of filters, such as target groups, geography, or other demographic information. This can give valuable cross-channel information, as well as reveal possibilities for new marketing opportunities.

- **Snapshot**
  Customer snapshot reports reveal sales figures by segment, both in the short term and over the customer lifetime. These reports are valuable for comparing both the number of sales and the size of sales among your various customer groups.

- **Segments**
  Customer segment reports help to compare the performance of specific segments. Sales counts, sales amounts over customer lifetime and in the last 30 days, as well as average sales per customer can be compared by segment. Overlaps between segments can also be very illuminating, suggesting future specials which might be coordinated between the groups, or even the need for a new, blended customer grouping.

- **Segment crossover**
  Segment crossover data can be so interesting, that sometimes it is valuable to cross-check it against even more data. Customer segment reports can compare all the data in the segment report, as well as average order size, and all segments and populations at once, rather than just two segments at a time (chart 4 - see next page).

- **Purchases**
  Customer purchase reports help you get a handle on which product groups are doing well with which target groups. Again, this information is invaluable when designing marketing, pricing, and customer personalization strategies (chart 5 - see next page).

- **Vintage.** Vintage reports reveal how many customers your site has had recently, and over various time periods, and correlates this information with how recently customers have made a purchase. This information will tell you if your lifetime value figures are likely to be healthy, and can also be an indicator of customer satisfaction and marketing success.

Customer Segment Crossover
Filter = None

Customer Segments	Customer Segments					
Number	All Customers	Gold Members	Corvette Club	Men Over 40	Teenage	First Time Buyer
All Customers	100,000	35,000	14,000	25,000	35,000	22,000
Gold members	35,000	35,000	11,900	15,400	3,850	-
Corvette Club	14,000	11,900	14,000	12,320	140	3,080
Men over 40	25,000	15,400	12,320	25,000	-	8,500
Teenage	35,000	3,850	140	-	35,000	11,550
First Time Buyer	22,000	-	3,080	8,500	22,000	22,000

Percent	All Customers	Gold Members	Corvette Club	Men Over 40	Teenage	First Time Buyer
All Customers	100.00%	35.00%	14,00%	25.00%	35.00%	22.00%
Gold members	35.00%	35.00%	11.90%	15.40%	3.85%	0.00%
Corvette Club	14.00%	11.90%	14.00%	12.32%	0.14%	3.08%
Men over 40	25.00%	15.40%	12.32%	25.00%	0.00%	8.50%
Teenage	35.00%	3.85%	0.14%	0.00%	35.00%	11.55%
First Time Buyer	22.00%	0.00%	3.08%	8,.50%	22.00%	22.00%

Chart 4

Customer Purchases
Filter = None

Units: Items purchases per customer

Customer Segment	Product Category				
Sum	Books	Music	Food	Beverages	Total
All Customers	157	112	3,527	2,986	6,782
Gold members	33	23	435	45	536
Corvette Club	43	23	445	434	945
Men over 40	45	34	3,434	3,434	6,947
Teenage	34	34	45	34	147
First Time Buyer	54	35	344	34	467

Row %	Books	Music	Food	Beverages	Total
All Customers	2.31%	1.65%	52.01%	44.03%	100%
Gold members	6.16%	4.29%	81.16%	8.40%	100%
Corvette Club	4.55%	2.43%	47.09%	45.93%	100%
Men over 40	0.65%	0.49%	49.43%	49.43%	100%
Teenage	23.13%	23.13%	30.61%	23.13%	100%
First Time Buyer	11.56%	7.19%	73.66%	7.28%	100%

Chart 5

Why are Customer Reports Important?

The cost of acquiring a new customer can be very high. As mentioned elsewhere, if your customers buy once and never return, your cost of acquisition will almost certainly prove to be ruinously high. When raising the return-to-buy rate only a few percentage points can have a major impact on your bottom line, it is imperative to monitor closely not only how many customers return, but which customers are returning.

Customer segment information, customer vintage reports, and cross-segmentation data all help in several crucial areas. The most important of these is in your personalization. When you examine your customer reports, you will be able to tell which customers would be the best candidates for a new sales campaign, which ones your new marketing efforts may be losing, and you may even be able to deduce why. Customer reports are one of your most important tools for directly evaluating which customers are satisfied, and which are not.

This can lead to good suggestions on which campaigns or personalization programs to try next.

4. Product Reporting

Product reports allow you to monitor the sales performance of specific products and product groups. You use product reporting because you need to keep track of your inventory levels and sales trends (overall popularity and target group interest) of your product lines.

What are Product Reports?

Product reports tell you how much of a particular item has sold. They will tell you how much of a particular category has sold, and also during what periods of time they sell well and when they sell poorly. They should also be able to tell you which items are in stock, which are out of stock, and which are back ordered. Some systems may be able to track which items are in stock in some stores, but not available in others.

What do Product Reports Tell You?

Product reports will help you monitor your inventory levels in real time. They should be able to reveal trends on a group (product category) as well as on an item-by-item level (by item number or SKU) Some examples of product reports include:

- **Snapshot**
  This report will list items individually, and give totals for units sold, amount sold, and average costs per unit, during a specific block of time.

- **SKU**

   An SKU report will list individual products by product number and give totals in units sold and total monetary value sold within a block of time.

- **Inventory**

   Inventory reports will list individual products by category and name, list whether the product is available or not (active or inactive), give the amount of inventory remaining, and show the minimum inventory levels that have been set. (Minimum inventory levels are a device used by some stores to ensure that online sales are never made that can't be filled if store sales deplete the inventory).

- **Sales Trends Reports**

Why are Product Reports Important?

Product reports will help you identify product categories that are selling well and should therefore be expanded. They can also help you identify products that sell particularly well with certain target groups, at certain times of the year, or when bundled with certain other products.

   When deciding which products to retain, and which to phase out, product reports for the past year will be invaluable. When deciding what products to use in a new marketing campaign, an incentive program, or a new discount package, product reports should give you the data you need to make effective choices.

5. Campaign and Promotion Reporting

Campaign and promotion reports are a necessary tool to evaluate the efficiency of your campaigns and specific marketing and promotional efforts. You use campaign and promotional reporting because you need to evaluate the success of your marketing and messaging.

What are Campaign and Promotion Reports?

All of the above-mentioned data can be especially powerful when organized by specific campaigns and promotions.

   Reports on the effectiveness of your campaigns are one of the most important kinds of Web reporting. Campaign reports are intended to answer questions such as: "What were the results of the 10% discount on product X over the time period of the campaign?" Campaign summaries are reports of the overall success of a particular campaign or promotion. This report displays information comprising all the pieces of the campaign, usually for a specified date range, and shows the sales in units sold and dollar amounts.

What do Campaign and Promotion Reports Tell You?

Campaign reports tell you how effective your marketing efforts are, and which techniques and approaches work best together.

Online promotional activities are tracked using a source code embedded in the digital coupon, URL, or Web address associated with each specific promotion. When a customer clicks through to your site using the hyperlink with the embedded code, your software stores that information in a transaction file. That information can then be used to send email announcements to those customers during subsequent campaigns.

The effectiveness of your offline campaigns can also be evaluated using the Web by providing radio listeners, hard copy catalogue browsers, newspaper readers, or TV viewers with a special Web address that will be picked up on your site and then connected to sales and customer records for that campaign. This serves the same purpose as an embedded code and is easily captured by the reporting system.

Campaign reports are designed to give you a way to measure the success of a promotional campaign. Some examples of campaign reports include:

- **Promotional report**
  Promotions can be stand-alone or part of larger campaigns. Designed to measure the effectiveness of promotions, this report shows sales for each particular promotion by time period or for the entire promotion.

- **Digital coupon sales report**
  This report gives the response in volume and sales dollars for digital coupons and measures the success of the coupons for specified date ranges. Coupons can be stand-alone promotions, or part of a larger campaign.

- **Digital coupon conversion report**
  This report gives detailed information on the success of specific promotions such as digital coupons. Abandoned orders, conversion ratios, number of items bought per order: all these things can be invaluable when later deciding which digital coupons had the desired effect.

- **Affiliate referral report**
  This report shows sales results from affiliate program referrals over the specified date or date range, and the resultant sales in dollars.

- **Campaign conversion rates**
  Campaign conversion rates are crucial in evaluating the success of a particular campaign. Campaigns can be evaluated by response rates, number of orders, order sizes, number of abandoned carts, and possibly other

criteria. Whether the campaign was a success will depend on what the goals for the campaign were, but all of this data will be interesting and useful information in planning the next campaign.

- **Cross-sell conversion report**
  When determining which cross-sells are effective, it is useful to examine not only which items sell well together, but how one item affects the others. Product A may have a high rate of convincing customers to buy Product B, but the reverse may not be true. (Ex: buying a candlestick may induce many people to buy candles that fit it, but buying candles may not necessarily convince customers to buy another candlestick). Where these relationships exist, it is important for future sales and merchandising campaigns to be aware of them, and how strong that influence is. Furthermore, different combinations of products will likely perform differently with different target groups.

Why are Campaign and Promotion Reports Important?

The Internet is an unparalleled medium for reaching existing customers and new prospects in a cost-effective way. It also provides unmatched capabilities for assessing the effectiveness of customer acquisition campaigns, often in real time. Online marketing campaigns can increase sales, enhance your branding and presence on the Web, increase affiliate relationships, and improve your customers' shopping experience across your product lines, product groups, and affiliates, as well as within your sales channels.

Campaign and promotion reports should be run and checked frequently, especially when testing out new campaign ideas. As responses come in, campaigns and promotions can be refined and/or corrected in near-real time. Unlike the brick-and-mortar world and print advertising, online ads and discounts can respond nimbly to indications that a current promotion has a serious flaw or is particularly successful. But to act quickly on these indications, reports must be made to reveal them. Check your campaign reports frequently and be prepared to respond.

6. Content Reporting

Content reports should be used to frequently evaluate the value and appropriateness of the content on your site. You use content reporting because you need to evaluate the amount of effort that your site should dedicate to content.

What are Content Reports?

You need to know which content is being viewed, and therefore which content is most important. Spend your time and effort on frequently updating and expanding only the content your customers care about, and also that which actually shows evidence of increasing sales.

Content reporting is intended to answer one critical question: What is driving sales on your website? A significant and critical investment for any e-business is the development and ongoing evolution of site content. Content is just as important as product because it encompasses virtually every facet of your website and your company's presence on the Web. It includes product information in the forms of text and graphics, navigational tools and links, informative articles, special offers, customer and affiliate testimonials, frequently asked question (FAQ) areas, product usage information, customer ratings, chat areas and bulletin boards, company e-zines, as well as customer service and feedback areas.

What do Content Reports Tell You?

Specific information about the value of articles, product information, FAQs and other site content can best be revealed in a path to purchase report. This report notes which content a customer viewed before deciding to put an item into the shopping cart, and at which point the final decision was made. Hit reports can also be examined to see which content is popular, but it is this report that will do most to reveal the impact your content is having on your sales.

Why are Content Reports Important?

While it is often overlooked by many retailers, how your content is designed, presented, and deployed on your site can have dramatic, positive effects on your sales. Interesting, appropriate, and compelling content can engage a visitor and maximize sales opportunities both now and in the future. A poorly organized site with meaningless clutter and inappropriate, dull content will quickly drive customers away. Research indicates that if a site cannot keep the interest of visitors for more than eight seconds they won't buy anything and usually won't return.

Your reporting system should not only tell you what content is being looked at the most, but also how specific content contributes to sales. Moreover, it should be capable of doing this dynamically, virtually in real time, so you can evaluate and adjust your content rapidly when you find that something is not working, or when you add new content, personalize features, or conduct various sales campaigns. If your content is designed to link visitors to products, then browse-to-buy conversion ratios can be uncovered for each item of content on your site by analyzing and reporting on a customer's click-through behavior.

- Page views—Content reporting can be as simple as tracking page views, or as complex as page-view/sales correlation analysis (see the path-to-purchase section for an example)

- Other content—In addition to articles and editorials, your site has a lot of content which should directly affect sales. You need to know which of these items (such as kickers, lifestyle images, extended product views, etc.) are being viewed, and if possible, determine which have helped lead to a sale.

7. Site-Gathered Data Reporting

Site-gathered data is one of your best tools for directly finding out what your customers think and feel. Only so much can be deduced from observed behavior while on your site. You use site-gathered data because sometimes the best way to find out what's important to your customers is to simply ask.

What are Site-Gathered Reports?

Any online survey, response form, or other information-collection tool on your site will generate some sort of data, even if it is only a simple radio button, two choices, and a "submit" icon. When used in conjunction with cookies and customer registration information, seemingly simple surveys and response forms can give surprising good feedback.

What do Site-Gathered Reports Tell You?

Any question that you can put in a survey or form could be collected on-site. Of course tact and sensitivity must be used as customers have every reason to feel cautious about what and how much they reveal to you. Questionnaires and surveys that are too long will be largely ignored. But if you can find the moment (and there usually is one) when customers are in the mood to give you feedback or are willing to answer a few questions in return for some incentive, you can gather a lot of very useful information. Further, that information can be cross-indexed against what information you already have about that customer.

Some examples of site-gathered data include:

- **Survey summary report**
  A survey summary report will list all the questions on your survey, the number of customers who selected each choice, and the percentage of the total that each represents. This is a good way to get an overview and first pass "feel" for the responses.

- **Survey by question report**
  A survey by question report allows you to view the same information as in the summary, but separated by question, and further filtered by other information, such as target group, new user versus return customer, referred-link customer, etc.

- **Survey cross-question report**
  The cross-question report allows you to compare directly which customers who answered question X a certain way also answered question Y a certain way. This can be very useful for identifying the outlooks and characteristics which define a target group.

8. Path-to-Purchase (Clickstream) Reporting

Path-to-purchase reports tell you what is selling to whom and when. You need to know everything you can find out about exactly what is working to make sales. You also want to be aware of which products are attracting which groups.

What are Path-to-Purchase Reports?

Path-to-purchase reports give sales numbers reported by which page's buy button was used to place an item in a cart. Or, it may record specific clickstream data such as the page viewed immediately prior to the product page. The level and depth of information will depend on your site's ability to track customer behavior and on how much data it can track at once in real time.

What do Path-to-Purchase Reports Tell You?

Path-to-purchase reports come in a variety of complexities and in the amount of computation needed to extract relationships. Some are as simple as seeing how many times a page is viewed. These reports can be simple but effective early warning systems: if no one is reading your articles or extra product information, it is not likely that these things are affecting sales. Other reports attempt to track a customer's most recent clicks just before selecting the buy button, or to correlate conversion rates with different kinds of data such as sales by product, target group, or kicker.

Some kinds of information require a lot of computation to gather, and you will want to run your analysis in the most efficient manner and at a time when the load generated by such a report will not negatively impact your website performance. Analysis of sales logs or end-of-month sales reports are often best done during off-hours. You may want to run other kinds of reports daily or even hourly if you need to keep a close watch on a special campaign.

Why are Path-to-Purchase Reports Important?

Path-to-purchase reports are essential, precisely because the point at which a sale is made is one of the most important ways to measure your success in selling. It also helps you track the success of your campaigns, messaging, and content in affecting sales – which is of course their primary purpose. Conversion ratios linked to customer behavior and page views help you to pinpoint those ways of selling, times to sell, and tools to sell with, that work best. Furthermore, you can gather seasonal data that will tell you how to best sell your products over time. Once you have identified the methods that work, you can start to generalize the successes across your site. When your conversion rates are high, you know that something is working – and your conversion reports will help to tell you what that something is.

Some examples of reports that give you information about your customers' buying and browsing habits are:

- **Search terms reports**
  One of the favorite ways for many people to navigate a site is to simply go straight to the search box and enter the terms that the customer hopes will lead her directly to the desired item. If you find that customers are entering certain words that are not assigned to some of your products, then use this as an indicator of how to update your search terms. In addition, it may give you data on what products customers would like you to stock.

- **Average page views by day**
  This report is a good snapshot view of your site's activity. Page views by day can tell you where customers are visiting most, and can help reveal the priorities of your major target groups. This information is later even more valuable when combined with conversion information

- **Content viewed / sales correlation report**
  How does the content viewed correlate to sales completed? While correlation is not a guaranteed indicator of causality, it is still valuable for examining which content may have led members of different target groups to buy something. In other words, there is no proof that the content caused better sales, but it is at least reasonable to assume that where high sales numbers and high content views occur together, the content may have helped to complete the sale. If your best customers are interested in a certain kind of content, then obviously providing that content is helping to keep them satisfied and coming back to your site – even if it doesn't directly cause them to buy one product over another.

- **Decision to buy reports**
  These are related to the conversion reports and will reveal not only how many products were bought in relation to products viewed, but also what information helped to induce the customer to buy. Such information can be very valuable in assessing the future need for site content, deducing what sort of promotions, kickers, and tools are most effective, and in general helping to shape the next revision of your site by allowing you to pinpoint what works and what does not (chart 6).

Sales - Decision to buy report
Filter = Time
From 10/1/2000 to 11/1/2000

Buy-Point	Orders	Sales	Average Order Size
Men's shirts	654	$57,552	$88.00
Women's shirts	882	$105,840	$120.00
Kid's shirts	286	$9,724	$34.00
On sale	1,121	$84,075	$75.00
Editorial article	976	$10,736	$11.00
Products search	4,445	$146,685	$33.00
Digital coupon	2,000	$76,000	$38.00
	10,364	$490,612	$47.34

Chart 6

The Future of Web Reporting

In the e-commerce environment, as in any enterprise, in order to understand and use your data effectively, you must first know what data is available and what that data means. In the Internet and e-business age, data collection from websites has never been faster or easier. Furthermore, we are also collecting different types of data. Both of these trends will continue and probably accelerate. At the same time, the challenge to make business sense out of all that data in a timely manner has never been greater.

In this environment, OLAP (OnLine Analytical Processing) techniques have quickly become the approach of choice for analyzing the increasingly large amounts of data collected on websites. OLAP techniques, along with data warehousing and other decision support approaches, were initially used in financial services areas and other businesses where very large amounts of data had to be analyzed. Their use in the Web world was a natural extension of this approach since large websites can generate gigabytes of data on a daily basis.

The great attraction to using OLAP methods for website data analysis is its multi-dimensional aspect: the ability to analyze large amounts of data rapidly, coupled with the flexibility of reporting on that data from many different perspectives. In addition, multi-dimensional OLAP data cubes can be broken down into smaller cubes that can then be compared to each other to find relationships within the data. This is typically referred to as drilling down or slicing and dicing the data to find relationships that pertain directly to customer personalization or Customer Relationship Management (CRM) issues like cross-selling, target marketing, customer acquisition, and customer loyalty.

While OLAP techniques are both fast and flexible, they may require substantial amounts of computing power. You may end up with an enormous data and report report log-jam if the reporting system is not properly integrated with your Web systems, or if the data and dimensions are not chosen carefully before processing and analyzing occurs. This can be a very real problem for larger websites since data is collected continuously and the sites themselves are being changed regularly in terms of their content, products, or promotional offerings. This leads to discontinuous data, new/multiple dimensions to reflect the changes, and a concomitant increase in the data processing demands placed on the OLAP system.

Even if the OLAP processing requirements become large, these can usually be overcome with better technology. The bigger issue is in reporting. As your database grows and changes, generating the right kind and number of reports in a timely manner may become impractical. In the brick and mortar world, you may have weeks to gather, analyze, and interpret data from a direct mail campaign, newspaper ad, or even a TV commercial. In the online world, you may only have hours or days. Pre-defined or canned reports may not capture or reflect subtle differences in the shopping behavior of visitors and the buying patterns of customers on your website. Further, it may not be possible to modify the reporting system fast enough to keep up with the changes to your website, those who visit it, and the buying/spending patterns of your customers.

OLAP techniques are the favored choice at this time, and are likely to remain so for the immediate future. Therefore, it is very important to make sure you don't end up either with a multitude of reports that don't support sales growth and personalization, or with spiraling processing costs. There are ways to minimize these problems, and some of these include:

- Keep your marketing and sales personnel involved in the Web reporting system at all times.

- Establish a flexible data analysis and report system, regardless of whether it is vendor-supplied or home-grown.

- Create a report review and revision process that remains in step with changes to your website.

- Keep the focus of your reporting system on customers and sales: things that will help your business, rather than general website traffic issues.

- Keep the number of reports reasonably small and as effective as possible.

- Don't let the Web reporting process, OLAP or not, turn into a traditional brick and mortar IT operation.

- Avoid having your Web reporting system tied to any proprietary architecture. Report systems based on Java™ methodologies are probably the most platform independent, scalable, and flexible at this time.

Finally, your Web reporting system should be fully integrated with your e-commerce and website management and development system. This will maximize your ability to have the reporting system working in concert with changes to your website, and help prevent the reporting system from becoming an independent entity unto itself.

A prediction: While OLAP and other extant data warehousing techniques represent the methodology of choice for today, the amount of data generated by e-commerce sites is completely unprecedented in the history of data processing. Since necessity is the mother of invention, it is very likely that in response to this exponential growth something new and quite different will replace this approach in the near future.

Chapter 11 Links
Reporting

http://www2.cio.com/metrics/
CIO Magazine site – research center for Metrics
Behind the Numbers – a look behind the numbers you need. Contains valuable and interesting articles and surveys on the use and interpretation of the statistics and metrics used to evaluate and measure website performance and design.

http://www.nua.com
NUA Internet Surveys
An online resource providing information on Internet demographics and trends. Their database contains over four years of freely accessible information gathered and collated by Nua, and Nua's weekly editorial articles.

http://sic.nvgc.vt.edu/
SIC: e-Business Systems Integration Center
See their Tutorial on Clickstream Data Analysis: "The Ultimate Starting Point for Clickstream Data Analysis":
http://sic.nvgc.vt.edu/SICstuff-Virtual/Heine/WWW/index.html

http://www.clickz.com/metrics/
Clickz Today
Comprehensive list of articles and white papers, on the topics of research and personalization. Including such subtopics as: ad measurement , ad metrics, customer metrics, online traffic. Keyword-searchable database with an impressive selection of material.

https://secure1.securityspace.com/s_survey/data/index.html
Security Space Online Free Reports
SecuritySpace provides comprehensive and detailed internet research reports. Although some of their material requires payment, a substantial section contains free material.

http://www.statmarket.com/
StatMarket
"The Recognized Authority in Internet User Statistics." Sign up for their free newsletter. Their "Featured Statistic" offers a free look at some of their most interesting latest research.

12

Multi-Channel Selling

In this chapter I will discuss:

- Multi-channel buying behavior on the part of customers is already remarkably well developed. Merchants who fail to account for this in their business plans do so at their own peril.

- 59% of online shoppers also bought from catalogs, and 43% also bought from brick-and-mortar stores.

- How to overcome the challenges to multi-channel integration: conflicting internal goals, inconsistent customer service across channels, lack of communication among data systems, and others.

- Your website can be the key to converting inter-channel competition into a cooperative effort to boost business across the board.

- Your website can stimulate sales in stores and catalogs through coupons available online, store locators, "request a catalog" feature, and many more.

- Use the same product photos, product descriptions, color schemes, logos, and promotional copy in your catalogs, in your stores, and on your website to promote a uniform customer experience.

The Internet: Growth of a Channel

Throughout this book I have repeatedly mentioned the importance of bringing all your sales channels in line so they present a uniform vision of your company, regardless of how the customer approaches it. You have already learned a lot about how to accomplish this, but in this chapter I will sum up the basic ways in which you can polish your company's multi-channel presentation.

Customers prefer to shop with companies that offer them the greatest range in choices not only in the products they buy but in the way they get them. Because Intelligent Selling means creating the optimal environment for your customers to find the products they want and need, smooth multi-channel integration is a vital part of the process. You owe it to your customers to make it work. And you will reap the rewards in the form of increased loyalty and sales.

Multi-channel selling is not new to the Internet era. For decades, even centuries, businesses with physical store locations have used a variety of other channels to increase sales, and to sell their products in the ways that are most satisfying to their customers.

The benefits of multi-channel selling are stronger than ever. The Internet now offers the promise of intelligently uniting the three primary sales channels — retail, catalog, and Internet — into an interrelated whole. With well-integrated organizational and technological changes, consistency and congruence across all channels will be a natural by-product of the way companies do business.

The Jupiter Media Metrix Online Shopping Index forecasts that, by 2006, 132 million U.S. consumers will shop online, representing 63 percent of the online population and 44 percent of the U.S. population. This is a huge leap from the 66 million U.S. consumers who were shopping online 2001. Forrester also released data confirming that online shopping continues to take hold with US shoppers but also that "fragmented sales mean that retailers must fight to defend their market share." A major goal for retailers should therefore be to de-fragment their sales through careful assimilation of the forces that tend to fragment it, in this case, the Internet and e-commerce.

The problem of assimilating a new sales channel is not new. A look to the past shows that as transportation and communication technologies evolved, entirely new selling techniques were invented and added to the mix of customer-merchant interactions available to the retailer. Door-to-door sales, in-home "parties", phone sales, mail-order, in-store kiosks, and many others are now part of the everyday shopping experience. Each new channel rarely replaces older ones entirely; they are just added to the retail repertoire. Sears and Roebuck may have become a household name in the 1800s by selling from their catalog, but their catalog never replaced their brick-and-mortar stores. It was incorporated into their overall business.

In this sense, e-commerce is merely one more technology that businesses must now accept and incorporate in their integrated sales and merchandising plans. But in another sense, the Internet does represent a substantial advantage in multi-channel interaction. Where once each new channel caused some degree of fragmentation in the merchandising capabilities of a business, the Internet model now shows the potential of reintegration and realigning a business's many channel options. The website can actually be the key tool in pulling all channels together and getting them to work in harmony.

The Internet is an information tool, and it is with information that integration takes place. In less than a decade, the Internet has become a "killer app" for modern culture. Combining the resources of dictionary, encyclopedia, telephone, ATM, and catalog, the Web allows the immediacy of face-to-face contact, the low-pressure environment of home catalog shopping, the exchange of detailed information as with an expert salesperson, and the advanced media potential of television ads or movie product placements.

Behaviors of Customers Purchasing From Multiple Channels

Research has shown that, given the tools to do so, most customers prefer to compare similar products and do their research before they buy. Increasingly, the most convenient tool for doing that research is the Internet. Even for those customers who prefer to buy in-store, many will first make comparisons or conduct research through a combination of catalogs, direct mailings, peer-referrals, and most recently, browsing on the Internet.

Results from a summer 2001 Boston Consulting Group (BCG) report show that "fully 88% of all Internet users in the six countries we surveyed, browse," which they defined to mean looking up products on the Internet for information and selection, even with no intent to buy. BCG believes that "to take full advantage of this enthusiasm, companies will have to look beyond online transactions to consider all the behavior that consumers exhibit on the Internet."

BCG found, for example, that of all Internet users who browsed online before purchasing offline, 37% stated that browsing online helps them get a better idea of the choices that are available. Furthermore, 85% of this group bought offline in the end, though they identified the brand and product online. 35% bought from a merchant they found online.

Most businesses are likely to see a clear distinction between each of their channels and the purchases made through them, but to most customers, the line between these channels has already blurred into invisibility. Suppose a customer buys something from a brick-and-mortar store or catalog after using the Internet to find what he wants. Does it make sense to call this sale a purely "in-store purchase?"

The Web has matured to the point at which it has to be considered a part of the mainstream business world, and part of any broad-based merchandising effort. It is no longer just a realm for computer aficionados and research communities.

A recent study by BizRate (an e-commerce rating service) and the J. C. Williams Group makes this abundantly clear. In their report "Channel Surfing: Measuring Multi-Channel Shopping," they found that multi-channel behavior on the part of customers is already remarkably well developed. Some of their results include:

Purchasing Across Channels

Online Shoppers who also bought from:
Store (59%)   Catalog (43%)

Store Shoppers who also bought from:
Catalog (21%)   Website (4%)

Customers not only buy from more than one channel, but many also use the resources from one channel to influence their decision to buy from another:

Cross-Channel Influence
(% of customers that looked for or purchased something previously seen in another channel).

Saw in store, bought in:
Catalog: 34%   Online: 27%

Saw in Catalog, bought in:
Store: 35%   Online: 51%

Saw Online, bought in:
Store: 34%   Catalog: 23%

Of particular note is the report's finding that online shoppers who also buy through a catalog will spend 36% more on the website than those who only buy on the site without use of the catalog.

The BizRate study suggests that you sell much more to your customers if you sell to them through multiple channels. No one channel has it all – personal service, detailed information, easy product location and perusal – so customers do a little bit of it all, and get the best of all worlds by using them together. Remember that your focus is your customer, so give them the experience they prefer.

Multi-Channel Selling Increases Overall Sales and Improves Retention and Loyalty

The basic, underlying reason to employ multi-channel methods is to increase sales, whether directly (by providing more buying opportunities) or indirectly (by improving the customer experience in such a way that customer loyalty, retention, and satisfaction increase).

Also found by the BizRate.com/J.C. Williams Group study:

- Store shoppers who also visit the retailer's website
  - spend 24% more per store visit.
  - have an 8% higher frequency of store shopping.

- Catalog shoppers who visit the retailer's website
  - spend 8% more per order.
  - order 11% more frequently from the catalog.

- Women are 45% more likely to make online purchases from a merchant with an offline store.

- Loyal customers are 26% more likely to purchase online from a multi-channel merchant.

Again, it's All About the Customer Experience:

Customers themselves seem aware of their own higher satisfaction with stores that have multi-channel options. BizRate found that customers had fairly strong opinions about the advantages of being offered both online and offline shopping. Customers surveyed gave the following reasons for enjoying multi-channel merchants:

1. Can shop online outside store hours: 76%

2. More customer support options (email, phone, online chat) 40%

3. Can check prices online before purchasing from store: 39%

4. Can return online purchase at store: 35%

5. More confident about order when merchant has a brick-and-mortar store: 31%

6. Can get product information from store before purchasing online: 26%.

A Summary of the Advantages of Multi-Channel Integration

In short, all the evidence suggests that offering customers as many options as possible is to the merchant's advantage, especially when those channels work closely together to serve the customer well. The advantages of multi-channel integration are:

- Unifying the customer's complete experience through consistent and satisfying service at all customer touchpoints.

- Serving customers based on their preferences, allowing them to choose the types and methods of interactions that fit their own lifestyles and personalities.

- Increasing overall sales and improving average order size and order frequency

- Strengthening customer loyalty and improving customer retention.

- Aggregating data for closer one-to-one marketing activities, improved customer service, better personalization, and improved business-wide efficiency.

Dangers in Implementing Multi-Channel Selling

There are dangers inherent in the lack of appropriate multi-channel integration. Businesses risk damaging customer satisfaction if their customers are denied services in one venue that they have come to expect from other channels. When services or policies offered in one channel are not available universally, the customer's perception of bad service is likely to outweigh their positive experiences in other channels, and poison their opinion of the whole organization.

Multi-channel models bring up a new and tricky set of balance issues. A deep rift between channels can leave merchants struggling to run what amounts to two or more separate businesses. Unless the website is inextricably integrated into the local and regional accounting system, with fair accounting for local influence on online sales, local channels can end up being penalized for their success in customer satisfaction and for the online sales they helped generate.

Mistakes Made in Multi-Channel Selling

It is obvious that, when well integrated, a multi-channel selling environment can be a great advantage to any business. But because the online channel is relatively new, many businesses have not yet fully integrated e-commerce into their organization, and those that have may not be benefiting from it as fully as they could.

The following are some of the most common mistakes made, and some basic advice on how to redress them. More detailed advice on improving inter-channel functionality is provided throughout the remainder of this chapter.

1. Lack of organizational alignment

The Internet portion of the business is frequently a "tacked-on" part of the organization. Little or no effort may be made to integrate Web capabilities into the organizational structure of the business as a whole. This can lead to serious internal conflicts that harm overall sales, branding, and customer satisfaction issues. Some elements of this problem include:

- **Conflicting internal goals**
  If the website uses sales tactics that draw business away from local stores, then the Web and retail channels will come into conflict. For example, if sales incentives are based on the success of individual channels and not on universal sales volume, then website management might find greater reward in "hoarding" customers than in passing them on to the appropriate channel. But if the most profitable way to sell is through local stores, then good business practices would dictate that the website direct customers to the local store when possible, and that your Web staff be given due credit and compensation for an increase in retail sales.

- **Lack of staff support**
  If compensation in the form of salaries, commissions, and profit and loss accounting is not fairly balanced between the online and offline branches of the business, the staffs of various channels will not work well together. Because of unintended competition for recognition and reward, there will be in-house resistance to the very programs you most need to work together. Again, all staff should be rewarded for an overall increase in sales.

- **Poor communications**
  If online and offline segments do not have clear methods of communicating, both in handling customers and in business and marketing issues, the organization as a whole will suffer. When sales leads, customer preferences, and responsibility for different aspects of customer service are isolated in different branches of the business, the customer will be frustrated and ill served as different branches of the business shuffle responsibility back and forth between departments, or fail to share information. The solution is a universal customer and product database that is accessible from every channel.

- **Lack of brand alignment**

  Brand Alignment is when a customer has a similar impression of the business and is treated consistently no matter which branch of the business is helping him. When there is no consistency, the customer usually remembers his most negative experience and uses that to judge the business. Some brand alignment problems include:

  - **Service levels not consistent across channels**

    If the polarization of your channels means that staff training, availability of resources, management style, and other important details vary from one branch of your business to another, this will filter down to the customer level and taint their perception of your business and brand. Customers may not get the service they have come to expect. The retail stores might have extremely knowledgeable staff, but no access to inventory information. Call center reps might have access to all the inventory and customer information anyone could need, but have no training in customer interaction. A pattern like this will frustrate and anger your customers. All branches should offer consistent service. Return policies, guarantees, the knowledge level of customer service representatives, and other service factors should be congruent across all channels.

  - **Quality of website does not reflect the brand**

    If your website is treated as a wholly separate channel, the result can be something that was put together too quickly, does not reflect well upon your business, does not have customer service capabilities that mesh with other channels, and may not even use the same imagery and language. This will dilute your brand, and leave your customers wondering if they are dealing with the right organization. The website should reflect the same care and investment as other channels. Products and services offered on the Web should be of the same high quality, be handled as carefully, and be backed by the same guarantees and return policies as other channels. Online graphic design and product shots should harmonize with the company's direct mailings, catalogs and in-store materials.

  - **Products vary across channels**

    Deep separation between channels can lead to separate merchandising strategies within each channel. The business will lose customers to other providers when they find that they cannot reliably get the same things in the store, through the catalog, or on the website. The same products should be available from all channels. While it may be acceptable to have a more limited set of products on one channel than the other, or to offer bargains in the channel which has lower operating costs, it is important to communicate at least some of the reasons for these differences to the customer so that there are no unpleasant surprises. And in any case, all channels should offer consistent quality of goods and services. Each channel must be aware of its equal responsibility to reflect well on the organization as a whole.

- **Messaging varies from channel to channel**
  Customers will become confused or suspicious when they encounter differing or contradictory information. All channels should project the same or nearly the same messaging. Whenever possible, increase customer recognition of products across channels by using the same or similar graphics, the same versions of your logos and mascots, and generally maintaining a similar "feel" across all venues.

- **Website is not consistent with campaigns or promotions used for stores or catalogs**
  Promotions in catalogs, stores, and on the website should be consistent and reflect similar graphic design and featured products. When promotions, campaigns, and other messaging such as seasonal changes occur in one channel, the same changes should appear in all channels.

- **Multiple channel usage is not promoted**
  When your channels do not support each other, it exacerbates all other problems and leaves the customer wondering if they are dealing with the same company. Print your URL on catalogs and merchandise bags, offer catalogs through the website and in stores, and put store locators on the website and in catalogs. Remember that the more points of contact you have, the more your customers will buy, and the more likely you will be to have a way of satisfying every customer's unique blend of needs and preferences.

2. Lack of staff training

If both online and offline staff are not consistently trained, customers will be given inconsistent and conflicting treatment, to the detriment of the business as a whole. Staff at your brick-and-mortar locations should receive Web training and become familiar with the services that the website offers. Online customer service reps should be familiar with the stores and even with store-only products if such exist. Cross-train all channels as much as is possible.

3. Inconsistent policies among channels

If policies across channels are not consistent, customers will find themselves effectively penalized for using one sales channel over another. Merchandise returns are a good example. When a customer returns something she bought, allow her to return it to any channel, regardless of how she purchased it.

4. Customers are handled differently among channels

Inconsistent treatment soon results in confused and frustrated customers, with their opinion of the organization as a whole based on their worst experience. Remember that to the customer, you are all one business, not several different departments. Strive for consistency across channels.

5. Lack of communication among data systems

Lack of communication among data systems results in slow or no proliferation of corrections to customer information, preferences, behavior, and past communications. Customers become angry and frustrated when the left hand doesn't know what the right is up to. Furthermore, you may not be able to identify your most valuable customers — those who spread their purchases among a variety of channels. Make sure that all channels share their data, and do your best to use this collective knowledge base when identifying customers with high value, in offering reward programs and incentives, and in crediting customers for cumulative rewards in loyalty programs.

6. Customers have access to more tools and information than employees

Since it is newer, your website may offer superior access to information and product updates. In-store staff is put in the unenviable position of having less access to inventory and other information because they are using outdated retail computer systems. When customers discover this, it reduces their respect for stores, their personnel, and the organization as a whole. This is another error that can be addressed by cross-training, and also by allowing in-store access to the store website. This can be accomplished either by actual web stations, or by in-store kiosks.

Mutual Channel Support: How to Get the Three Main Channels Working Together

To truly support a multi-channel business, your three main retail channels should support each other in all possible combinations (Fig. 1.)

1. Your Internet channel should support your catalog and your stores.

2. Your stores should support catalog and Internet sales.

3. Your catalog should support both the Internet and your stores.

And finally, there should be promotions or campaigns in which all three work equally together to support a common overall goal, such as customer service, or other business imperative.

The tools you use to accomplish this can be anything that helps your organization achieve a specific goal. They may be a process, an online program, or sometimes just a rule of thumb. But each of these tools can be very useful in increasing your effectiveness across channels. The following list is not exhaustive, but should give you some useful starting places for seeing how the channels can cooperate rather than compete.

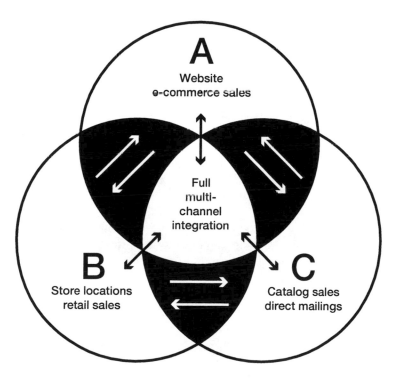

Figure 1

Each of the three primary channels can be used to boost sales in the others, and all three work together to support overall sales through multi-channel integration.

1. How the Internet can help increase store and catalog sales

Stores:

- **Store Locators:** Offer a store finder on the website which locates the store nearest to the customer. Parameters should be country, state, city, or zip code.

- **Promotional Coupons:** Provide online coupons that customers can print out and take to a local retail location. Use them to promote sales of items that are not as efficient to sell via mail order, or which have a higher conversion rate when viewed in person.

- **Event Listings:** On the website, publish lists of upcoming regional events, such as location-specific sales, close-out and remainders sales, seminars, and in-store demos. If pre-registration is required, allow customers to sign up online via online forms or email. If classes have a cost, allow customers to pay online and offer a discount and "no wait" entry and seating for early registration. By offering incentives for online registration, your stores can get a better idea of attendance in advance, and plan space and resources more efficiently.

- **Notification:** Your website can provide email reminders to customers who opt to be notified of sales, seminars, and other events. If your site has a calendar feature, program it to automatically list the events that they have signed up for. Offer a "tell a friend" feature to help spread the word.

- **Purchase Option Button:** For any purchase, you may choose to allow customers to select how and where to buy an item. When items are available on both the website and in the walk-in location, offer a "purchase option" button so customers can choose to buy from your store or from the website. Set it up so they can pay online and pick up their merchandise at the store, place something on "hold" so they can go to the store and pay for it and bring it home, or simply find out which store near them has the desired item in stock.

Catalogs:

- **Request a Catalog button.** Allowing online customers to request a print catalog does a couple of important things. First of all, it gets the catalog to the customer, who may be more comfortable browsing for products offline. Second, it gives the customer a practical incentive for giving you their demographic information (address, email, and a small amount of other information).Add a "save your info" button on the catalog request form, explaining that it will save them time when they return. Even if your registration forms include a lot of other data, you can save this starter information and give the customer a log-on name and password. Your site will recognize the customer during future visits, and you may later convince the customer that it is worth their time to complete a full registration.

- **Send a Catalog to a friend.** Give your customer the option to enter a friend's address and email address, so you can send them a catalog. You should send the friend a single email, informing this person that a catalog will be arriving. Do not add the friend to your opt-in list yet. This one brief but interesting email gives you the opportunity to provide a few helpful links in the footer of the email, offering your new prospect an easy way to contact you on their own. To further help catalog sales, the email could offer a promotion, or an email coupon code for a special discount on a catalog order.

2. How your stores can help increase Internet and catalog sales

Internet:

- **Store loyalty programs.** Collect email addresses whenever customers in your stores sign up for your various loyalty programs. Use them in your website's email promotions for online sales, discounts, and so forth.

- **In-store contests** do not require emails, but you should include an input line for emails for those customers willing to volunteer the information. Offer to notify contest winners by email to increase willingness to give you their email address, and sometimes it may even be appropriate to offer an opt-in box for your store newsletter.

- **Print your Web address** on in-store signs, merchandise bags, newspaper and magazine ads, and on packaging for your branded items. Use it in television and radio ads.

- **Train sales staff** to try the website when local stores do not have specific items in stock. If the store has Web access or kiosks, store staff should help the customer order online.

- **Use special "hang-tag" codes.** Put them on price tags along with your usual SKUs and other information. Program your website to recognize these codes so your customers can go home, enter the hang-tag code, and have online access to the same product line. They would then have the option of ordering their chosen item in a color or size that may not be available at the store, without having to do extensive searching throughout the site.

- **In-store gift registries**, such as bridal or baby registries, should be accessible online. This allows registrants to make changes from home after their initial store visit, and shoppers have the convenience of shopping from home or in the store.

3. How your catalog can help increase store and Internet sales

Internet:

- **Catalog Quick-Order** gives your catalog customers an easy way to shop online. This feature lets your website accept item numbers from your catalog and to serve up product detail pages with information and images identical to those in your catalog. Include a buy now button that takes the shopper directly to the shopping cart. Other systems may simply offer a search or order box where the customer can type in the product number from the catalog, and be taken directly to the check-out page, bypassing the product detail step (fig. 2).

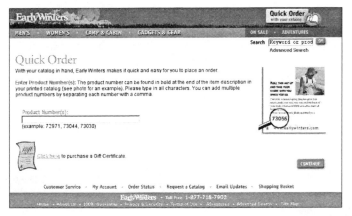

Figure 2

Stores:

- Catalogs can help store sales by referring customers to your online store locator feature, or by including a list of all retail locations.

Brand Support Tips

Aside from simply supporting and boosting sales in other channels, all your channels can work better together to support your brand and public image. The following tips have a primarily indirect effect on sales, but they can have a huge impact on how your customers view and react to your business.

Maintain a consistent look and feel across channels

- Change your website design to reflect changes in retail or your catalog. Keep graphics and product images the same wherever possible.

- Promote your channel alignment. Let your customers know that your channels all work in concert. If there is a sale at your retail stores, announce it online. Allow returns of Web-purchased goods at your retail locations.

- Make sure your promotions on your website and in your stores or your catalog are similar.

- Keep all your policies consistent regardless of channel. For example, it should be easy to return or exchange merchandise regardless of how it was purchased, and a member of a premium customer club should get the same benefits whether they log onto your website, call your phone center, or walk into a retail store.

- Use similar graphics, mascots, icons, etc across all channels to create an instant feeling of consistency whenever a customer encounters your brand. On Walmart's website they use graphics and design similar to those used in their stores, catalogs, and mailers, and they organize their website in a way that reflects the layout of their stores.

Simulate the in-store or catalog experience online

- If you publish a printed catalog, it is probably already one of your strongest brand support tools. Simulate this online by allowing your shoppers the double convenience of browsing the catalog and ordering online 24 hours a day. Catalog tools can work in a variety of ways. One lets the customer input a catalog SKU number and pull up a product page directly. Another streamlines the process even further by letting the shopper enter multiple product numbers and then generating a full shopping cart page already populated with the items they chose. Other catalog tools may simulate catalog page spreads, or send the customer to special search pages depending on the catalog code they enter.

- Decision wizards simulate an in-store experience by emulating the "question and answer" style of an experienced sales person. The shopper uses the Web interface to answer a number of questions about their preferences and needs, and the decision wizard serves up a number of products calculated to please. The Art Matcher from Visualize (fig.3) is one example.

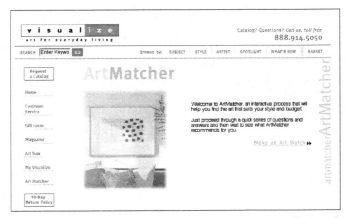

Figure 3

- Provide virtual model technology to let the customer "try things on." This helps bring the store right into the home by helping to show how garments will look when the shopper is wearing them.

- Offer services that show full integration of your channels, such as home delivery or local pickup of catalog and on-line purchases.

Organizational Structure: Getting Channels to Work Better Together

Your business will most likely need to make some organizational decisions in order to really embrace multi-channel integration. It may require that you change the very way your organization conducts its business. When channels are not integrated as part of an overall business-wide strategy, then the business as a whole can suffer as competing channels cannibalize each other. The following are some tips for reorganizing and setting company policy that will help your channels work better together.

Empowerment of Employees

- **Embrace the "Moment of Truth" philosophy**
  The Moment of Truth philosophy refers to the retail practice of trusting the staffer who is on the spot to deal with customer concerns and complaints immediately – without having to refer the customer to a frustrating escalation of levels of management and delays. This requires a certain amount of autonomy and expanded training for all staff, but the rewards can be enormous as processes are streamlined and customer satisfaction rises.

- **Integrate Web training into in-store sales training**
  All stores should have access to the Web, and personnel should be trained on your website's features. Tutorial classes are a good idea.

- **Update training often as website features change**
  It is never a good idea for your customers to know more about your website's features than your own staff. As changes are made, train your store and call center staff on the new material. Make sure that they understand how the Web channel integrates with their own.

- **Pop quiz with prizes**
  Demonstrate the importance you put on your Web channel, and inspire your staff in other channels to become conversant with the Web features, by having after-hours "pop quizzes" with prizes and rewards for good scores.

- **Computer purchase program**
  One of the best ways to increase staff familiarity with the Web is to help employees get their own home systems. Large-group purchase plans can help employees get the best possible price, either directly through a store program or in association with an affiliate store.

- **Provide Web Access in every store**
  Make sure there are Web-enabled machines in the stores and call centers so employees can pull up information and use the online tools while at the store. When possible, also provide kiosks for customers so they can pull up

information on products, access their reminders and wish lists, or even print shopping lists or product specs.

Fair Assignment of Responsibility and Credit

Research has found that approximately 25% of online purchases are returned. Of the items not returned, 41% of customers keep the merchandise even though they did not want it. This is very damaging to long-term customer satisfaction and retention, because customers who get products they are unsatisfied with but cannot easily return are unlikely to buy from that store again.

Surprisingly, only 50% of online retailers accept returns offline. This causes the stores to miss many excellent opportunities to turn a potentially negative experience into a positive one. Customers who return an item at a store are much more likely to select a new item rather than opt for a straight refund. Also, they can get the benefit of in-store sales advice, they often buy other items as well, and they may use the experience to visit a store for the first time.

- One complaint that many stores have is that online sales returned to store locations count against their sales figures. Encourage store enthusiasm for your Web channel by separating accountability for these items from the local stores. Maintain a separate P & L (profit and loss record) for the Web sales and returns, rather than charging such items against the stores.

- Use your website to generate RMAs (Return Merchandise Authorizations). If your returns actually require RMAs, this will have to be integrated into your page programming, but even if you do not actually require the RMA, generating some sort of RMA form for the customer to fill out can help streamline the process and help inform and reassure the customer on the policies and procedures involved.

Tie Compensation for Web and Other Marketers to the Performance of the Company as a Whole

- Look at the whole picture, so channels do not end up being rewarded for cannibalizing each other. At the same time, share credit for multi-channel efforts wherever appropriate.

- Credit Web sales back to the local store or service center. Use the customer's zip code to determine which store is nearest them, and give the store a small bonus for every Web purchase, whether the lead originated in the store or not.

Use Appropriate Talent for Appropriate Tasks

- Your store and catalog merchandising experts should drive your Web merchandising. Use your specialists for execution of tasks specific to the Web channel (e.g. email marketing).

Use Your Website to Drive Direct Purchasing

- Store finders are simple online tools that use the customer's zip code or city to locate nearby brick-and-mortar stores. Other more advanced tools may involve marketing tie-ins between special store events and regionalized Web pages.

- Customers signing up for events through the website might be offered a discount coupon to be printed out from the website and brought to the store, or for simply mentioning the website at time of purchase. Use such activities to measure the influence of the website on the event's participation and success. Whenever possible, track the individual who initiates successful customer contacts or transactions, and reward them appropriately.

Infrastructure for Making Multi-Channel Integration Possible

Re-organizing your company to take advantage of multi-channel integration is one step. Implementing the proper technology is another. There are a number of software and hardware applications available, most notably an assortment of business-wide Web-enabled e-commerce engines. An in-depth discussion of these is beyond the scope of anything in this book, but in general their underlying struc-

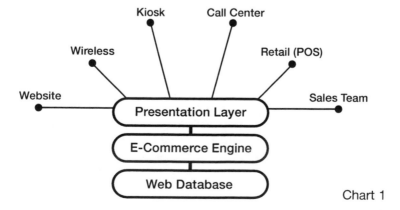

Chart 1

ture can be sketched as in Chart 1.

When an integrated solution with a single data source and real-time access is used, everyone with a stake in the transaction will have their own properly secured window on the data that makes the whole process work. This includes sales staff, customer service representatives, affiliates, point-of-sale kiosks, Business-to-Business clients, and the customers themselves. Maintenance becomes logistically easier as changes to business rules, policies, and other data proliferate naturally throughout the system after being entered into that central data source from any one of these touch-points.

New businesses just starting out have an advantage; they can start up from day one with a fully-formed integrated system in place, giving them advantages in response time and marketing agility and a subsequent leg-up over older, established businesses.

Retro-fitting or converting old systems into a workable integrated structure is not impossible, and established businesses may actually have years of data in legacy systems that can suddenly come to life and provide powerful marketing and selling clues when made available for new analysis and use. Data from customer service records, sales teams, point-of-sale reports, etc. can be quickly correlated and combined to provide powerful new insights.

The difficulty lies in finding the best way to make these connections happen. A lot depends on the flexibility and scalability of existing systems. Sometimes the best solution will be to import data from old systems into a new, turn-key system and start fresh; for other businesses, a network of older and newer systems may be able to work together. The important thing is to get them all talking together and updating (and sometimes correcting) each other. Access control and supervision is important, of course. But the power of data centralization and integration can electrify the way your organization does business, and radically increase your bottom line.

The Ultimate Goal of Intelligent Multi-Channel Selling: Business-Wide Channel Integration

Research indicates that cross-channel shoppers tend to be among a store's very best repeat customers. Such buying behavior strongly points out the need for stores to seamlessly integrate their policies, practices, prices, and philosophies. Because the Internet itself relies on computers and communication between them, it is the perfect tool to get all your channels communicating smoothly.

When businesses use the Internet to coordinate all their varied channels, their customers benefit from the strongest advantages of each channel. A seamless integration of channels allows each channel to use its own strengths to balance the weaknesses of the others, giving customers the impression of always dealing with you when you're at your best.

An example is the business that offers:

- Detailed search and look-up information on its website.

- A printed catalog, which can extend browsing to any place and any time.

- Television ads for promotion of sales and other in-store events.

- Phone representatives for good customer service and order placement.

When all these channels are available to the customer and information is fully shared between them all, then a customer's needs and preferences are very likely to be met. This is the kind of integrated service that customers look for when choosing where their loyalties will be assigned.

When all data and business logic are controlled from one central location, then the whole organization benefits – marketers, managers, customer service, salespeople, and many others. Instead of becoming a potential communications and logistics nightmare, the Web channel brings about needed consistency and congruence across all channels as a natural by-product of the way the organization does business.

A Final Look at the Advantages of Multi-Channel Integration

The Boston Consulting Group believes that businesses with online venues "should treat the Internet not as an independent channel or a stand-alone business but rather as an integral component of a multi-channel strategy for attracting and deepening relationships with high-value customers. Because many consumers are already using the Internet to decide on offline purchases, store-based companies with well-run online sites can begin to profit immediately and gain competitive advantage by delivering a superior multi-channel experience."

The *E-tail Economic Study*, a study by McKinsey & Company with Salomon Smith Barney, found that "retailers who sell to their customers across multiple channels, through stores, catalogs and online significantly increase their chances of generating healthy returns, and emerging intact amid the growing e-tail shakeout."

According to Sean Kaldor, Vice President of Analytical Services at Netratings, leading off-line brands who have started up online stores (such as Walmart.com, JCPenny.com, Target.com, and Sears.com), have proven that they can convert offline customers to online customers, "even matching and exceeding 34% year-over-year growth of online giant, Amazon.com." These sites have proven that customers will indeed buy products online that were previously very difficult to sell through a website.

According to Jupiter Media Metrix, the reason that these strongly multi-channel venues are succeeding is that customers like to do all their shopping, browsing, and comparing online, but make the actual purchases offline. Indications from their study showed that this behavior was especially popular among teens, a strong indication that the future generation of young adults will continue to prefer multi-channel shopping.

Such consumer habits make it all the more important that there be tight integration among a business' channels to manage inventory, commissions, credit for total sales, and other business evaluations. Furthermore, it highlights the great need for businesses to integrate customer data and make the full data picture for each customer available equally to each channel as it comes in contact with the customer.

Chapter 12 Links
Multichannel Integration

http://researchcenter.zdnet.com/
ZDNet's Research Center
ZDNet's Research Center. Use their search tool with multichannel and marketing for some excellent research and articles on making your multiple channels work together with e-commerce.

http://www.etailersdigest.com/search/archive_search.htm
Etailer's Digest – Retail Today
Read recent articles, or use the search feature to find articles in the archive. Be sure to check out the special report on multichannel sales at http://www.etailers-digest.com/resources/Specials/Energy_Slow_Down.htm

http://www.business2.com/webguide/0,1660,39296,00.html
Business 2.0: Multichannel Retailing
Comprehensive archive of articles and research. This section specifically contains its latest articles on retail selling through a variety of channels.

http://b2b.ebizq.net/shared/white_papers.jsp
ebizQ.net
The Portal for e-business integration. Contains white papers, articles and links on a variety of e-business topics. Be sure to read their article on multichannel integration:
http://b2b.ebizq.net/ebiz_integration/thompson_1a.html

http://www.clickz.com/
Clickz Today
Comprehensive list of articles and white papers, on a wide variety of topics. Keyword-searchable database: enter the keyword "Multichannel" for a wide range of excellent articles on this subject.

http://www.allnetresearch.com
Allnetresearch.com
Allnetresearch is a comprehensive site which searches multiple databases for articles and whitepapers which fit your keywords. Use their search tool with the term "multichannel integration."

13

Intelligent Email Marketing

In this chapter I will discuss:

- How to develop a brand-centric e-mail campaign strategy that works for your company.

- Measuring and analyzing e-mail campaigns for continual improvement.

- Creating effective e-mail messages that begin selling the moment they enter your recipient's in-box.

- Avoid the many hazards inherent in e-mail by knowing your brand and being true to it, and by respecting the wishes of your customers.

- Personalizing your e-mail campaigns: targeting your messages for maximum effect without getting in over your head.

- How to build your e-mail list with quality opt-in names.

Why is Email so Powerful?

Although email is not strictly one of the Intelligent Selling components, it is so powerful and its use is so widespread that it is an indispensable part of the Intelligent Selling approach. Used alone or in conjunction with other aspects of online or offline campaigns, it can add a new dimension to the marketer's ability to plant powerful messaging in the minds of recipients, communicate brand identity, build relationships with customers and prospects, and spread the word about offers and promotions. Forrester estimates that U.S. marketers will send 209 billion emails a year by 2004, a quantity that testifies to email's utility and makes forward-thinking marketers wonder how they will manage to be heard above the din.

Proper and effective execution of email campaigns requires careful consideration of overall strategy and the use of some special tactics. This paper outlines the practices that help online marketers maximize the return on their email investment, support the integrity of their brand, build better relationships with their customers, and improve their businesses overall.

Email is fast, effective and relatively inexpensive. It reaches out to customers directly, which makes it active, rather than passive. It can be highly personalized and individually configured, and can even contain images, color, and movement. And yet it incurs only the costs of the email management and delivery of bandwidth, making it far more cost-effective than printed media. It can be modified at the last moment, allowing you to respond quickly to events and customer feedback.

As an interactive medium, email has a great advantage over print or broadcast advertising; it allows and even encourages recipients to take immediate action by providing a mechanism of direct linkage to your store. Imagine a direct mailing letter that included a card upon which was written "Press Here," and which, when pressed, instantly transported the customer into your store with coupon pre-clipped and wallet in hand.

Email Hazards

But that very power brings with it a number of hazards and responsibilities. Email's low cost and the simplicity with which it can be sent means that customers are often swamped by unwanted emails. Many customers already use filters and sieves to pre-sort their "real" mail from the unsolicited mail (called "spam"). To be welcome, an email must either be permission-based, or extremely interesting to the recipient.

Another danger is the erosion of a carefully constructed brand identity through ill-considered messaging tactics. Just as with any other marketing campaign, every item sent via email must be designed to support your company's overall marketing strategy, or you risk diluting or even contradicting the marketing message you so carefully build up through your other channels. Here are some tips on what to do and what not to do:

- Don't send unsolicited bulk email. If you must send unsolicited email, make it very short, to the point, and make it clear how to be removed from all future mailings. If you cannot base your campaign entirely on customers who have asked for contact, at the very least, check all lists against the Direct Marketing Association's (DMA) "Do Not Pander" list (look for links to the DMA in the list of websites at the end of this chapter). Such customers have clearly stated their desire to be excluded from all non-permission-based mailings and you ignore their wishes at your own peril.

- If you use third-party lists it is very important to cross-check them against all your other lists of current customers, past customers, or other email contacts who have asked to be removed from your list. If customers know that you can be relied upon to honor such requests, they are much more likely to consider signing up at a later time if you can convince them of the value of doing so. But once trust is lost, it can be incredibly difficult to regain.

- State your confidentiality policy prominently. Also, clearly state that email addresses will be used only in-house and will never be shared, sold, or rented. If this is not true, inform customers of your policy up front.

- Make it easy for people to say "stop." Include clear instructions on how to unsubscribe. Your messages should include a link that when used, automatically places the recipient on your "opt-out" list. Removals should take effect promptly, within minutes or hours, not days, and these people should never be contacted again unless they opt-in for emails again at some later date. If possible, check each unsubscribe request for other database entries with different email addresses for the same person. Avoid spam-like phrases such as "opt out" and "remove list." Preferred terms are "subscribing" and "unsubscribing," or even "opt-in."

- Make the first contact an acknowledgment. Thank your customer for signing up to receive whatever it is you are sending to remind him of how and where he signed up. An effective message might be something like, "Thank you for requesting email delivery of our newsletter."

- Keep records of each registration. You must be able to determine how a user registered, even years afterward. Some users forget, and the best way to handle complaints such as "I never signed up for this" is to reply with the details of the original registration. If they still wish to be removed from your list, do so immediately.

- Appoint a real person to handle problems. Include a toll-free phone number in your messages so customers can reach a staff member who monitors and fields email inquiries, including opt-out requests and complaints.

- Personal responses take time, so use an automailer to give an immediate response to all inquiries. If you have the appropriate software, email analysis can allow a machine to make a first-pass approximation at an appropriate response. Many questions can be answered by a short FAQ list and important contact information and phone numbers. Make sure that any automatic message includes information on when (and whether) the automatic response will be followed up by a real person. Check your systems frequently to be sure that the volume of your responses does not exceed your system's capacity.

- Keep your lists secure. Protect the email addresses from misuse. Make sure recipients can't see each others' email addresses or send "reply" messages to the group.

- Your email must be useful and readable to clearly communicate your intent as soon as your reader opens the message. Make sure your email deployment technology supports accurate delivery segmentation for text, HTML, and AOL formats. Do not rely upon graphics or HTML to carry the weight of your marketing message, since many people do not have HTML email capabilities. Even customers that accept HTML email may not always have images turned on. Very few people will wait for large images to load. So rely upon plain text and good copy to communicate your core message, and interested customers will follow up in their own way.

- Don't start your email with a message like "Jim told us you might be interested in our offer." Phrasing like this is typical of spam messages. People are also wary of this kind of thing because many computer viruses are sent with friendly greetings similar to this. If you use a Tell a Friend feature (discussed later in this paper) announce up-front that the message is from you, and refer to the friend's name in the first line of the email body.

- Never use any deception at all in your emails. Always be truthful. If your offer cannot stand on its own, it is not worth sending. A common violation of this rule occurs when a marketer promises a "free gift" as an incentive. Rather than laying out the offer and then describing the incentive, deceptive marketers lead off with a message like "Free gift for you," followed immediately by a glowing description of the gift, with the terms for receiving the gift—usually full payment for a purchase or subscription—buried in a large block of fine print. You may get some buyers, but chances are excellent that you will alienate a far larger number of viable prospects. Put your legitimate offer up front, and back it up with the gift: "A great offer from ABC Mobile Services, plus a gift for you."

- Protect and support the integrity of your brand. Make sure that every email your company sends—whether it announces a discount, confirms an order, or delivers a newsletter—speaks with the same voice and delivers the same message about your company as the strategically planned campaigns you execute through other media. For example, an established and respected clothier should avoid making itself look like the close-out king through repeated email announcements of bargain-basement prices. This may start as an inexpensive way to move some old stock, but initial success may tempt even the best marketer to rely on this more and more. Customers will soon learn that everything can be had at a discount if they just wait, and they will wonder what happened to that steadfast supplier of style and substance they had come to trust. It is true that discounts and clearances are an extremely useful tool that most marketers can benefit from, but they must be presented with caution and forethought if they are to move your business in the direction it needs to go.

Note that most of these issues pertain directly to maintaining a positive image before your customers. This is because no email campaign has the faintest hope of success if it does not show respect for the recipients' time, privacy, and interests. Email messages are extremely easy to delete without reading, and very few people have the time to read the complete text of every email that shows up in their inbox. As soon as a message is perceived as being irrelevant, annoying, invasive, or disrespectful in any way it is deleted and the sender is marked as unworthy in the recipient's perceptions. Future emails are likely to suffer instant deletion. Base your campaigns on respectful messages that are conspicuously relevant to the recipient's interests. Tips on making your messages relevant are included later in this paper.

With email, the high road is the effective road. But failure to adhere to basic email etiquette may carry a far greater cost than the ill-will of some of your recipients.

Blacklisting

Blacklisting may occur when the sender of marketing email is perceived to send spam, or unsolicited or annoying promotional email. Blacklists are lists kept by Internet Service Providers (ISPs) for the protection of their customers. If a marketer gets placed on a blacklist, the ISP will block delivery of that marketer's emails. Though very useful and effective in preventing spam incursions, many legitimate marketers unknowingly and unjustly wind up on blacklists through innocent mistakes or ignorance. Even the actions of a third party (such as an email management service) can place an otherwise ethical marketer on a blacklist, whether they were aware of their offense or not. The key factor in blacklisting is the recipient's perception of the marketer's activities.

Some of the primary causes of blacklisting are:

- Failure to offer easy and quick unsubscribe

- Disregard for unsubscribe requests

- Failure to provide, publish, and uphold a strict privacy policy

- Disrespectful or outwardly offensive messaging

- Misleading or dishonest advertisements

Removing your company from a blacklist is possible, but it can be tedious and time-consuming. It is far better to be diligent about the quality of the messages you send in the first place.

If you suspect your company has been blacklisted, first determine where you are blacklisted and for what reason. Contact the ISP, discuss the problem, and find out what they objected to. Once the ISP is convinced that you are legitimate, they are likely to remove your company from the blacklist. Just make sure to heed their instructions regarding proper email etiquette or you could wind up on the same blacklist again with your next email campaign.

Email Strategy

Your email strategy must support your overall marketing and branding strategy. Because email is so flexible and cost effective, it can be adapted to a wide number of marketing initiatives. However, these same characteristics make it very easy for email to get out of control, with too many mailings put together too quickly without adequate consideration of the strategic consequences. Your brand identity and the strategies that support it should be well-defined before your first email goes out, and then every email should be consistent with your brand image. It is only with brand consistency that email can build a successful long-term relationship with your customers. Without that consistency, your messaging can become confusing or contradictory, jeopardizing the customer's trust in you. That said, here are some of the strategic initiatives that email can support:

- **Customer acquisition**
Email gives you an opportunity to express to customers exactly how a visit to your website will fulfill a need. A compelling offer, a carefully selected list of opt-in email recipients, and a link directly to the product page can result in an admirable conversion rate. Having a one click way to get that customer to your site can have a profoundly positive effect in the long run. Once the first sale has been successfully completed, chances are much higher that the customer will return to shop again.

- **Customer retention**
Since the first visit possibly resulted in a sale, chances are good that participating customers also chose to register at your site, starting their own account. Throughout the normal process of sales fulfillment you will have a number of opportunities to keep in contact with the customer through order confirmations, package tracking information, newsletters, or other appropriate contacts. Each one of these opportunities gives you yet another chance to message to the customer, show him or her the high quality of your service and the helpful way that you do business, and in general reinforce the customer's impression of your site as an establishment worth doing business with. Entire email campaigns can be constructed specifically to enhance customer retention.

- **Customer loyalty and satisfaction**
Some campaigns are specifically intended to increase customer loyalty and satisfaction, rather than creating short-term sales. One example is a campaign that provides your existing customer base with special content or a special discount. Another could be the announcement of "members only" access to a special area of the site: "Because you have been a regular customer we are giving you access to our Preview site where you can view our new fall line."

- **Customer service awareness**
Use email to make your customers aware of the services you offer. If your site offers live webchat with your customer service representatives, phone assistance, bulletin boards, browsing help via page-pushing, or other special services, you will want your customers to know about it. A brief email message about these features and services can support your more product-oriented sales efforts.

- **Multi-channel promotions**
Promote any multi-channel capabilities through targeted emails. Use email

to announce sales and promotions taking place in retail locations, through your catalog, or on your website. You can generate interest in an upcoming catalog drop or mailer by announcing it through email a few days in advance, especially if you include images of the cover of the catalog to visually tie the two together. Send electronic coupons that can be redeemed through any channel. This helps your channels all support each other in making sales and serving customers, and improves your customers' awareness of any integration you offer between channels. Studies have shown that customers who use more than one channel of a store buy more, and buy more often, so your overall business will benefit if you can include other channels in your email campaigns. Email can be very influential in generating interest in people who prefer to make their actual purchases over the phone or at your retail locations. The technology does not yet exist to easily track such cross-channel purchasing, but once it does, marketers will likely discover that a surprising number of their customers are purchasing in this way. An important caution: if you intend to promote catalog drops via email, specialized integration of back-end with front-end may be required. Also, make sure you understand and work in harmony with your company's catalog circulation plan to properly synchronize mailing dates and to get the maximum messaging impact. Also, be aware of your email server's and website server's capacity and space out your emails accordingly. Sending out half a million emails in one day may overwhelm your email system's capacity, and a heavy response could knock out your website. Staggering a single large mailing over a week could be a wise choice. Consult with your IT department to determine what will work best.

- **Event-related campaigns**
  Email can alert local customers to events on your website, in your stores, or at other venues. Celebrity chats, gallery exhibitions, in-store readings, brand sponsored concerts and races, and many other events can benefit from email announcements. You could tie your email in with online registration, email notification, gateway page ads, and other campaign elements to increase participation and the success of your event.

- **Reinforce your brand**
  The main aim here is not sales but the image of the business itself. This sort of campaign may be tied in with a contest, event, special sale, or customer service options. Success for this campaign would be not in how much product was moved, but in how many new potential customers became aware of your website or your services and products. Emphasize good inter-channel practices, such as cross-channel product returns and

customer service. Track and evaluate the results of each of your campaigns in terms of their effect on your overall strategy. Refine your offers and messaging as needed to bring the results in line with what you want.

Creating an Effective Email Message

Though appropriate email strategy and etiquette are important parts of the equation, they do not necessarily lead to an effective campaign. Your messages need to start selling from the moment they enter your recipient's in-box. As with all marketing messages, email has to be clear, timely, appropriate, and compelling if it is to be effective. Your e-commerce provider should be able to help you develop email campaigns that address the following important tactical considerations:

- **Put some punch in your subject line**
  Grab their attention right away through a subject line with a clear, specific incentive to read on. Good subject lines might be "Free Shipping on Your Next Order," "15% off on gifts for Mother's Day," "Holiday Savings: 10% discount on all orders made by December 22," and so forth. Focus on the interests of the recipient, and emphasize the benefits to them. If your email is going out to different segments of your database, follow up on your good subject line with messaging designed to appeal to each target group.

- **Call to action**
  As with any good marketing effort, your message should make it perfectly clear what your customers should do. Tell them you want them to visit your site, and include a link and digital coupon. Tailor your call to action to the strategic goal of that particular campaign.

- **Create a compelling offer**
  Give your customers a good reason to click through. Sales, discounts, free shipping, free gifts, and other incentives are a time-honored and effective way to get your target customers' attention, and in the age of email this means higher click-through rates. Let them know when your offer is specifically for email customers. Track responses by embedding a unique source code in your message, or by providing a special URL for the landing page.

- **Plan and write your copy carefully**
  Write your copy specifically for your email messages, keeping in mind that people are far quicker to click the "delete" button than they are to toss a direct mail piece in the trash. The copy that works well in a direct mail piece may not work at all in email, especially if that copy was written to go

with specific images or a certain look and feel unique to that mailer. In addition, email can be written to take advantage of its instantaneous nature; you can send an offer on Monday announcing a sale that ends at noon on Wednesday, and be fairly certain that your recipients will receive it in time.

- **Use digital coupons**

  Make it easy for your customers to take advantage of your promotions by sending them digital coupons. Digital coupons are simply pieces of code embedded in your emails. They typically carry special source codes that your website can recognize and track. Suppose your customer receives an email from you with a digital coupon worth 20% off any fall sweater. When they click the link back to your site, they are brought directly to a landing page that presents the products, the discounted prices, and links to details about each item. This is the kind of convenience and attention to customer needs that generates sales and gains customers.

- **Balance between content and commerce**

  Messages with content of interest to the user are more likely to be read, and at times well-written content can generate more interest than a discount offer. Make your messages clear and to the point, and use the first line of your message to entice the recipient to read the rest. Research has shown that many emails get deleted before the customer has read the second line so even though you may think you may have a paragraph or two of "must read" content, distill that down into the most important point or two and put it up front. If anyone is really interested they will keep reading, and maybe click through to your site. Some email campaigns may not be based upon a discount offer at all. Many merchants have gotten a better return on community-oriented emails which emphasize the sharing of information than from purely promotional messaging, however good the offer. For example, a travel goods provider could position itself as an expert resource for travel information (and by extension, travel products) with a campaign that offers free reviews of popular resorts. A few well-placed links to beachwear or luggage will pull the reader right to the website, their purchasing interest stimulated by the images conjured up by the informational content. Any other kind of interesting online content can be used to generate click throughs. The possibilities are endless.

- **Personalize the email for successful conversion**

  People respond best to offers that pertain directly to their own interests, and Web technology makes it possible to personalize virtually everything about your email messages to increase the likelihood of making a sale. By using what you know about your customers you can personalize the offer you send them, the email message that expresses what you have for them, the landing page that welcomes them when they click through to your site, and the messaging they read when looking at the offered products. Personalization is a large topic on its own, and will be discussed in greater detail in chapter 4.

- **Determine frequency of emails**
  The frequency of your emails can have an effect on whether customers will respond. Too frequent, and customers will feel inundated and be driven away. Too seldom, and your customers may forget about you. Appropriate frequency depends a lot on the source of the email list, the nature of your business, and what promises you may have made to your recipients about how often they can expect to hear from you. If you have promised to keep it reasonable, be sure that the customer is only receiving as much mail as she feels she committed to. Customers who have responded enthusiastically to email offers may be open to more frequent contacts than those who seldom respond. When possible, offer a choice to your registered customers, and let them tell you if they are comfortable being contacted weekly, monthly, quarterly, or only in response to customer requests. Watch your opt-out rates to gauge how your email volume is received by your customers. If a sudden rise in opt-out rates corresponds with a recent increase in frequency, then it is likely that you are sending too often. As a general rule, you should send emails whenever you have something relevant to say but again, be wary of overdoing it. Once a month is a good rate at which to start. Modify your schedule as your response rates indicate.

- **HTML vs. Text**
  Advanced HTML email capabilities can add interest and real value to your message, when used appropriately and when sent to the right customers. According to Jupiter Communications, customers respond to HTML messages twice as often as they do to plain text messages. On the other hand, only about 60% of email users are capable of, or choose to receive HTML mail. Always create an alternate message for customers whose access is limited by their hardware, software, connection speed, or personal settings.

- **Sound and video files**
  Caution is required when adding audio or video to your marketing emails. Many customers will not have the plug-ins required to play them, and

many do not want to install them. Your customers' sound systems vary too, and it is likely that even carefully-created sound files will not work well for everyone. In addition, sound files can create a bad impression or embarrassment by blaring out at the wrong time, so never set files for audio, video, or other advanced content to launch automatically. Provide a button or a link that allows customers to choose whether or not they play this material.

Executing an Email Campaign – Technological Issues to Consider

Email campaigns are often run from the same machines or web farm that hosts the website itself, and without proper preparation the extra load can lead to performance problems with the site. It is a good idea to make some special considerations and take some extra precautions to make sure your site continues to run efficiently while it sends all the messages for your email campaign and handles the responses. Your e-commerce provider should be able to help you assemble technologically solid campaigns.

- Determine overall effect on your Web servers, bandwidth, connection speeds, and other hosting issues. When possible, send your email during the lowest traffic times possible, or (even better) from separate machines.

- One way to avoid the extra load on your own resources is using a third party service provider.

  Advantages: you get out-of-the-box functionality, allowing you to add appropriate email capabilities without extensive development and integration times. Third parties also may offer opt-in lists to help you expand your email list.

  Disadvantages: you have less control over the process, and are dependent on your provider to execute your mailing in a responsible way that upholds your company's respectable image. Also, you may not have access to the lists used and therefore you may not know if customers are receiving multiple copies of your messages.

- Send "ping" checks to everyone on your list to find out which contacts are no longer good and will "bounce" (fail to connect). A ping is a test message that connects with your recipient's server but never actually shows up in their inbox, allowing you to spot bad or discontinued addresses and remove them from your lists without disturbing the intended recipients.

- Be very careful about using multimedia (video and audio) in emails. This can greatly increase the file size of each message sent, adding a potentially huge load to your servers.

- Test your entire email process before sending anything out to customers. Some email applications and services have testing routines built in. Test for proper delivery and function of plain text, AOL, and HTML emails through all the most popular email client applications and operating systems (Mac, Unix, and Linux included.)

Measuring the Success of Your Email Campaign

Another enormous advantage email has over other marketing methods is its measurability. With proper preparation you will be able to determine the effectiveness of each campaign, and use what you learn to improve future mailings.

The nature of your campaign will largely determine what you measure. For example, if your goal is to increase sales, you would do well to determine how many people opened your messages, used them to link to your site, and actually made a purchase. If your goal is to increase brand awareness, you will want to know how many new customers clicked to your site as a result of receiving your email.

The statistics available to you depend on what email management software and reporting tools you use. In general, these are some of the most useful measurements:

- **Average order size**
  An important carryover from the traditional direct marketing arena, average order size is a good indicator of the overall effectiveness of your campaign, and the degree to which your offers, messaging, and products appeal to you customers. Calculate this by dividing total demand by the number of orders, or

  average order size=demand ÷ orders

- **Response rate**
  Another important metric from direct marketing, response rate is a calculation of the number of orders received per a given number of messages sent. This is extremely useful in determining the overall effectiveness of your message and the appropriateness of your offer. Also referred to as conversion ratio.

  response rate=orders ÷ circulation

Average order size and response rate are important carry-overs from the direct marketing world. Besides these two mainstays, the following measurements are now commonly used to evaluate email:

- **Open (view) rate**
  If you are sending HTML email, you can determine how many people opened your email by including a small, transparent pixel in the email. The number of times that a unique visitor hits that image file will tell you exactly how many emails have actually been opened – though not whether they have been read.

- **Click-through rate (CTR)**
  Click-through rates measure how many unique visitors actually clicked on a link in the email and visited the site. It will not report the number of customers that read the email and then entered the site from a bookmark or other method.

- **Bounce rate**
  The bounce rate will tell you how many emails were refused by the ISPs to which they were addressed. The reasons for bounces may vary, but most are caused by high server volume, the customer's account no longer being valid, or because the ISP has determined not to accept emails from your server (see the section on Blacklisting earlier in this paper.) Fortunately, you are apprised of every bounce so you can continually clean up your database. For this reason, the bounce rate should decrease over time.

- **Unsubscribe rate**
  This is the proportion of customers who opened the email and chose to unsubscribe from your list rather than participate.

- **Cost of email campaign**
  Add your cost for sending the emails and any loss you may take on an offered product.

- **Cost per message**
  This measures the cost of each individual message sent. Simply, it is the cost of the email campaign divided by total number of emails sent.

  cost per message=cost of email campaign ÷ total number of emails sent

- **Total revenue generated**
  This is the total gross amount of sales that can be attributed to the email campaign.

- **Cost per response**
  This is an acquisition measurement. To measure it, divide the total cost of the email campaign by the total number of visitors.

cost per response=cost of email campaign ÷ total number of visitors

Cost per sale
This is a conversion measurement. To measure CPS, divide the cost of the email campaign by the number of sales attributable to the email campaign. Note that it does not do any weighting by size of sale: the cost is per transaction, whether small or large.

cost per sale=cost of email campaign ÷ number of sales from campaign

ROI (Return on Investment)
Total of all the profit made on sales attributable to the email campaign.

Personalized Email Campaigns – Taking the Next Step

Even without personalization an email campaign can do a lot to promote your brand and advance your business goals. But when you are able to create offers and messaging tailored to every customer group in your database then the results can be truly impressive. Personalization enables you to send pertinent offers to every individual in your database, increasing sales, average order size, conversion rates, and customer satisfaction. Your personalization strategy should center around creating long-term trust with your customer file and building your brand.

Keep in mind that the most effective personalization extends not only to your email messages but to the pages of your website that your customer is likely to visit. The same personalization methods discussed here can be used in campaigns that involve channels other than your website and email.

Personalization begins with an in-depth analysis of your customers' behavior as represented by the data in your customer databases. Database analysis and personalization are huge topics in themselves, and will only be summarized here.

Typically, customers are placed in one or more customer groups or segments, each sharing a specific quality or qualities. Groups can be small or large, few or numerous, depending upon the marketer's resources and the abilities of their data handling software. A segmentation strategy does not need to be complex to start yielding results. Most marketers should start simply and add complexity as their experience increases.

Customer groups can be based upon any measurable characteristic, but some of the most commonly used groups are determined by:

- Frequency of purchase.

- Date of most recent purchase.

- Average purchase size.

- Types of products purchased.

- Age and gender.

- Geographic location.

- Answers to survey questions.

Customers will typically belong to several groups. Once you know what your groups are, you can begin actively targeting them.

- **Personalize the offer**
  Develop special promotions, products, and pricing relevant to each group. This improves the odds of any individual receiving an offer that is pertinent to their interests. Consider an online pet supplier. Their two largest groups might be those who buy dog-related items and those who buy cat related items. They would send a promotion for dog food to those who apparently own dogs, and a cat food offer to the cat owners. Their offers could be split further by sending the dog food offer only to those who typically buy dog food online, and a doggie toy offer to those who usually buy doggie toys. A more generic offer could be sent to those customers with no clear buying pattern.

- **Personalize the message**
  Using your database information, messages can be easily crafted to include the customer's name, and even their local region. If the customer is near a local store, the message could be regionalized with local store sales and/or events as well. Depending on the target group, the spin you place on your offers is likely to vary. A clothier's messaging might emphasize style and quality for big spenders, and monetary savings for bargain hunters. For a preseason winter sale, they might promote overcoats to customers in Chicago and light jackets to those in Florida.

- **Personalize the landing page**

  Use landing pages to enhance customer click-through and conversion. A landing page is the first page your site presents to a customer when they click a link in your email message. For each target group or special campaign segment, a special landing page could be made that presents information, graphics, and messaging specific to that offer. Source codes embedded in your emails can tell your site which group this customer is from, and therefore which landing page to serve up. Studies have shown that if people click to a site in response to an offer, but do not immediately see the offer on arrival, over 75% will click away again immediately.

- **Customize all site messaging**

  Support your promotions and the promises you make in your campaigns by changing all appropriate messaging. If your website supports it, home pages, landing pages, relevant search and product pages, and even content, customer service, and thank you pages could be customized with messaging that pertains to the current offer or promotion. Try to provide pertinent information and integrate your campaign anywhere on your site where the customer is likely to go. The goal is to emulate the attentive service one would find at a reputable retailer. At this time, most websites do not have the technological foundation to make in-depth customization like this possible. This requires an advanced e-commerce engine with the ability to build pages on the fly according to business rules set by the merchant.

You do not need to dive into complete personalization of everything on your website to make your initial email campaigns a success. Start simply. Begin with well-tailored offers and customized landing pages to steer customers in the right direction. Start with two or three large customer groups, and split them into smaller, more numerous, more refined groups as your email experience grows. Try different approaches to find out what works best to get your customers to respond to your brand in the way you want them to. Measure the response from each campaign carefully and begin plotting a course for your future email strategy. Add more personalization to your site as you refine your capabilities and become accustomed to marketing in this way. But be forewarned: you are likely to need an entirely new website if you are going to add extensive personalization. So master the basics first, and make them work for you. Don't take on extensive and expensive modification or replacement of your website until you ascertain that your return on investment will make it all worthwhile.

In addition, provide the functionality that lets the customer update her profile and preferences at will. Most regular customers will appreciate well-targeted email messaging and site personalization. But customer interests evolve over time, and they will appreciate it more if they can actively tell you what their new interests are so you can send them material that is more relevant.

How to Build Your Email List

No one registers to receive email simply for the sake of receiving email. Anyone who agrees to receive email from a profit-driven company will expect more than an inbox full of promotions. There must be more value for them in this exchange if they are going to sign up. Here are some proven ways to make your emails more useful and relevant to everyone who receives them, and to encourage more and more to opt in.

1. Enlist all your channels in a list-expanding campaign

The boundaries between sales channels are becoming increasingly blurred, allowing marketers to bring to bear the resources of other sales channels in their efforts to grow their email lists.

- Your catalog order forms should have a line for the customer's email address, and check-boxes where they can opt in for emails on topics that appeal to them: newsletters, announcements of sales and discounts, new products in specific categories, and so forth.

- Phone center Customer Service Representatives should be trained to ask for email addresses during every exchange with customers who have none on record, and to offer to sign everyone up for mailings pertinent to the subject at hand. So when a customer calls to check on order status, the CSR should ask if she would like to receive order status notification through email. When she places an order, the CSR should offer to sign her up for email notification when similar products are on sale.

- Retail stores can gather the same information by asking for it with every sale, by offering a coupon that is redeemable online if the customer fills out an online registration, or by collecting them through contest or sweepstakes sign-up forms.

- Hybrid email lists that contain email and standard mail contact information are available for rental, and you could use them in campaigns that involve email and direct mail.

The value to the customer: improved service and convenience.

2. Rent an email list

Just as in the world of printed mailers, a carefully constructed offer and message sent to a well-targeted rented list can generate some very positive results. Be very careful to rent a list that is likely to yield good results. Confirm that the list is composed 100% of opt-in addresses. Follow your list rental agreement carefully. As with direct mail, incorporate the responses into your database, keeping track of the source of the lead and any preferences the respondent indicated regarding their interests and wishes. Include opt-out requests in your database as well, in a special category, and do not ever send anything to them again. As is true in the traditional direct marketing arena, email list selection is a complex issue, and is beyond the scope of this paper.

The value to the customer: depends upon the offer you present.

3. Contests, prizes, and sweepstakes

Use your website, retail locations, catalog response cards, and phone centers to announce contests, prizes and sweepstakes, and to collect your respondents' names, email addresses, and even information about their interests, buying habits, and other demographics. Announce your contests via email as well, through a mailing to your existing opt-in recipients, and encourage them to forward your message to their friends and family. You might also consider using banner ads on carefully targeted sites that relate closely to your business. Remember that a response to a contest announcement does not constitute a blanket opt-in for all your promotional emails. To generate legitimate opt-in contacts, send all respondents a message thanking them for their interest, and include a discount offer or digital coupon to encourage them to visit your site. As usual, include a way for them to opt in for future mailings, and don't send anything else to those who do not respond.

The value to the customer: "something for nothing," excitement, no risk.

4. "Tell a Friend": Word of mouth online

Any time you send something special via email, such as contest entry forms, announcements of sales, newsletters, or other promotions, include a link so the recipient can easily send your announcement to someone else. This link should open a special page on your site where your contact can type their friend's name, email address, and a brief message. Your original promotion is sent to the new contact with clear messaging indicating how you got their name, and an easy way to unsubscribe from your list. This is perhaps the most widely used of the viral marketing methods.

Keep correspondence with "tell a friend" leads low-key to avoid generating friction between your two contacts, and to prevent an angry backlash directed at you. Leads generated this way are most safely considered opt-out until they actually click through to your site. A comprehensive, clear, respectful privacy policy and your determination to adhere to it are vital to maintaining your company's good name when prospecting in this way.

The value to the customer: a friend's opinion. "If Sally liked it, it must be good."

5. Register your website users for access to special content
If your site offers non-product specific content, consider making some or all of it available only to registered users. Registration must be easy, and require only their name and email address. Send a single email to confirm their registration, and give them the opportunity to opt in to receive updates on content and products of interest to them so you can better target future mailings.

The value to the customer: privileged access.

6. Clubs
Clubs are similar to the registered user example above. Clubs can be set up for groups of users with specific similar interests, or for regular preferred customers. Offer registrants announcements of promotions or content specially created for them.

The value to the customer: privileged access, reduced prices, rewards for loyalty, content specific to their interests.

7. Newsletters
Send regular newsletters via email. Provide an initial digital coupon for a discount as a thank-you gift, and an opportunity to opt-in for announcements of content and products that are of interest to them. After this initial pitch, hold back and let your newsletter do the talking. You might include an occasional digital coupon or announcement of a sale as part of the newsletter, but keep this low-key and pertinent to newsletter content. Newsletters are primarily intended to build a relationship with your readers, and to be informative and not promotional. They will see through you immediately if you try to turn it into an ad spread.

The value to the customer: information with no pressure applied.

8. Notification of discounts and clearance sales
The offer of a deep discount will attract buyers who might respond to little else. Offer them email notification so they can get first crack at your clearance sales and see how many sign up. Not only will you move some of that clearance merchandise faster, but you will also have an addition to your list with clearly stated demographics and interests — you can know what will attract them in the future and use this information to personalize future offers.

The value to the customer: early notification, deep discounts.

9. Affinity or incentive programs

Encourage people to let you keep track of their purchases so they can eventually receive an award: gifts, discounts and the like. Such prospects are likely to welcome your promotional emails, because they will find more things they want to buy and thus get closer to their goal all that much faster. There are several third-party systems and applications available to help you with this.

The value to the customer: membership, lower prices, and rewards for loyalty. Getting something very few others have.

10. Virtual greeting cards and post cards

Similar to the "tell a friend" feature, this allows someone to send a visually appealing greeting via email. They enter their friend's name, email address, and a brief message, select an image, and your email system assembles the virtual card and sends it on its way. Not only do you get a new name and email, but the recipient receives a pleasant and extremely low-key item which promotes your business. This could be very effective for businesses that sell visually-or lifestyle-oriented products like artwork, greeting cards, sports and recreation equipment, and so forth. This is another viral marketing approach.

The value to the customer: a pleasant experience, the personal touch from a friend.

11. Include opt-in links on all your customer service emails

Every email you legitimately send for order confirmation, shipping notification, order update, or other administrative purpose can contain a discrete offer for someone to opt-in for newsletters, product updates, and so forth. Put the copy for your offer at the bottom of your message so it does not interfere with the true purpose of your email. Phrase your offer in terms of added customer service.

The value to the customer: convenience, better service.

Non-Responsive Email Addresses

It is likely that many of your recipients have seldom or never made a purchase from your website, though they have not opted out either. The question naturally arises as to what to do with these names. The first step is to mark non-responders as a segment of their own. The second is to put together a strategy that breaks the pattern of non-response. There are several ways to accomplish this:

- Increase the value of your messages by sending them offers targeted specifically at them, in an effort to convert them to buyers. Give them a offer they can't refuse to get them into your website.

- Scale back your mailings, under the assumption that the recipients are not very interested in hearing from you. Lower volume means lower likelihood of your customer getting tired of seeing your messages and eventually deciding to opt-out entirely.

- Increase the number of emails you send them, in the hopes that with more volume they are more likely to see an offer that appeals to them. Be careful with this one. It usually has a low success rate, and could actually lead to higher opt-out rates.

- Keep sending them the same kind of emails you have been, since they have not actually opted out, and since they could be actively buying through another channel unbeknownst to you.

- Send them an electronic survey form which asks what they expect from the emails you send them, and what products they are most interested in hearing about or are planning to buy in the future. Emphasize your intent to serve their needs and interests by finding out what they want. Your survey form should be multiple choice, with a space for them to type in messages of their own. One question should be whether they have bought anything from you recently through your website, catalog, phone center, or retail store. There should be an opt-out check box as well, in a place that is easy to find. Whatever their response, you will know for certain what that particular person is getting out of your emails, and what customer segments you should include them in for future mailings.

    As with any change in email tactics, try your new approach on a small but representative group to gauge their responses. Adjust your tactics accordingly. If you see a dramatically increased number of opt-outs, re-examine your tactics, your offers, and your messaging, and try again.

How to Get Them to Click Through

Finding someone to send a promotional email to is not difficult. Finding someone likely to be interested in your offer is a little harder. But the toughest part of all is sometimes just getting them to click through to your site and take a look around. Here is a collection of tips—taken from this paper and from other sources—that can help improve your click-through rates.

- Promote your catalog in your emails, especially those that will be mailed in the near future. Provide a special link to a "sneak preview" part of your site with highlights of new products featured in the upcoming catalog.

- Provide good compelling offers tailored to the interests of your customers.

- Be repetitive. Keep sending the offers, even though your customers may not have responded as you want them to. Repetition breeds familiarity. And one day you might send them the offer they like. But don't drown them, or they are likely to opt out.

- Keep your copy short and to the point, to encourage people to read it all and recognize the benefits in your offer.

- Use images where appropriate to generate interest and excitement, but don't overdo it.

- Be honest and use a respectful tone when addressing your customers.

- Provide existing customers special access to content or promotions.

- Announce sales, discounts, free shipping, free gifts, and other promotions.

- Include links to interesting articles, surveys, polls, and other content.

- Include a link to an "update your profile" feature, where customers can give you more information about their latest preferences, or opt out entirely.

- Include a digital coupon.

- Put your "must-read" copy right at the top of the email.

- Announce events happening at your retail locations, and provide a link so customers can sign up online.

- Announce a contest or sweepstakes, and include a link to your online sign-up form.

- Make the subject line clear and powerful, and include an appropriate call to action.

- In an HTML email, include thumbnail images of products you are offering, and link them directly to the product pages on your site.

- Experiment with the frequency of your emails until you optimize the click-through rate.

- Give customers a choice as to the nature and frequency of the emails you send them. Some might only want announcements of discounts, others might only be interested in specific categories of your product line, and some might only want your newsletter.

- Include images, sound, and video to generate interest. Such content must be pertinent to the products or content you are promoting. Do not set sound and video to play automatically.

- Include a picture of your catalog's cover to spur instant recognition and interest.

- Personalize your emails with the recipient's name, and if possible, with messaging and offers calculated to be of interest to them.

- Send a newsletter with low-key links to the products mentioned.

- Create some new segments and send targeted emails to them. Track the results and refine further efforts.

- Don't overdo it with any of these, particularly in regard to the number of emails you send to any given customer. Select a few techniques that reflect best on your brand and your company's style, and see what kind of results you get.

- Write your email message copy specifically for your emails. Do not just use the copy from your direct mail, since people read and respond to email differently.

- Send time-sensitive offers. A message such as "you only have two days left to take advantage of our Winter savings" can generate significant response, since it only takes a couple of seconds to link to your site.

- Send follow-up emails after the customer has placed an order. Thank them for their order and give them a tracking number, and include links to a couple products or articles that may be of interest to them.

- In your follow-up email, include a link to an order tracking system or even a "past orders" page. Customers value links like this and are likely to save them as a bookmark.

- Be truthful in all your emails and your contacts will learn to trust you.

- Send a "tell a friend" link so the customer can easily forward your offers to someone else. Honor any digital coupons that may have been forwarded in this fashion.

- If your customer has not purchased in a long time, invite them back with special messaging and offers for long-time customers.

- Solicit their input on your quality of service and your product line. Many people appreciate the chance to provide a compliment, suggestion, or complaint.

- Follow the rules of good e-commerce etiquette and don't get blacklisted.

Email could be the biggest revolution to hit the marketing scene since the first promotional phone call was made. It is likely that we have only seen a small degree of email's complete potential. Yet it is not a cure-all. Email is only as good as the thinking that goes into its use. It is not enough to simply put together an offer, put your Web address on it, and send it to every address you can lay your hands on. Like any marketing tool, it can only reach its full potential when integrated with a brand-centric campaign designed to support the overall strategies and goals of the business.

Chapter 13 Links
Intelligent Email Marketing

http://www.the-dma.org
The Direct Marketing Association (DMA)

In recent years the DMA has become increasingly involved in e-commerce issues, and the organization's website has a lot of very valuable material regarding email and selling online. Take a look before you solidify your own marketing plans. Though some material is reserved for use only by DMA members, plenty is accessible to everyone. These sections of their site are particularly useful to email marketers:

- Professional Development: in particular their guidelines on ethics.

- Consumer Help: see what the experts are teaching the public about their rights, privacy, and safety.

- Library: includes news, white papers, research resources, and other valuable material. The section on privacy is especially useful.

- Government Affairs: information on legislation.

http://www.imarketing.org
Association for Interactive Marketing (AIM)

AIM is a non-profit trade organization devoted to helping marketers use interactive opportunities to reach their respective marketplaces. AIM is an independent subsidiary of the Direct Marketing Association.

http://www.retailing.org
Electronic Retailing Association (ERA)

The ERA is the trade association for companies who use the power of electronics to sell goods and services to the public. The purpose of ERA is to foster the growth, development and acceptance of the rapidly growing electronic retailing industry worldwide.

http://www.nrf.com
National Retail Federation (NRF)

The world's largest retail trade association. NRF's mission is to conduct programs and services in research, education, training, information technology, and government affairs to protect and advance the interests of the retail industry.

http://www.shop.org
Shop.org
The leading trade association for online retailers. Shop.org, the E-Retailers' knowledge exchange, now serves as the NRF's online retailing arm.

http://industryclick.com
Primedia Business Magazines and Media
Publisher of a number of titles, including Catalog Age Magazine. When you get to the main Primedia site, click on the Marketing link in the main part of the screen and you will be presented with links to Catalog Age, Direct, and others. Though not specifically about email, these magazines regularly publish articles about email marketing.

http://researchcenter.zdnet.com/data/rlist?t=busofit_10_30_26_10
ZD Net Research Center
ZD Net covers virtually everything about the integration of technology with business. This link takes you straight to the section containing research and white papers on email marketing.

http://www.ecommercetimes.com
Ecommerce Times
A part of News Factor Network, one of the largest e-business & technology news publishers in the U.S. News and comment about e-commerce issues.

http://www.catalogsuccess.com
Catalog Success Magazine
This magazine is directed at catalogers, but it regularly publishes articles about email marketing.

http://www.internet.com
internet.com
Internet.com serves as an index to a wide number of other Internet-related sites. Visit their Marketing section at:
http://www.internet.com/sections/marketing.html.

http://www.targetonline.com
Target Marketing Magazine
Target Marketing has a large number of current and archived articles on their site, many of them about email marketing strategy and execution.

http://www.digitrends.net
Digitrends
News and articles about everything to do with the Internet. See their section on email marketing within their Advertising & Marketing section. A useful 5-part series on finding an email provider is at http://www.digitrends.net/marketing/13640_15061.html

http://www.nua.com
NUA Internet Surveys
An online resource providing information on Internet demographics and trends. Their database contains over four years of freely accessible information gathered and collated by Nua, and Nua's weekly editorial articles.

http://www.ilpf.org/
Internet Law and Policy Forum (ILPF)
The Internet Law and Policy Forum is dedicated to promoting global growth of e-commerce by contributing to a better understanding of the particular legal issues which arise from the cross-border nature of the electronic medium.

http://www.gahtan.com/cyberlaw/
Cyberlaw Encyclopedia
A portal site providing a collection of links to legally-oriented material online.

14

It's All About the Customer

Adapting to Customer Needs as the Market Changes

By now you have learned something about the art and science of looking at your customer from all angles and using as many tools as possible to stimulate their interest. You also understand that the evolving nature of the Internet and Web tools will constantly change the way in which your customers look at you and also the way in which you can relate to your customers. The future belongs to those companies that can embrace this kind of change and adapt their methods and techniques to suit the interests of the customer.

Anyone doing business online will have to keep a close eye on trends in the Web-using population, and their goals and habits in using it. Businesses will particularly need to watch two things: new technologies being incorporated into e-commerce, and the special needs and behaviors of their customers. Fortunately, because of its solid grounding in direct marketing principles, the Intelligent Selling approach already provides the paradigm for successful growth and adaptation as these and other trends take shape. Its eight key aspects are not technologies in and of themselves, nor are they reliant on any specific technology. Rather, they are interrelated concepts that are part of the overall Intelligent Selling philosophy:

- **Personalization:** the guiding force that makes your site relevant to each individual user.

- **Dynamic merchandising and messaging:** the way you guide your customer through the optimal path to purchase and stimulate sales by careful selection of the messaging and product offers you provide them.

- **Campaigns:** the orchestrated use of all appropriate aspects of your business to obtain a specific goal.

- **Customer loyalty:** designing your site and your services in such a way that customers find value in them and choose to return to your site to shop again and again.

- **Customer service:** the use of good site design, the incorporation of a customer-centric attitude throughout your business, and a willingness to resolve problems or conflicts to the customer's benefit.

- **Content:** product and non-product information carefully chosen to support the sale, acquire and retain the customers' interest, and help them find what they are looking for.

- **Data and analytics:** careful tracking of all customer information for more accurate personalization and division of your database into customer groups.

- **Multichannel selling:** the deliberate unification of all sales channels to present a consistent view of your business to the customer regardless of how he or she approaches you.

Used appropriately, Intelligent Selling gives you greater power to satisfy your customers throughout all your interactions. It helps you build a 360 degree relationship cycle, wherein you are better able to acquire site visitors in the first place, convert them to paying customers, and retain them as customers after they have made their first purchase. They will keep coming back to you because your relationship with them is the best they have found. And the most profitable businesses are those which typically have a high degree of customer return.

You'll Meet Your Goals If Your Customers Meet Theirs

Employing the techniques outlined in this book will help you:

- increase conversion rates

- increase average order size and frequency of purchase

- improve customer loyalty and retention

- reduce abandoned cars rates

- decrease customer service costs

- improve overall customer experience.

The time to start attaining these goals is now, because they will only get more important in the future. The Internet is opening up new worlds to people in all walks of life, and will continue to do so. This is especially true because of the growth in new technologies that make access far easier than it is now. Portable phones, PDAs, Web terminals in stores, and even Internet-enabled household appliances will move the Internet from the desktop computer to almost every aspect of everyday life. This means far greater access for everybody, including those who don't own computers or have a hard time using them because of disabilities. I guarantee that as this happens, customer expectations will rise and it will become more important than ever that companies engineer a smooth integration between the retail, customer service, and data aspects of their business.

Imagine the difficulties of conducting business in an environment like this without a way of taking a unified look at your customers, your data, or your policies. Your customers will be coming at you from so many different angles and through so many different kinds of technology that in the absence of philosophies or methodologies that allow you to handle this diversity, the only result could be chaos and a breakdown of the ability to serve those customers. Regardless of the number of channels a business uses, customers expect them all to behave as one store and not as independent business units. Businesses will no longer be able to tolerate scattered and unintegrated data on their customers, products, and policies. Customers will soon come to expect that clerks in stores, customer service representatives, and web locations will all have access to the same information.

Intelligent Selling: A Toolkit for Future Success

While we may be some years away from being able to call home and tell the refrigerator to put the roast in the oven, it is just as clear that the Internet is becoming a fully-integrated part of American life. By applying the principles of Intelligent Selling, merchants with e-commerce channels will be able to make the most of new opportunities as they arise.

While this book is full of specific tips and suggestions, it is the nature of Intelligent Selling to undergo constant transformation. As technologies and population trends change, specific bits of advice may become more applicable or less so. But the principles behind Intelligent Selling will always remain valuable.

Always remember that everything you do is for your customers. Design your site and your services for their benefit. It is really their website after all, since they are the ones who will be using it. And they will quickly drop it and find a new one if it doesn't work.

Intelligent Selling is a dedication to success—to learning the skills of self-evaluation, to engaging in results-oriented decision-making, and to developing the eagerness and clarity of vision that allows growth and change when necessary. Master the principles of Intelligent Selling, and your business will be ready to grow and thrive, even as your tools, resources, and customer base undergo constant evolution.

About the Author

Ken Burke began developing his vision for successful e-commerce in the mid-1990s, before most people had even heard of the Internet and before most companies had a Web presence. In 1995 Ken founded Multimedia Live, the company that would put his pioneering vision to the test and in the process grow into one of the most successful and longest-lived e-commerce technology and development companies in the U.S. Starting with only $500 and the computer he used in college, Ken built the company with sweat equity and the determination to make successful online selling a reality. The past eight years has seen Multimedia Live develop thousands of e-commerce sites, each one helping to refine the company's principles of effective e-commerce Web design. This vision is now known as Intelligent Selling™, and is the driving force behind websites for some of the best-known brands in the cataloging and retailing arena: General Motors, Playboy, Keds, Norm Thompson, L-Com, The Limited Too, Wine Enthusiast, and The Swiss Colony to name a few. Under Ken's guidance, Multimedia Live has developed MarketLive™, the groundbreaking e-commerce application that powers these and many other merchandising websites. Ken is a sought-after media source for industry insights, a frequent speaker at Internet and e-commerce conferences, and a regular contributor to industry magazines. Through a series of educational seminars, he has personally trained over 10,000 entrepreneurs how to do business on the Internet. He studied multimedia and the Internet at the University of Southern California, where he completed a BA in Marketing and earned honors as an MBA graduate in Venture Management and Entrepreneurship.